GOOGLE INCOME:

How ANYONE of Any Age, Location, and/or Background Can Build a Highly Profitable Online Business with Google

By Bruce C. Brown

Google Income: How ANYONE of Any Age, Location, and/or Background Can Build a Highly Profitable Online Business with Google

Copyright © 2009 Atlantic Publishing Group, Inc.
1405 SW 6th Avenue • Ocala, Florida 34471 • Phone 800-814-1132 • Fax 352-622-1875
Web site: www.atlantic-pub.com • E-mail: sales@atlantic-pub.com
SAN Number: 268-1250

ISBN-13: 978-1-60138-300-6   ISBN-10: 1-60138-314-2

Library of Congress Cataloging-in-Publication Data

Brown, Bruce C. (Bruce Cameron), 1965-
  Google income: how anyone of any age, location and/or background can build a highly profitable online business with Google / by Bruce C. Brown.
     p. cm.
  Includes bibliographical references and index.
  ISBN-13: 978-1-60138-300-6 (alk. paper)
  ISBN-10: 1-60138-300-2 (alk. paper)
  1. Google (Firm) 2. Internet marketing. 3. Internet advertising. I. Title.

  HF5415.1265.B7648.2009
  658.8'72--dc22
                          2009009593

Printed in the United States

PROJECT MANAGER: Melissa Peterson • mpeterson@atlantic-pub.com
COVER DESIGN: Meg Buchner • megadesn@mchsi.com
INTERIOR DESIGN: Holly Marie Gibbs • hgibbs@atlantic-pub.com

We recently lost our beloved pet "Bear," who was not only our best and dearest friend but also the "Vice President of Sunshine" here at Atlantic Publishing. He did not receive a salary but worked tirelessly 24 hours a day to please his parents. Bear was a rescue dog that turned around and showered myself, my wife Sherri, his grandparents Jean, Bob and Nancy and every person and animal he met (maybe not rabbits) with friendship and love. He made a lot of people smile every day.

We wanted you to know that a portion of the profits of this book will be donated to The Humane Society of the United States. *–Douglas & Sherri Brown*

The human-animal bond is as old as human history. We cherish our animal companions for their unconditional affection and acceptance. We feel a thrill when we glimpse wild creatures in their natural habitat or in our own backyard.

Unfortunately, the human-animal bond has at times been weakened. Humans have exploited some animal species to the point of extinction.

The Humane Society of the United States makes a difference in the lives of animals here at home and worldwide. The HSUS is dedicated to creating a world where our relationship with animals is guided by compassion. We seek a truly humane society in which animals are respected for their intrinsic value, and where the human-animal bond is strong.

Want to help animals? We have plenty of suggestions. Adopt a pet from a local shelter, join The Humane Society and be a part of our work to help companion animals and wildlife. You will be funding our educational, legislative, investigative and outreach projects in the U.S. and across the globe.

Or perhaps you'd like to make a memorial donation in honor of a pet, friend or relative? You can through our Kindred Spirits program. And if you'd like to contribute in a more structured way, our Planned Giving Office has suggestions about estate planning, annuities, and even gifts of stock that avoid capital gains taxes.

Maybe you have land that you would like to preserve as a lasting habitat for wildlife. Our Wildlife Land Trust can help you. Perhaps the land you want to share is a backyard—that's enough. Our Urban Wildlife Sanctuary Program will show you how to create a habitat for your wild neighbors.

So you see, it's easy to help animals. And The HSUS is here to help.

THE HUMANE SOCIETY OF THE UNITED STATES

2100 L Street NW • Washington, DC 20037 • 202-452-1100 • www.hsus.org

DEDICATION

To Vonda – for giving me the best 25 years of my life. I can't wait to start the next 25.

"God has a plan. He has a plan for everything and everyone."

– Number Six

"How do you know?

I mean, how do you really know that you can trust me?" **– Sharon**

"I don't. That's what trust is." **– Adama**

Table of Contents

Chapter 3: Optimizing your Web Site for Google — Generating Web Site Traffic & Income 57

Chapter 4: Introduction to Pay-Per-Click Advertising 135

Chapter 5: Using Google AdWords............... 151

Chapter 6: Creating an Effective Google Pay-Per-Click Advertising Campaign: Keywords, Key Phrases, & Your Google AdWords Budget 199

Chapter 7: Increase Profits by Combating Fraud with Google AdWords 213

Chapter 8: Increase Profits & Generate Income with Google AdSense 233

What is Findability?

On the Internet, findability is being found at the right time and in the right place on a search engine or other Internet site. The challenge and art to being "findable" is knowing when and where in the searching process to insert yourself in front of the searcher. Businesses must understand this concept fully and embrace the multitudes of products and services offered by Google™ to truly capture the power of business on the Internet. Bruce C. Brown has undertaken the task of giving you a wealth of options for properly managing your "findability" by harnessing the power of Google™ products and services.

Beware of Your Internet "Ego"

Business owners time after time state their frustrations with Search Engine Marketing professionals and the disappointing results they have experienced. The key reason they fail is because they do not take ownership of how they want to be found, nor do they understand what buying customers are typing into the search engines when looking for that company's product or service. Business owners often hold tight to a concept I call "ego keywords."

Ego keywords are the broad search terms owners get a physical rush over when thinking about seeing their name listed on the first page of the search results, such as "television, stationary, florist, etc." These terms get searched hundreds of thousands of times each month, and we get dizzy thinking about all that fantastic exposure. As business owners who want to run a successful search marketing campaign, we must release our ego and get in touch with our target customers online (specifically our target customer who is willing and ready to buy). Traditional marketing – print, radio, and television – has brainwashed us into thinking that a massive amount of exposure is fundamentally a very positive goal for a campaign. However, it is important for successful entrepreneurs to realize the Internet is a completely different ball game, and in the world of search engine marketing, you have to let go of the premise that the largest search volume number WINS! Instead, it is important to realize that 100 customers ready to buy your service trump 100,000 click-happy consumers who are just as likely to buy your television as download the latest YouTube video of a demented teenager microwaving a television. The tragedy here is that business owners do not realize that, unlike traditional marketing, when they bid on ego keywords, they are targeting the wrong customer and making it impossible for the right customer to find their site. You must utilize the amazing tools and resources in *Google™ Income: How Anyone of Any Age, Location, and/or Background Can Build a Highly Profitable Online Business with Google™* to truly understand how your perfect customer searches and when to enter yourself into their consideration process through Google™ search results and other Google™ services. Only then will you start to realize the power of Google™ and harness the potential of earning real, stable income via the Internet.

Dominate Your Search Results Pages...By Keyword Phrase

As Search Engine Marketers, our job is never done. We are always looking for the best tools, the expert secrets, and the one thing that will propel our clients to the top of search results pages. The most successful Search Engine Marketing campaigns understand it is not just one tactic such as Pay-Per-Click (PPC), Search Engine Optimization (SEO), and other powerful Google™ tools that will make or break your Internet success. It is how they all "dance" together on the search results pages. If you have a paid ad, an organic SEO listing, and a blog post all on the first search results page under an important keyword for your business ... **You Win!** You are the only game in town and they have no choice but to click on your search results. It is about the sum and not its parts. Remember, your job as a business owner with a Web site is to be found – the search engines will not do it for you. You have to use whatever search products and services are available that will position your business as the obvious expert on the page. Of course, your job is not done – the Web site must then deliver a conversion rich environment in order to get the purchase, download, or contact form you desire. Google™ Income will give you the tools and education to do just this ... dominate the search results and make the income you always wanted. Bruce has written a book that will take you there quickly and successfully.

Keep making every click count for your business and never stop learning.

Lutze Consulting
14 Inverness Drive East, A212
Englewood CO 80112
303-841-3111
hlutze@lutzeconsulting.com

Foreword Biography

A nationally recognized speaker, trainer, and consultant in search engine placement, cost per click models, natural search, and ad campaign tracking, Heather Lutze's speaking engagements are conducted in the same irreverent style of her book, *The Findability Formula*, delivering equal parts good information and good entertainment to audiences nationwide. Heather taught Yahoo! Advertiser Workshops for two years for Yahoo! Search Marketing across the U.S. from 2006-2007.

Heather is a member of the National Speaker's Association, the Colorado chapter of the NSA, and the Meeting Industry Council (MIC). She is a Certified Google™ AdWords Professional (one of only three in the country), has her Yahoo! Search Marketing Ambassador Certification, and is a Lead Trainer for the prestigious PPC Summit. She is also a Senior Editor for the Search Engine Marketing Journal (SEMJ) and is the author of *The Findability Formula, the Easy, Non-Technical Guide to Search Engine Marketing*, published by John Wiley and Sons, Inc., publishers of the tried and true CliffsNotes and the famed "For Dummies" series of reference books.

Heather began her Internet career as a Web designer and then became a Paid Search Manager at a large dot com in Denver, Colorado, where she was responsible for a multi-million dollar paid search budget.

Heather's favorite anecdote from the early days of business Web sites is this: "If I heard, 'If you build it they will come' one more time, I was going to scream, because it wasn't true. People didn't automatically come to a Web site; you had to figure out how to get them there."

In July of 2000, Heather founded Lutze Consulting in response to all the Web site owners who had paid for Web sites that were not performing. Indeed, it was her clients' frustration with getting traffic to their sites that was her inspiration for learning and mastering the art and science of search engine visibility. Heather became an expert at what works and what does not in producing consistent search marketing success.

PREFACE

According to **www.internetworldstats.com**, as of June 2008, 90.1 percent of the U.S. population had internet access. This is a growth rate of 130.9 percent from the year 2000.

Google™ has 62.9 percent of the U.S. market share as of September 2008 and during the month of September 2008, Google™ received over 7.4 billion search queries, according to comScore, Inc.

If you have a business or want to start a business, you need to know how to take advantage of Google™'s popularity by knowing how Google™ works and how to get your site better placement so that more people can find your Web site. This can be one of the most valuable skills that you can learn. A relatively small number of people really understand how Google™ works and how to use Google™ to make their business successful, until now.

Inside Bruce C. Brown's *Google Income*, you will find a reference for every part of your business planning process from how to start your business on Google™ and improve traffic flow to your site all the way to making it a profitable adventure and collecting payments.

It is a fact that you need to have your business listed as high as possible on Google™. This book can give you the necessary information on how to become a Google™ master and can also be used as a guide for finding out about anything on Google™. Because there is so much information out there it can be quite overwhelming and Google™ Income is designed so you can quickly find the areas that you need to learn and apply them. This book can also be used to gain a basic understanding about Google™ so that if you hire someone to help you improve your ranking on Google™, you will have a better understanding of what they are doing and people will be less likely to take advantage of you.

Getting started on Google™ is almost as easy as tying your shoe. All you need is a credit card, $5.00, and a basic understanding of computers and you can begin advertising your products and/or services to the world in about 15 minutes. Google™ is as complicated as it is easy-to-use. Just like watching a professional athlete perform, it looks very easy to do, but really is not. Anyone can pick up a football or baseball or kick a soccer ball just as anyone can open up a Google™ account; what separates the professional that is getting paid millions from the average person is the hard work, skill set, experience, understanding, and ability to learn. Bruce C. Brown will give you the information and tools you need in order to know what it takes to become a professional on Google™. The book itself will not make you a millionaire, but if you follow the advice and are dedicated to learning, then you will have all the tools you need to know how Google™ works and what it will take to make your Web site profitable.

Chris Hickman, founder and co-owner of Silver Scope Promotion, LLC.

9139 E. Milton Avenue

St. Louis, MO 63114

Phone: 314-497-9644

Company E-mail: info@SilverScopePromotion.con

Chris Hickman's E-mail: Chris@SilverScopepromotion.com

Preface Biography

Chris Hickman is the founder and co-owner of Silver Scope Promotion, LLC., one of the world's leading search engine marketing firms. Silver Scope Promotion has helped thousands of clients worldwide to have an effective and profitable online presence. A very small number of firms worldwide have the status that Silver Scope Promotion has, being a Google™ Qualified Company and Yahoo Search Marketing Ambassador. Chris provides search engine marketing and consulting services in pay-per-click advertising, search engine optimization, Web site analytics, split testing, consumer behavior improvement, landing page development, and copy writing. Starting the company while in college, Chris graduated from the University of Missouri St. Louis with a Bachelor's degree in Management Information Systems and a minor in Math. Chris has almost eight years of search engine marketing experience.

INTRODUCTION

This book was a tremendous challenge to me. This is the eighth book I have written, six of which were related to online marketing, blogs, e-mail marketing, Google™, and pay-per-click advertising. The number of tools, services, and applications Google™ offers is mind-boggling. Building an online business is a tremendous, yet rewarding challenge. I know, I have built successful online businesses and helped others to achieve success.

The power of Google™ is a critical component to obtaining success on the Web. We know that Google™ is an incredibly powerful search engine, and the world's most popular. This book is intended for using Google™ in establishing, promoting, expanding, and developing your business, while harnessing the power of Google™ to maximize your income stream. We will cover a variety of applications from Google™ that you can use to generate income, such as AdWords and AdSense, and we will also explore how other Google™ applications can be used to generate Web site traffic and help you with marketing, analysis, promotions, and increased revenue streams. We will spend considerable time exploring, understanding, and explaining how search engine optimization for the Google™ Search Engine can yield dramatic results in how "visible" your Web site is to the search engine and teach you how to ensure you are consistently at the top of the Google™ Search Engine results rankings.

One of the most incredible facts about Google™ is that most of the Google™ applications are absolutely free to use, including the Google™ Search Engine. Obtaining success when starting an online business and achieving high search engine rankings involves a combination of many factors, starting with excellent overall Web site design with proper search engine optimization techniques, culminating with an effective Web site marketing strategy that maximizes your potential for high rankings and ultimately increased revenues or Web site traffic. My goal is to reveal how you can leverage Google™ to start your own online business, increase your income, and ensure consistent search engine rankings through the Google™ Search Engine. High rankings in search engine results equate to increased Web site traffic, which should lead to a growing customer base, corporate growth, and profitability.

In this book, we will explore pay-per-click advertising through Google™, as well as a variety of other tools and applications available from Google™. Pay-per-click advertising is simply a marketing and advertising technique where you are allowed to place your advertisements on Web sites and major search engines' results pages. We will explore Google™™ AdWords, AdSense, Google™ Gmail℠, Google™ Book Search, Google™ Base, Google™ Product Search, Google™ Desktop, Google™ Labs, YouTube, the Google™ Search Engine, and much more.

Who this Book is For

This book is written for anyone who has a business or is considering developing an online business, or companies with an established online presence who wish to expand their marketing campaigns by using the power of Google™ to help them gain customers and increase Web site traffic and income. This book is a practical, hands-on guide for how to harness the power of Google™. As with all my books, my primary goal is to provide you with a ready reference that you can refer to often as you achieve success in the online marketplace.

How this Book is Organized

This book is broken down into manageable chapters that cover a variety of topics and products relevant to Google™. Here is a brief summary of what is contained in this book:

Brief History of Google & Online Marketing

A condensed version of the history of Google™ and how it grew to be the world's most popular search engine. Additionally, we will discuss the evolution of online marketing and the different types of campaigns/marketing strategies employed by Web site operatosrs to promote their businesses through search engines, free marketing, and pay-per-click marketing programs.

Developing a Successful Marketing Plan with Google

A brief presentation and review of how to develop a marketing plan for an online business and incorporate the wide variety of Google™ functions into your business plan.

Optimize your Web site for the Google™ Search Engine to Generate Traffic & Income: Practical, proven advice on how to generate Web site traffic with Google™, increase overall Web site visibility, generate Web site traffic, and achieve higher results rankings in the Google™ Search Engine.

Introduction to Pay-Per-Click Marketing

An introduction to pay-per-click marketing, how it works, how it compares to other marketing techniques, and how to effectively design a pay-per-click marketing campaign to achieve maximum financial success. We will walk through the process of how pay-per-click works, what happens when a site visitor clicks on an advertisement, how it is tracked, and how this generates traffic and ultimately increases income.

Using Google AdWords

This chapter is a comprehensive introduction to Google™ AdWords, Google™'s pay-per-click application. This chapter includes instructions for detailed setup, campaign design, and management of all your Google™ AdWords campaigns.

Creating an Effective Google Pay-Per-Click Advertising Campaign: Keywords, Key Phrases, & Your Google AdWords Budget

This chapter focuses on how to effectively choose keywords and key phrases to maximize the effectiveness of Google™ AdWords pay-per-click marketing campaigns and how to manage your pay-per-click budget.

Increase Profits by Combating Fraud with Google AdWords

A comprehensive guide to help you understand pay-per-click fraud, identify it, combat it, and preserve the integrity and financial stability of your pay-per-click campaign. Fraud is the No. 1 problem facing pay-per-click marketing campaigns, and we show you how to be successful in combating it in conjunction with Google™ AdWords.

Increase Profits & Generate Income with Google AdSense

Google™ AdSense is a good application that lets you generate income by allowing others' pay-per-click advertisements to be placed on your Web site. This no-cost Google™ program is an excellent way to increase income, if you do not mind some ads on your Web site.

Google Base & Google Product Search

Free Tools to Generate Income and Promote your Products and Web site: Google™ Base is a place where you can easily publish virtually anything online, such as books, manuscripts, resumes, and recipes. Google™ Product Search, formally called Froogle, lets you list products for sale and search for the best prices on products. Google™ Base and Google™ Product Search dramatically improve exposure of your virtual storefront to unlimited markets. We will show you how and why you should be using both of these applications.

Proven Methods Using Google to Generate Income through Traditional and Affiliate Marketing

This chapter is an introduction to traditional marketing methods that you can use in conjunction with Google™, as well as how to effectively deploy an affiliate marketing campaign. When used in conjunction with an effective Google™ AdWords pay-per-click or other Google™ search engine optimization program, these methods will increase Web site traffic and generate additional revenue by harnessing the power of the Google™ search engine.

Google Web Services & APIs: Harnessing the Power of Google

An introduction to Google™ Web Services, the Google™ API, and how you can use the Google™ API to build better custom search results. While APIs are designed for developers, this chapter introduces you to what APIs are available for which applications, in the event that you wish to expand and automate your web services with Google™ applications.

Google and Blogs: A partnership to Generate Income

Use the power of Google™ and Google™'s free blog application, "blogger," to create sophisticated blogs to complement your Web site and use the phenomenal power of blogs to promote your online business and products. Blogs are an amazingly effectively marketing tool, which Google™ lets you use for free.

More Tools to Harness the Power of Google

Google™ is so much more than "just a search engine." This chapter opens the door to how you can leverage Google™ and other applications to empower your Web site, expand business lines, increase Web site traffic, and generate income. This includes GmailSM, Google™ Checkout, iGoogle™, Orkut, Google™ Talk, Google™ Chrome, Google™ Local Business Center, and more.

Interviews with Google Industry Experts

I spent countless hours seeking out and interviewing world-renowned Google™ experts and captured their insightful interview responses in this chapter. Learn from the best, and apply their advice to your Google™ development and marketing plans.

Google Case Studies

How did others succeed? Read some case studies and realize the potential power, success, and possibilities you too can achieve with Google™.

Recommended Reference Library

This is my list of "must have" reference books to help you develop your "portfolio" for success.

Glossary

Glossary of relevant terms and definitions.

This book will provide you with the tools and knowledge to harness Google™ to achieve increased Web site traffic and generate income for you and your business, empowering your marketing and advertising campaigns to be efficient and effective. You will learn how to optimize your Web site and blog for the best possible rankings in search engine results on Google™, as well as all other search engines. After reading this book and applying the principles and techniques contained within, you will empower your business and business Web site to achieve the ultimate goal of increased Web site traffic and increased income by tapping into the resources readily available from Google™.

I provide you with all the tools and steps you need to take to maximize and harness the power of the Internet to promote and market your business and products through Google™, as well as the formulas for success in developing your overall Web site strategy, design philosophy, and Search Engine Optimization and alternative marketing strategies. If you follow the guiding principles contained in this book, you will be successful in harnessing the impressive power, flexibility, and cost-effectiveness of Google™.

A Brief History of Google & Online Marketing

This chapter is not intended to be a history lesson, but there is some value in understanding how Google™ came to be the industry giant they are now. Founded in a garage, Google™ has grown to dominate the search engine industry and has expanded well beyond the boundaries of simply being a good search engine. We all use Google™ applications, daily whether it is Google™ Maps, Google™ Product Search, Gmail, YouTube, or another application.

Google™ was founded by two college students while attending Stanford University. It literally started out in a garage and grew quickly to the giant among search engines. From there, Google™ has since expanded beyond it's original mission of creating the best search engine to what it is today. In 1996 Larry Page and Sergey Brin created Google™ as a research project to prove that their methodology for search engine rankings based on relationships between sites versus results based strictly on search terms would return better results. In 1998 Google™ incorporated (still operating out of a garage) and quickly took over the internet as the most popular search engine. Throughout this book we'll discuss how Google™ is much more than just a powerful search engine, boasting an array of applications and tools which are all designed to improve your Web site visibility in the Google™ search engine, generate Web site traffic and create revenue streams for you.

Development of Online Marketing

Online marketing techniques have been around since the invention & creation of the World Wide Web. As Web sites were developed into online businesses targeting increased revenues for traditional brick and mortar business, the importance and prominence of online marketing became a dominating force in the industry. Just as the Google™ Search Engine rose in prominence to become the world's most popular engine, businesses adapted marketing plans to achieve the highest possible Google™ rankings. Today, there are hundreds of thousands of businesses who exist solely on the Internet and do not maintain a traditional retail brick-and-mortar storefront. To fully understand how to take advantage of Google™ in conjunction with the development of advertising and marketing campaigns, it is important to understand the development of online marketing and the variety of Web-based marketing techniques employed to increase market share.

Marketing and advertising for a traditional brick-and-mortar business can be a costly venture. Postage and mailing costs are high, and return rates on mailings are typically a dismal 1 percent or less of the total mailing.

Internet Marketing

Internet marketing is simply the fusion of traditional marketing which includes public relations, customer service and retail sales, with Web-based electronic commerce, and other forms of online advertising such as pay-per-click, affiliate marketing and more. In the early 1990s, Internet Marketing was a new frontier in advertising and sales. Typically, commercial Web sites were nothing more than a corporate public relations presence with generalized information about a company and/or its products and services. As technology improved, along with the understanding of the Hyper Text Markup Language (HTML), the predominant language for the creation of Web sites improved, and commercial Web sites evolved into little more than online brochures and catalogs of corporate product lines. These were designed to allow a potential customer to do research and explore the products online, and then go to the brick-and-mortar retail outlet or place a phone call order to the company.

Since credit card payment processing was readily available in retail outlets, and there was no security available online for processing credit cards, deployment of online sales was minimal. Thousands of companies allowed customers to place credit card orders using basic HTML order forms, which captured the unencrypted credit card information, recklessly sending potentially harmful personal financial information throughout the Internet. As awareness of credit card fraud and theft increased, savvy Web customers refrained from placing credit card orders online for fear of comprising personal financial data.

Everything changed with the development of encryption methods and secure site technology. Data could be captured securely and transmitted over the Internet in an encrypted format to protect data online. Since the development of encryption technology, online purchasing has exploded, and it is expected to grow exponentially in the future. Small startup companies like Amazon have grown into online sales powerhouses.

Internet Advertising

Advertising may be defined as any paid form of communication about an organization and its products and/or services by an identified, and typically paid, sponsor. Online marketing and advertising campaigns were designed to replicate existing advertisement, which was designed for traditional advertising outlets, including print media, such as newspapers, books, and magazines, and multi-media advertising, such as television and radio. With the expansion of the Internet, and realization of the potential impact on customer sales-base and revenues, online advertising was born, and the Google™ search engine has been powering that explosive growth.

In 2008, online advertising and marketing matured and became quite refined, largely due to Google™ and their suite of applications, such as AdSense and AdWords. Technology, population growth, and the increasing number of households with broadband Internet access have pushed advances in technology in the online advertising world, generating billions of dollars in sales annually. Despite recent downturns in the economy, online sales have been dramatically less impacted than traditional retail storefronts.

Types of Online Advertisements

Three major areas that continue to own the majority of the online market share are:

- Paid search advertisement (Pay-Per-Click)
- Banner advertisements
- Classified ads

Understanding Banner Advertising

Banner Advertising is simply a form of online advertising where Web developers embed an advertisement into the HTML code of a Web page. The idea is that the banner advertisement will catch the attention of Web site visitors, and they will click on the ad to get more information about the products or services advertised. When clicked, the banner ad will take the Web browser to the Web site operated by the advertiser. A banner ad can be created in a variety of formats, such as .GIF, .JPG or .PNG. Banner ads can be static images, or they can employ a variety of scripting codes, Java, or other advanced techniques, such as animated .GIFs or rollover images, to create rotating banner advertisements, which change every few seconds. Over the past five years, Shockwave and Macromedia Flash technology have become increasingly popular to incorporate animation, sound, and action into banner advertisements. Banner ads are created in a variety of shapes and sizes, depending on the site content and design, and are designed to be placed unobtrusively in the "white" space available in a traditionally designed Web page.

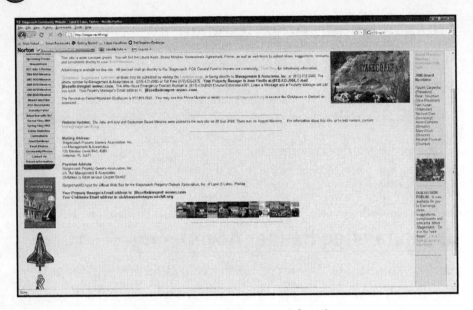

Sample Web Page with Banner Advertisements
Reprinted with Permission, Bruce C. Brown

When a page is loaded into a Web browser, such as Microsoft®
Internet Explorer or Mozilla Firefox®, the banner is loaded onto
the page, creating what is called an "impression." An impression
simply means that the Web page containing the advertisement
was loaded and potentially viewed by someone who is browsing
that Web site. Impressions are important to advertisers to track
how many visitors loaded that particular page (and banner ad)
in a set period of time. If the impression count is low, it is logical that the click-through rate, and subsequent sales, will also be
extremely low. When the Web site visitor clicks on the banner ad,
the browser is navigated to the Web site it is linked to, and the
Web site is loaded into the browser. The process of a site visitor
clicking on a banner ad with their mouse is commonly called a
"click-through."

Click-throughs are important to advertisers to track how many visitors actually clicked on a particular banner ad, and how many resultant sales are generated by the banner ad in a set period of time. Unfortunately, a high click-through rate does not necessarily guarantee or equate to high sales. We will discuss many techniques on how to properly design your Web site and maximize your search engine optimization techniques for the Google™ search engine. Banner ads can be made static (embedded within the actual HTML page) by the Webmaster, or may be "served" through a central server, which enables advertisers to display a wide variety of banner ads on thousands of Web sites with minimal effort.

Most banner ads currently work on a per-click system, where the advertiser pays for each click on the banner ad, regardless of whether that click results in a sale. Originally, advertisers simply paid for the ad space on a Web site — usually for a preset period of time, such as a week or month — and hoped that someone would see the banner ad and click on it to visit their site. Banner advertising is typically a low-cost investment per click (usually less than 10 cents per click), and the banner provider or hosting company then bills the advertising on a pre-determined basis, such as monthly. The key difference between banner advertising and pay-per-click advertising is that banner advertisements are placed within the content of Web pages, while pay-per-click advertising is not image based, and may be dynamically generated based on a search results.

Banner Advertising was extremely popular in the 1990s and early 2000s, and is still commonly used today; however, it is less effective and even less popular than other advertising techniques, such as pay-per-click advertising. Banner advertising is commonly used today with affiliate marketing techniques and is designed to inform potential customers or consumers about the products or services offered by the advertiser, just like traditional print advertising. However, banner ads offer the advantage of allowing advertisers to track individual statistics and performance at a level not possible with print media advertising.

Sample Banner Advertisements
Reprinted with Permission Atlantic Publishing Group, Inc.

When banner ads were originally created, they were highly successful, but as Web surfers became Web savvy, these ads were viewed as annoying and often distracted from the actual Web site content. Web browsers such as Windows® Internet Explorer and Mozilla Firefox® contain built-in pop-up blockers designed to suppress banner advertisements. If you choose to pursue banner ads on your Web site or through others to generate revenue and traffic, you will want to follow the guidelines outlined for proper Search Engine Optimization with the Google™ Search Engine.

Static Versus Dynamic Web Sites

Many Web sites are "static" in content. They are simple to build and maintain, but offer no "interactive" type of experience. Internet advertising was primarily limited to static, server-based, banner advertising served up to static Web pages. The development of database-driven Web sites created an entirely new experience for Web site visitors, enabling them to enter data into a Web site and receiving dynamically generated content based on their query.

Rich Media has evolved in the past year into the recycling of television advertisements and incorporating full TV commercials onto the Internet. Floating and expanding banners are increasingly popular, and equally frustrating to the Web site visitor. Floating and expanding ads use motion and appear to float across the screen, blocking the view of the actual Web site content, and often requiring a click to close the ad, although most disappear based on a time interval. Sound embedded in banner advertisements is becoming increasingly common. Podcasts, blogs, and RSS broadcasts have also become prevalent.

You should now have a general understanding of the variety of advertisement campaigns in existence and how they relate to the Google™ Search Engine. Throughout the remaining chapters, you will put much of this information to use as you develop marketing and advertising business plans to harness the power of Google™, increase Web site traffic, and generate income.

CHAPTER 2

Developing a Successful Marketing Plan with Google

While this book is not designed to teach you how to design an effective marketing plan, it is critical that you at least have the fundamentals of a marketing plan in place. An essential step before you begin to implement Google™ Marketing on your Web site is crafting a well-thought-out marketing plan for your business. I firmly believe that a Marketing Plan is critical for you to map out your future goals. Writing a marketing plan is a fairly straight forward process requiring you to set clear objectives and methods for achieving them. In our case, we will tie our action plans to achieve our objectives to the tools and applications offered by Google™.

A marketing plan must be achievable, realistic, cost-effective, measurable, and flexible. With Google™, the process of creating an online marketing plan is simplified, since Google™ offers a wide array of products that will assist you with developing a comprehensive marketing plan, including Google™ AdWords, Google™ AdSense, and Google™ Product Search.

One of the main objectives in developing a marketing plan is to establish your budget. Your marketing plan may consist of:

- Market Analysis

- Business Objectives

- Marketing Strategies

- Steps to achieving business objectives

- A realistic budget

- A realistic schedule

Performing a Market Analysis

You need to be flexible, considering your budget, marketplace competition, business objectives, and internal and external influences. Essentially, market analysis helps you determine whether there is a need for your supplies or services. Understanding the marketplace — the desire for your products and competition — helps you determine the key information that will be essential to establishing a successful business in a competitive environment. If there is no need for your products, you will likely fail unless you establish your presence in the marketplace. Likewise, if there is a high level of competition, you must develop a marketing plan that allows you to compete with significant competition in product, quality, availability, or price. Knowing the marketplace's needs and how they are currently served provides you with key information that is essential in developing your product or service and marketing plan. You must separate yourself from your competition by price, service, quality, or other characteristics that make you desirable in a highly competitive marketplace.

Web designers will design a Web site to your specifications and set up an e-commerce enabled site for you to sell your products, but you cannot realistically expect customers to find you. The next chapter on search engine optimization is critical for all Web sites, particularly for new Web sites, to achieve search engine rankings and indexing with Google™ and all other major engines. But even if you achieve fantastic search engine ranking results, if there is no demand or desire for your products or services, you will ultimately fail. Marketplace analysis must be done in advance to ensure there is a viable market for your products or services.

The following questions will help you to perform a basic market analysis:

- What market am I trying to enter?

- What is my current competition?

- How successful is my competition?

- What is the market share of my competition?

- Is the market saturated or open?

- What is the market size? Is there room to grow?

- Is there stability in the market or is it volatile?

- How are my competitors marketing their goods or services?

- What do customers seek in regard to my products? What is most valuable to them?

- What are customers willing to pay for my products or services?

- What do I offer that my competition does not?

- What effect will the current economy have on my business goals?

You should analyze current or previous marketing strategies, as well as those of your competition, both successful and unsuccessful. Understanding failure is as important as understanding success. These questions may help you analyze your potential for success in a competitive marketplace:

- Am I offering a new product line, new service, or unique product?

- What marketing strategies have I (or my competition) used successfully? What was unsuccessful? Have I used online marketing in the past? What was the success rate or return on investment?

- Have I evaluated the results of previous marketing plans (e.g., print advertising, pay-per-click, and e-mail marketing)? What was the impact on sales?

- Are we using any strategies currently?

- What strategies are my competitors using currently?

- How much money is allotted in my current budget? How much am I currently spending? How much was my marketing budget in the past?

- Why would someone choose our product over our competition?

- What do we do to distinguish ourselves from our competition?

- Why would someone trust us more than our competition?

- Who are our customers?

- Where do our customers come from?

You must perform primary and secondary research. Primary research includes phone interviews, surveys, Web-based surveys, focus groups, and other information-gathering techniques based on the marketplace. Primary research will give you the most current information available. Secondary research is data that has already been collected for other purposes, but may assist you with your market research. Examples of secondary research may be libraries, blogs, or other resources.

Since we are concentrating on generating increased income through Google™, and your primary area of concern is competition from other online businesses, it makes sense that most of your market analysis would be performed by using the Internet. The Internet contains a wealth of analytical information, and may prove to be your greatest ally in performing market analysis.

Establishing Business Objectives

Many new businesses will fail within the first few years of their launch. Although this statistic also applies to online businesses, you do have some distinct advantages over traditional brick-and-mortar businesses, as well as some overarching challenges. You may have fewer employees, less building space, and, most importantly, less overhead. However, without the traditional storefront, you also do not have a physical presence; instead, you have a virtual presence online. You need to develop a long-range business plan that will map out your path toward success. You may have heard this called a strategic plan, or strategic goals. This plan is simply your goals, objectives and timelines in a written format. This document is intended to be "living," and can be easily adjusted based on the current operating environment. You will need to complete your market analysis for assistance in preparing your long-range business objectives. The point of business objectives is not to predict the future, but to establish the desired course of action, setting strategic goals along the way. Your objectives should be attainable, and they must be measurable so you can evaluate your success in meeting (or failing to meet) them.

If you are an existing business, you should first perform a comprehensive evaluation of your current business state. What have you or have you not accomplished? Are you profitable, or operating at a loss? What and who is your competition? What are the industry trends in relation to your products or services? Use resources to help you research and establish your business objectives, such as the Small Business Administration, Chamber of Commerce, and industry associations. Similar research and market analysis must be completed for new online businesses as well.

Document your initial findings and business objectives. Review goals with your employees, as they may provide input or ideas you have not thought about. Ensure your plan addresses all aspects of your organization, such as sales, marketing, human resources, advertising, customer service, and information technology.

Develop a mission statement for your company. A mission statement is a statement that captures your organization's purpose, customer orientation, and business philosophy. Share your mission statement with employees, and post it prominently. You must have employee "buy-in" to your mission statement if you want employees to share your vision and help you achieve your strategic objectives.

Ensure that you update your business objectives at least annually, perhaps even semi-annually, during your initial operating years. Remember, your business objectives must be realistic, attainable, and flexible.

Establishing Marketing Strategies

You must establish a clearly defined, written strategy and marketing plan for your online business. You must consider all marketing strategies and implement those that are most relevant to your business operations and offer the most potential for increased customer base and return on investment. Your marketing strategy must be realistic and measurable. If you do not measure the results of your marketing campaign, you cannot evaluate its effectiveness or be ready to implement a shift in strategy. At a minimum, your marketing strategy should include:

- A profile of the target consumer

- Competitive market analysis

- Distribution plans for your products

- A product price strategy

- An advertising budget

- Advertising & marketing strategy analysis to evaluate potential methods

- Your corporation's vision and business objectives

- Brand uniqueness or image for your products

- Evaluation of your products and services

- Distinction of your company/products from competitors

Implement and evaluate your marketing strategy as it relates to achieving your corporate business objectives. Some marketing plans may take significant time and investment: think long-term, and do not be quick to change your objectives because you are not realizing the goals in your specified schedules. Be flexible, but allow your marketing strategies time to grow and mature.

Your online marketing plan does not need to be overly complex and should not be a time-consuming process; however, it is important to map out your objectives, budget, and critical success factors so you can measure and evaluate your success in achieving them. An average marketing plan may be less than a couple of pages in length and is a "map" for your company to achieve success on the Internet.

Media exposure is a key component in your successful marketing profile and strategy. Your customers will form their opinions (positive or negative) based on what they hear and see in the media. Recognizing the importance of media exposure, and dedicating resources to promote your online business, can boost the sales of your products or services. That positive media exposure is also a major step toward maintaining credibility in your online marketplace and ensuring that you compel visitors to channel more traffic to your Web site — ultimately increasing volume and revenue for your online business.

Developing a tactical approach to media exposure should be part of your overall business objectives and marketing plan. There are several things you can do to promote your offline media exposure, including the following:

- Approach your local chamber of commerce and request that they write a short article about you and your business; even if you are an online-only business, the local exposure is helpful. You can then take that article and publish it on your Web site as another promotion tool or use it in an online e-zine campaign.

- Offer to be a speaker at a seminar or lead a workshop in your area of expertise. This is a good way to gain media exposure that is incredibly positive and community oriented, thus building you credibility and trust among potential clients. Circulate your URL and business information at the seminar; put your Web site URL on everything you distribute, such as flyers, promotional items, business cards, and letterhead.

- Follow up any correspondence or phone calls from the media with a letter or phone call. Make sure to leave your Web site URL on their voice mail. This strategy builds you media exposure by building a reputation as a conscientious, courteous entrepreneur.

Share your knowledge by writing articles and professional opinions for online publications, and upload them to automated, e-zine syndication sites. These syndication sites are perfect for having immediate hotlinks back to your Web site and other specific landing pages. Remember to include your e-mail or picture in the byline as well as brief biographical information on yourself and your business. The more exposure you generate, the more successful your business will become. Give permission to authors to use your articles in their books, magazine, or publications, and be sure to require them to include a corporate biography and contact information in exchange for the permission.

Develop tactics to make media exposure and coverage work for you. Make media friends wherever and whenever the opportunity presents itself, all in an effort to increase media awareness and promote public relations. You are going to have to earn media exposure, but the time and effort you expend will be rewarded when you create a positive public profile, both on- and offline.

Most columnists will give their e-mail address in their byline at the conclusion of their article. Send them a note with your comments and views, while offering your expertise as a source for future quotes. Optimize your media exposure whenever possible; the returns for your business will be substantial.

Gaining the Trust of Clients

Gaining the trust of your customers is extremely critical in developing a continuing relationship that rewards your online business with repeat customer sales. The one-time sale may boost your immediate sales numbers, but it is returning customers who take your business from mediocre to fantastic profits. Your goal is to build quality customer relationships and then maintain them. Gaining media exposure, both online and offline, opens the doors to a potentially long-term relationship with customers by using implied third-party credibility, thus legitimizing you as the expert in your field. Once you attract the prospects, you still have to deliver your goods/services and ensure that the customer is completely satisfied. One of the major advantages of using Google™ marketing tools is that Google™'s reputation is superior, and you can leverage that reputation and trust in your marketing campaigns.

Increasing Your Public Profile

The more positive your public profile, the more success you will have. Your public profile is your trademark for success and profits, and your online profile and business rating is critically important to how customers perceive you. Your local and state Better Business Bureaus are good organizations to join and obtain positive ratings with. Other online business profile ratings services worth considering are **www.resellerratings.com**,

www.epinions.com, and **www.consumerreports.org**. Do not underestimate the impact of a review of your business and/or products and services. Many decisions have been made based entirely on the review of others in regards to purchases. You must ensure 100 percent customer satisfaction in both service and product quality to ensure you gain only positive reviews for your company.

You want to establish a successful, upbeat profile that is based on your confidence and credibility, supported by your products, services, and superior customer service and satisfaction. You can increase your public profile by taking advantage of opportunities that allow you to use your services and knowledge in a variety of venues, thereby gaining public awareness and online marketing exposure, without spending your own funds on relatively expensive advertising.

Positioning yourself, and becoming an expert in your market, takes time, patience, and confidence. Just knowing the advantages of effective marketing is half the battle. It is the combination of media and marketing that communicates the benefits and unique aspects of your business, which in turn drives customers to your Web site. When you establish yourself as an expert in your market, others will be drawn to you for advice, sponsorship, professional opinion, and branding — all of which will have dramatic, positive impacts on your online business.

Your goal when it comes to sharing your expertise is to publish for free, thereby allowing many other organizations, news services, and other publications or magazines to distribute your article throughout their network in return for Web site links back to your Web site and direct product promotions to thousands of potential new customers. There are ways that you can publish a full-page ad promoting yourself and your business without spending a dime. Contact editors of publications and offer them your press release to add content to their next publication. Many editors are looking for useful, relevant content so they can meet deadlines. Take advantage of this opportunity by creating the perfect article for publication. Always ensure that you require a corporate biography and full contact information to be published with your articles.

You should target newspapers, magazines, newsletters, Web sites, and Web magazines as ideal opportunities for displaying your article. Magazines that have both an offline and an online image are excellent for increased exposure for driving customers to your Web site. Knowing your products, market, competition, and other factors before you begin to develop your Web site, marketing, and promotion plans is a critical success factor. Being armed with marketplace knowledge in advance will help you achieve success in the marketplace.

Optimizing your Web Site for Google — Generating Web Site Traffic & Income

To achieve success with the Google™ Search Engine, you must achieve high rankings in search results. Often, the most over-looked factor in Web site development is the optimization of your Web site for search engines. This chapter focuses entirely on the Google™ Search Engine, but when you get your site op-timized for Google™, you will reap the benefits from all major search engines. I feel one of the most critical steps in designing and implementing a successful Web site and marketing campaign is to invest in a search engine optimization plan for your Web site to ensure that it is designed to work effectively with all major search engines. Search engine optimization should be an ongo-ing process that you begin and consistently re-evaluate on a pe-riod basic. There are over two billion Web pages on the Internet, meaning that there are many Web sites that are directly compet-ing with yours for potential customers — often, your competitors may be selling identical products to yours. You need to take real-istic, time-proven measures to ensure that your online business gets noticed and obtains search engine rankings that will deliver the results you desire.

Search engine optimization (SEO) consists of a variety of proven techniques that you can use to push up the ranking of your Web site within your target market on the Internet by using keywords that are relevant and appropriate to the product or services that you are selling on your Web site. You should design your site with SEO in mind — building it right is much easier and more effective than building it wrong and having to retrofit it to meet World Wide Web Consortium (W3C) compliance and SEO optimization standards.

W3C produces the guidelines and standards by which Web pages should be created, constructed, and maintained. Essentially, these are the "best practices," and industry recognized standards. A W3C compliant Web site ensures that it is accessible, navigable, works across multiple browser platforms, and can be read by readers, PDAs, mobile devices, and displays properly regardless of monitor size, browser type, resolution, or type of monitor (standard versus widescreen). Detailed information can be found at **www.w3.org**.

Another term you will hear commonly now is Web 2.0. Web 2.0 is not an application or a physical standard. Instead, it is a generalized term to describe the Web "movement," or the latest trends and direction for using technology and Web site design to improve communication sharing, collaboration, and data exchange. Web 2.0 is synonymous with the expansive popularity of YouTube, Orkut, Facebook®, MySpace®, and other social networking sites.

When you implement an SEO plan, you make sure that your Web site is "visible" in search engines, and is subsequently found by potential customers. SEO accomplishes this by taking the keywords that people may use to search for your products or services on the Internet using a search engine and placing them in title pages, meta tags, and the content of your Web site. Additionally, there are many other factors that affect the indexing and ranking of your pages in each search engine.

When you properly use SEO and optimize your Web site based on sound Web design principles, you know that your site is ready to be submitted to search engines and that you will significantly increase its visibility and ranking within the search engines. Focus on the content on each Web page, and strive to include at least 200 content-related words on the pages of your site. Integrate your keywords into the content you place on each page, but be cautious of "keyword stuffing," which is where you over-load the pages with keywords, which may result in being blacklisted from major search engines.

Google™ uses PageRank™, which measures the quality of a Web page based on the incoming and outgoing links from that page. This led to a huge increase in the emphasis on links to and from Web sites, in an effort to increase one's PageRank™ score. Google™ has since changed its algorithm to eliminate links it deems low in quality, lacking Web content, or not relevant topically (e.g., linking your cosmetics Web site to a Web site that sells parts for John Deere tractors). PageRank™ is not just based upon the total number of inbound links. PageRank™ considers some links more important than others; therefore, all links do not count equally. The ranking algorithm for Google™ is complicated, but in general, a higher PageRank™ score equates to better search engine placement in the Google™ Search Engine — therefore, quality inbound links are critical.

You can check out the ranking for any Web site, page, or domain name at **www.prchecker.info/check_page_rank.php**.

Successful Search Engine Optimization

Understanding the concepts and actions necessary for successful SEO can sometimes be confusing and hard to grasp when you are first starting out using SEO techniques. There are several steps that need to be followed so that you get the most out of your SEO. Some of these steps include:

- Making sure that your Web site is designed correctly and set up for optimal SEO

- Choosing the right keywords that are going to bring the most hits to your Web site

- Using the right title tags to identify you within search engines

- Ensuring appropriate content writing on your Web site

- Using properly formatted "meta tags" on your Web site

- Choosing the right search engines to submit your Web site to

- Understanding free and paid listing service options

- Having quality inbound links to your Web site

- Ensuring that every image on your site has an "ALT" tag

Once you know which areas to focus on, your ranking in search engines will increase dramatically. The main problem with SEO, and the #1 reason most site builders fail to properly ensure a site is optimized, is that it requires significant time investment and patience to obtain high rankings in search engines. SEO will not get you immediate visibility in search engines. You need to be realistic in your expectations — expect it to take months to see tangible results.

Meta Tag Definition and Implementation

Meta tags are a key part of the overall SEO program that you need to implement for your Web site. There remains controversy surrounding the use of meta tags and whether their inclusion on Web sites truly impacts search engine rankings, but I am convinced they are still an integral part of a sound SEO plan, and some search engines do use these tags in their indexing process. You will find conflicting guidance on whether Google™ uses them or ignores them. You do need to be aware that you are competing against potentially thousands (or more) of other Web sites, often promoting similar products, using similar keywords, and employing other SEO techniques to achieve a top search engine ranking. Meta tags have never guaranteed top rankings on crawler-based search engines, but they may offer a degree of control and the ability for you to impact how your Web pages are indexed within the search engines.

When it comes to using keywords and key phrases in your meta-keywords tag, use only those keywords and phrases that you have included within the Web content on each of your Web pages. It is also important that you use the plural forms of keywords so that both the singular and the plural will end up in any search that people do in search engines using specific keywords and key phrases. Other keywords that you should include in your meta keyword tags are any words that are the misspelling of your keywords and phrases. Since many people commonly misspell certain words, and you want to make sure that search engines can still find you.

Do not repeat your most important keywords and key phrases more than four to five times in a meta keyword tag. Another thing to keep in mind is that if your product or service is specific to a certain location geographically, you should mention this location (e.g., Washington DC, District of Columbia) in your meta-keyword tag.

Meta tags comprise formatted information that is inserted into the "head" section of each page on your Web site. To view the "head" of a Web page, you must view it in HTML mode, rather than in the browser view. In Internet Explorer, you can click on the Toolbar on the VIEW menu and then click on SOURCE to view the source of any individual Web page. If you are using a design tool, such as Adobe® Dreamweaver® CS3, Microsoft® SharePoint Designer® 2007, or Microsoft® Expression® Web Designer, you will need to use the HTML view to edit the source code of your Web pages. You can also use Notepad to edit your HTML source code.

This is a simple basic layout of a standard HTML Web page:

```
<!DOCTYPE HTML PUBLIC "-//W3C//DTD HTML 4.01//EN"

<HTML>

    <HEAD>

        <TITLE>This is the Title of My Web Page</TITLE>

    </HEAD>

    <BODY>

        <P>This is my Web page!

    </BODY>

</HTML>
```

Every Web page conforms to this basic page layout, and all contain the opening <HEAD> and closing </HEAD> tags. Meta tags will be inserted between the opening and closing head tags. Other than the page title tag, which is shown above, no other information in the head section of your Web pages is viewed by Web site visitors as they browse your Web pages. The title tag is displayed across the top of the browser window and is used to provide a description of the contents of the Web page displayed. We will discuss each meta tag that may be contained within the "head" tags in depth.

The Title Tag

This is the first tag a search engine spider will read, and therefore, it is critical that the content you put in the title tag accurately represents the content of the corresponding Web page. Whatever text you place in the title tag (between <TITLE> and </TITLE>) will appear in the reverse bar of an individual's browser when they view your Web page. In the example above, the title of the Web page to the page visitor would read as "This is the Title of My Web Page." Titles should accurately describe the focus of that particular page and might also include your site or business name.

The title tag is also used as the words to describe your page when someone adds it to their "Favorites" list or "Bookmarks" list in popular browsers, such as Windows® Internet Explorer or Mozilla Firefox®. The title tag is the single most important tag in regard to search engine rankings. The title tag should be limited to 40 to 60 characters of text between the opening and closing HTML tags. All major Web crawlers will use the text of your title tag as the text they use for the title of your page in your listings as displayed in search engine results. Since the title and description tags typically appear in the search results page after completing a keyword search in the Web browser, it is critical that they be clearly and concisely written to attract the attention of site visitors. Not all search engines are alike: some will display the title and description tags in search results but use page content alone for ranking.

The Description Tag

The description tag enables you to control the description of your individual Web pages when the search engine crawlers, which support the description tag, index and spider the Web site. The description tag should be no more than 250 characters. This is an important meta tag, since all major search engines use it in some capacity for site indexing. A page's description meta tag gives Google™ and other search engines a summary of what the page is about. Also, you need to be aware that Google™'s Webmaster Tools provides you with a content analysis section, which will notify you if your meta tags are too short, too long, or duplicated too many times.

It is important to understand that search engines are not all the same, and that they index, spider, and display different search results for the same Web site. For example, Google™ ignores the description tag and generates its own description based on the content of the Web page. Although some major engines may disregard your description tags, it is highly recommended that you include the tag on each Web page, since some search engines do rely on the tag to index your site.

The Keywords Tag

A keyword is simply a word that may be used by Internet users when searching for information on the Internet; it is also a critical component to developing your pay-per-click campaign, which we will discuss in detail in later chapters. The keywords tag is not used much anymore, as it has been heavily abused in the past. Today, your page content is critical, while your keywords tags are limited or not used at all by spiders indexing your site. However, I recommend you do use the keywords tag in moderation. Using the best keywords to describe your Web site helps get those searchers to find your site in search engines. The keywords tag allows you to provide relevant text words or word combinations for crawler-based search engines to index.

The keywords tag is only supported by a few Web crawlers. Since most Web crawlers are content based (meaning they index your site based on the actual page content, not your meta tags), you need to incorporate as many keywords as possible into the actual content of your Web pages. For the engines that support the description tag, it is beneficial to repeat keywords within the description tag that appear on your actual Web pages — this increases the value of each keyword in relevance to your Web site page content. You need to use some caution with the keywords tag for the few search engines which support it, since repeating a particular keyword too many times within a keyword tag may actually hurt your Web site rankings.

If you look at the example earlier, you will notice that the keywords tag is the one that says <meta name="keywords" content=." The keywords you want to use should go between the quotation marks after the "content=" portion of the tag. It is suggested that you include up to 25 words or phrases, with each word or phrase separated by a comma.

To help you determine which keywords are the best to use on your site, visit **www.wordtracker.com**, a paid service that will walk you through this process. Wordtracker's suggestions are based on over 300 million keywords and phrases that people have used over the previous 130 days. A free alternative for determining which keywords are best is Google™ Rankings. We will go into keywords in depth in later chapters.

The Robots Tag

The robots tag lets you specify that a particular page within your site should or should not be indexed by a search engine, or links that should not be followed by search engine spiders. To keep search engine spiders from indexing a page, add the following text between your tags: `<META NAME="ROBOTS" CONTENT="NOINDEX">`. To keep search engine spiders from following links on your page, add the following text between your tags: `<META NAME="ROBOTS" CONTENT="NOFOLLOW">`. You do not need to use variations of the robots tag to get your pages indexed since your pages will be spidered and indexed by default; however, some Web designers include the following robots tag on all Web pages: `<meta name="robots" content="ALL">`.

Other Meta Tags

There are many other meta tags, but most provide amplifying information about a Web site and its owner and do not have any impact on search engine rankings. Some of these tags may be used by internal corporate divisions. In our example earlier, you can see some examples of other meta tags that can be incorporated (note that this is not a complete list of all possible meta tags):

```
<meta name="language" content="en-us">

<meta name="rating" content="SAFE FOR KIDS">

<meta name="distribution" content="GLOBAL">

<meta name="contentright" content="(c) 2009 APC Group,
Inc">
```

```
<meta name="author" content="Gizmo Graphics Web Design">
```

```
<meta name="revisit-after" content="30 Days">
```

```
<meta http-equiv="reply-to" content="info@crystalriver-
house.com">
```

```
<meta name="createdate" content="4/8/2009">
```

You may also use the "comment" tag, which is primarily used by Web designers as a place to list comments relative to the overall Web site design, primarily to assist other Web developers who may work on the site in the future. A comment tag looks like this:

```
<!-begin body section for Gizmo Graphics Web Design>
```

ALT Tags

The ALT tag is an HTML tag that provides alternative text when non-textual elements, typically images, cannot be displayed. The ALT tag is not part of the "head" of a Web page, but proper use of the ALT tag is critically important in Search Engine Optimization. ALT tags are often left off Web pages, but they can be extremely useful for a variety of reasons, including the following:

- They provide detail or text description for an image or the destination of a hyperlinked image

- They enable and improve access for people with disabilities (see Section 508 of this chapter for more information on accessibility)

- They provide information for individuals who have graphics turned off when they surf the Internet

- They improve navigation when a graphics-laden site is being viewed over a slow connection, enabling visitors to make navigation choices before graphics are fully rendered in the browser

Text-based Web content is not the only thing that increases your ranking in the search engines: images are just as important, because these images can also include keywords and key phrases that relate to your business. If any visitors to your Web site have the image option off, they will still be able to see the text associated with your images. ALT tags should be placed anywhere where there is an image on your Web site. It is key to avoid being too wordy when describing your images, but include accurate keywords within the ALT tag. The keywords and key phrases that you use in the ALT tag should be the same keywords and phrases that you used in meta description tags, meta keyword tags, title tags, and in the Web content on your Web pages. A brief description of the image, along with one or two accurate keywords and key phrases, is all you need to optimize the images on your Web pages for search engines.

Most major Web design applications include tools to simplify the process of creating ALT tags. For example, in Microsoft® Expression® Web, right-click on the image and choose "properties" and the general tab, and you can enter ALT tag text information. Most Web site development applications actually prompt you for ALT tags as you add images.

To enter ALT tag information directly into a Web page, go to the HTML view and enter them after the IMG tags in the following format:

```
<img border="0" src="images/cftec.jpg" width="300"
height="103" alt=" ChefTec Software helps you save mon-
ey"></b></font></p>
```

Using the Correct Keywords in Your Content

When it comes to keywords, you need to choose the words or word combinations for which your potential customers are searching when they look for products or services using a search engine. If you start to optimize keywords that are incorrect, you may be wasting your time as your potential customers search using keywords that do not put you in the top rankings of search engines. You will need to do some market research to find out what keywords are being used by people in search engines to find similar products or services to what you are selling. There are software tools on the market that you can use to find out just what these keywords are so that you can implement them into your Web content and meta tags.

The use of keywords in your pay-per-click advertising campaign is critical, and we will discuss pay-per-click keywords in depth later. The key to finding the right keywords or phrases is to understand how people will search for your products or services in the first place, then use those key phrases or key words embedded in your Web site to raise your search engine rankings. One very important concept to consider is that the goal of a search engine is to deliver results based on the searched key words or key phrases. Your goal as a Web site owner is to get your Web site into those matching results, in particular, for someone who has never heard of your company or Web site.

Here is an example. If I am looking for a book about restaurant management, I might type in "Restaurant Management hand-book." It brings back results in which the top five search results are for Doug Brown's book, *The Restaurant Managers Handbook*. Amazon is the #1 listing, and the rest are for other sites. Now, if I already knew the title of the book I wanted, I could have just typed in, "The Restaurant Managers Handbook," which returned a different results set. Of course, if I already knew that the book I wanted was published by Atlantic Publishing Company, I could just search for "Atlantic Publishing Company," or simply go to **www.atlantic-pub.com**. The point is that you want to target people who do not know who you are. When they start searching for a product, your site is pushed to the top of the relevant results so they find your site without specifically looking for it. This is how you use the Google™ Search Engine to draw in new business and increase your income level.

SEO means that every page of your Web site will be optimized to the greatest extent possible for search engines. Keywords will vary based on the individual Web page content. By using the wrong keywords, you risk sending your potential customers in an entirely different direction from your Web site. Always keep in mind that if you are not listed in the top rankings of search engines, your customers may have difficulty finding you, and your competition will have an edge over you. Unfortunately, there is no magic formula to developing search-engine-optimized, effective search phrases. Keywords that work for some of your Web pages may not work for others, which is why you need to constantly assess how your SEO campaign is progressing, and be prepared to make changes along the way.

A good way to keep on top of effective keywords is to keep an eye on your competition. Use a search engine yourself and use some of the keywords and phrases that you know target your type of product or service. Take a look at the top-ranking Web sites and view the source HTML code, as well as the keywords that they have used in their meta tags. The HTML code will show you the keywords that the site's creator used. You will be able to come up with more keyword ideas and keep up with your competition so that you rank at the top of search engines as well.

Keyword density is another factor that affects your search engine results. Keyword density is defined as the number of times a keyword or key phrase is found within the text of a single Web page. This is typically ranked in relative order to the other words on the page, so each word is compared to other words, the number of times a single word or phrase is used, in contrast to all the other words factors into the total density of that particular word or phrase. When writing Web page content, consider increased keyword density as a goal to achieve. Balance this against keyword stuffing (adding excessive keywords to a page) and remember, it is relative to other page content, so five keywords in a one-hundred-word page are less dense than five keywords in a fifty-word page.

Optimization of Web Page Content

Web page content is by far the single most important factor that will affect and determine your eventual Web site ranking in search engines. It is extremely important that you have relevant content on your Web pages that is going to increase the status of your Web site in search engine rankings. The content on your Web page is what visitors are going to read when they find your site and start to browse your Web pages, whether they browse to a page directly or via a search engine. You need to optimize your Web site with all the right keywords within the content of each Web page so that you can maximize your rankings within search engines. You can use software tools to find out what keywords people are using when they search for certain products and services on the Internet, and we will provide some of those to you throughout this book.

Not only are the visitors to your Web site reading the content on these pages, but search engine spiders and Web crawlers are reading this same content and using it to index your Web site among your competitors. This is why it is important that you have the right content, so that search engines are able to find you and rank you near the top of the listings for similar products that people want to buy. Search engines are looking for keywords and phrases to categorize and rank your site; therefore, it is important that you focus on just as many key phrases as you do keywords.

The placement of text content within a Web page can make a significant difference in your eventual search engine rankings. Some search engines will only analyze a limited number of text characters on each page and will not read the rest of the page, regardless of length; therefore, the keywords and phrases you may have loaded into your page may not be read at all by the search engines. Some search engines do index the entire content of Web pages, but they typically give more value, or "weight," to the content that appears closer to the top of the Web page.

How the Google Search Engine Works

All search engines use "spiders" or "crawlers" to index your Web site. They find a page, follow the links to your Web pages, follow links to other pages, and "crawl" the Web in search of all Web pages, indexing each one as they go. One of the first questions I am asked after building a new site is, "How will I be found by Google™?" (When will I be found is #2). Well, you can submit your URL to Google™ yourself by simply visiting **www.Google. com/addurl.html**, or Google™ finds your site by following a link from another site it is crawling to your site, thus indexing it into its database, or by submitting a site map through Google™ Webmaster Tools, which we will explore later. Another way is to sign up for Google™ AdWords, which triggers an indexing of your site as well. Because higher "PageRank™" equates to better search engine placement in the Google™ Search Engine, quality inbound links are critical.

Optimizing Your Web Site

To get the best results from search engines, here are some tips that you should follow to optimize your Web site.

- Make sure that you have at least 200 words of content on each page. Although you may have some Web pages where it may be difficult to put even close to 200 words, you should try to come as close as you can, since search engines will give better results to pages with more content.

- Make sure that the text content that you have on your Web pages contains those important keywords and key phrases that you have researched, that you know will get you competitive rankings, and that are the most common phrases potential customers might use to search for your products or services.

- No matter how much content you have after incorporating keywords and phrases, make sure that the content that you have is still understandable and readable in plain language. A common mistake is to stack a Web site full of so many keywords and phrases that the page is no longer understandable or readable to the Web site visitor — a sure way to lose potential customers quickly.

- The keywords and phrases that you use in the content of your Web site should also be included in the tags of your Web site, such as meta tags, ALT tags, head tags, and title tags.

- Add extra pages to your Web site, even if they may not at first seem directly relevant. The more Web pages that you have, the more pages search engines will have to be able to find you and link to. Extra pages can include tips, tutorials, product information, resource information, and any other information or data that is pertinent to the product or service that you are selling.

Optimizing your Web content and Web pages is one of the most important tips that you can use to ensure the success of your Web site. If you are unable to optimize your Web site yourself, you should hire an expert so that you get the most out of your Web content.

Web Site Optimization Tips, Hints, and Secrets

It is critical that you explore and implement the wide range of tips, suggestions, and best practices we have provided in this book to give your Web site the most competitive edge and obtain the highest possible rankings with search engines, and ultimately, in conjunction with your pay-per-click advertising campaigns. The following pages contain various best practices, tips, and secrets:

- It is important to use your keywords heavily on your Web pages. Use key phrases numerous times, placing them close to the top of the page. Place key phrases between head tags in the first two paragraphs of your page and in bold type at least once on each page. Repeat keywords and phrases often to increase density on your pages.

- Design pages so they are easily navigated by search engine spiders and Web crawlers. Search engines prefer text over graphics and HTML over other page formats.

- Never use frames. Search engines have difficulty following them, as will your site visitors.

- Limit the use of Macromedia Flash® and other high-end design applications, as most search engines have trouble following them, hurting you in search engine listings.

- Consider creating a site map of all pages within your Web site. While not necessarily the most useful tool to site visitors, it does greatly improve the search engine's capacity to properly index all your Web site pages.

- Many Web sites use a left-hand navigational bar. This is standard on many sites, but the algorithm that many spiders and Web crawlers use will have this read before the main content of your Web site. Make sure you use keywords within the navigation, and if using images for your navigational buttons, use the ALT tags, loaded with appropriate keywords.

- Ensure all Web pages have links back to the home page.

- Use copyright and "about us" pages.

- Do not try to trick the search engines with hidden or invisible text or other techniques. If you do, the search engine may penalize you.

- Do not list keywords in order within the content of your Web page. It is fine to incorporate keywords into the content of your Web pages, but do not simply cut and paste your keywords from your meta tag into the content of your Web pages. This will be viewed as spam by the search engine, and you will be penalized.

- Do not use text on your Web page as the page's background color (e.g., white text on a white background). This is a technique known as keyword "stuffing," and all search engines will detect it and penalize you.

- Do not replicate meta tags. In other words, you should only have one meta tag for each type of tag. Using multiple tags (such as more than one title tag) will cause search engines to penalize you.

- Do not submit identical pages with identical content with a different Web page file name.

- Ensure that every Web page is reachable from at least one static text link.

- Ensure that all of your title and ALT tags are descriptive and accurate.

- Check for broken links and correct HTML.

- Try using a text browser, such as Lynx, to examine your site. Features such as JavaScript™, cookies, session IDs, frames, DHTML, or Flash® keep search engine spiders from properly crawling your entire Web site.

- Implement the use of the robots.txt file on your Web server. This file tells crawlers which directories can or cannot be crawled. You can find out more information on the robots. txt file by visiting **www.robotstxt.org/wc/faq.html**.

- Have other relevant sites link to yours. This is an often overlooked but extremely important way of increasing your search engine rankings, especially with the Google™ search engine. This is also known as back-linking, and is critically important to gaining search engine visibility.

- Design Web pages for site visitors, not for search engines.

- Avoid tricks intended to improve search engine rankings. A good rule of thumb is whether you would feel comfortable explaining what you have done to a Web site that competes with you. Another useful test is to ask, "Does this help my users? Would I do this if search engines did not exist?"

- Do not participate in link schemes designed to increase your site's ranking. Do not link to Web spammers, as your own ranking will be negatively affected by those links.

- Do not create multiple pages, sub-domains, or domains with substantially duplicate content.

- Do not use "doorway" pages created for search engines.

- Consider implementing cascading style sheets into your Web site to control site layout and design. Search engines prefer CSS-based sites and typically score them higher in the search rankings.

Web Design and Optimization Suggestions

Establish Links with Reputable Web Sites

You should try to find quality sites that are compatible and relevant to your Web site's topic, and approach the Webmasters of those sites for link exchanges. (Note: do not link to your competitors.) This will give you highly targeted traffic and will improve your score with the search engines. Your goal is to identify relevant pages that will link to your site, effectively yielding you quality inbound links. You need to be wary of developing or creating a "link farm" or "spam link Web site," which offers massive quantities of link exchanges, but with little or no relevant content for your site visitors or the search engines.

How to Establish a Reciprocal Link Program (Backlinks)

Begin your link exchange program by developing a title or theme that you will use as part of your link request invitations. Your title or theme should be directly relevant to your site's content. Since most sites use your provided title or theme in the link to your Web site, be sure you include relevant keywords that will improve your Web site optimization and search engine rankings. Keep track of your inbound and outbound link requests. Begin your search for link exchange partners by searching a popular engine, such as Google™, and entering key phrases, such as link with us, add site, suggest a site, or add your link. If these sites are relevant, they are ideal to being your reciprocal link program, since they too are actively seeking link partners. Make sure that the Webmasters of other sites actually link back to your site, as it is common that reciprocal links are not completed. If they do not link back to you in a reasonable time, remove your link to them, as you are only helping them with their search engine rankings.

You may want to use **www.linkpopularity.com** as a free Web source for evaluating the total number of Web sites that link to your site.

Free Link Popularity Report for
Atlantic Publishing Company
(www.atlantic-pub.com)

Google™	981 links
MSN	680 links
Yahoo!®	661 links

Establish a Web Site Privacy Policy

Internet users are becoming increasingly concerned with their privacy. You should establish a "privacy" Web page and let your visitors know exactly how you will be using the information you collect from them. You may also wish to develop a P3P Privacy policy. This may be necessary to solve a common problem of blocked cookies on Web sites, as well as with shopping carts and affiliate programs. Details may be found at **www.w3.org/P3P/ usep3p.html**. This page should include the following:

- For what do you plan on using their information?

- Will information be sold or shared with a third party?

- Why do you collect their e-mail addresses?

- Do you track their IP addresses?

- Notify site visitors that you are not responsible for the privacy issues of any Web sites you may be linked to.

- Notify site visitors that you have security measures in place to protect the misuse of their private or personal information.

- Provide site visitors with contact information in the event that they have questions about your privacy statement.

Establish an "About Us" Page

An "about" page is an essential part of a professional Web site for a variety of reasons. One reason is that your potential customers may want to know exactly who you are, and second, it is a great opportunity to create a text-laden page for search engine visibility. An "about" page should include the following:

- A personal or professional biography

- A photograph of yourself or your business

- A description of you or your company

- Company objectives or a mission statement

- Contact information, including your e-mail address

Establish a Testimonials Page

Another way to develop credibility and confidence among your potential customers is to include previous customers' testimonials. You need to make sure your testimonials are supportable, so include your customers' names and e-mail addresses for validation purposes.

Establish a Money-Back Guarantee

Depending on the type of Web site you are operating, you may wish to consider implementing a money-back guarantee to completely eliminate any potential risk to customers in purchasing your products. By providing them with a solid, no-risk guarantee, you build confidence in your company and products with potential clients.

Establish a Feedback Page

There are many reasons to incorporate a feedback page into your Web site. There are times when potential customers will have questions about your products and services or may encounter problems with your Web site, and the feedback page is an easy way for them to contact you. Additionally, it allows you to collect data from the site visitor, such as name, e-mail address, or phone number. A timely response to feedback is critical to ensuring customers that there is a "living" person on the other end of the Web site, and this personal service helps increase the likelihood that they will continue to do business with you.

Establish a Copyright Page

You should always display your copyright information at the bottom of each page. You should include both the word Copyright and the © symbol. Your copyright should look similar to this:

Copyright © 2009 Bruce C. Brown, LLC.

How Search Engines Work

There are several different types of search engines, including: crawler-based, human-powered, and mixed. We will discuss how each one works so you can optimize your Web site in preparation for your pay-per-click advertising campaign.

Crawler-Based Search Engines

Crawler-based search engines, such as the Google™ Search Engine, create their listings automatically. They "crawl" or "spider" the Web and index the data, which is then searchable through Google™.com. Crawler-based search engines will eventually revisit your Web site; therefore, as your content is changed (as is that of your competitors), your search engine ranking may change. A Web site is added to the search engine database when the search engine spider or crawler visits a Web page, reads it, and then follows links to other pages within the site. The spider returns to the site on a regular basis, typically once every month, to search for changes. Often, it may take several months for a page that has been "spidered" to be "indexed." Until a Web site is indexed, the results of the spider are not available through the search engines. The search engine then sorts through the millions of indexed pages to find matches to a particular search and rank them in order based on a formula of how it finds the results to be most relevant.

Human-Powered Search Directories

Human-powered directories, like the Open Directory, depend on humans for their listings. You must submit a short description to the directory for your entire site. The search directory then looks at your site for matches from your page content to the descriptions you submitted.

Hybrid or Mixed Search Engines

A few years ago, search engines were either crawler-based or human-powered. Today, a mix of both types is common in search engines results.

Using a Search Engine Optimization Company

If you are not up to the challenge of tackling your Web site's SEO needs, it may be to your benefit to hire an SEO company so that the optimization techniques that you use are properly implemented and monitored. There are many SEO companies on the Internet that can ensure that your rankings in search engines will increase when you hire them. However, be wary of claims of anyone who can "guarantee" you top-ten ranking in all major search engines; these claims are baseless. If you have the budget to hire an SEO company, it may be extremely beneficial for you to do so since (a) you will know that the experts at SEO are taking care of you and (b) you can focus your energies on other important marketing aspects of your business. To find a good SEO company, follow these basic rules:

- Look at the business reputations of the SEO companies that you are considering. Ask the company for customer references that you can check out on your own. You can also contact the Better Business Bureau in their local city or state to confirm their reputation, at **www.bbb.org**.

- Do a search engine check on each company to see where they fall into the rankings of major search engines, such as AOL®, MSN®, and Google™. If the company that you are considering does not rank high in these search engines, you cannot expect them to launch your business to the top of the ranks.

- Choose an SEO company that has people working for them, not just computers. While computers are good for generating the algorithms that are needed to use search engine programs, they cannot replace people when it comes to doing the market research needed to ensure the company uses the right keywords and phrases for your business.

- Make sure that the SEO company uses ethical ranking procedures. There are some ranking procedures that are considered to be unethical, and some search engines will ban or penalize your business Web site from their engines if they find out that you, or the SEO company that you have hired, are using these methods. Some of these unethical ranking procedures include doorway pages, cloaking, or hidden text.

- The SEO company you hire should be available to you at all times by phone or e-mail. You want to be able to contact someone when you have a question or a problem.

Once you have decided to hire an SEO company, it is important that you work with the company instead of just handing over all the responsibility to them. How much control of your Web site you should allow your SEO company is, but since you will be controlling your pay-per-click advertising campaign, you must have control over your SEO efforts. Use these tips to work effectively with your SEO provider:

- Listen carefully to the advice of the SEO account manager. They should have the expertise for which you hired them and be able to provide factual, supportable recommendations. SEO companies are expected to know what to do to increase your ranking in the search engines; if they fail to deliver, you need to choose another company.

- If you are going to be making any changes to your Web site design, let your SEO account manager know. This is because many times, any changes you make can have an effect on the already optimized Web pages. Your rankings in search engines may start to plummet unless you work with your SEO account manager to optimize any changes to your Web site design that you feel are necessary to make.

- Keep in mind that SEO companies can only work with the data and information that you have on your Web pages. This means that if your Web site has little information, it will be difficult for any SEO company to pull your business up in the search engine rankings. SEO relies on keywords and key phrases that are contained on Web pages that are filled with as much Web content as possible. This may mean adding two or three pages of Web content that contain tips, resources, or other useful information that is relevant to your product or service.

- Never change any of your meta tags once they have been optimized without the knowledge or advice of your SEO account manager. Your SEO company is the professional when it comes to making sure that your meta tags are optimized with the right keywords and phrases needed to increase your search engine ranking. You will not want to change meta tags that have already proven successful.

- Be patient when it comes to seeing results of SEO. It can take 30 to 60 days before you start to see yourself pushed up into the upper ranks of search engines.

- Keep a close eye on your ranking in search engines, even after you have reached the top ranks. Information on the Web changes at a moment's notice, and this includes where your position is in your target market in search engines.

Search Engine Registration

It is possible to submit your Web site for free to major search engines, including Google™. However, when you use paid search engine submission programs, you the process of listing will be faster, but results are often unacceptable, as many search engines are rejecting automated Web submissions. Other than pay-per-click and similar advertising programs, such as Google™ AdWords, it is not necessary to pay for search engine rankings if you follow the optimization and design tips contained in this book and have patience while the search engine Web crawling and indexing process takes place. At the end of this chapter, we have provided a wealth of tools and methods to submit your Web site to search engines for fee. If you do decide to hire a third-party company to register you with search engines, we have provided some basic guidance to ensure you get the most value for your investment.

Submitting to Human-Powered Search Directories

If you have a limited advertising budget, you will want to make sure that you have at least enough to cover the price of submitting to the directory at Yahoo! (called a "directory" search engine because it uses a compiled directory), which is assembled by human hands and not a computer. For a one-time yearly fee of approximately $300, you will be able to ensure that search engines that are crawlers will be able to find your Web site in the Yahoo! directory. Crawlers consistently use directory search engines to add to their search listings. If you have a large budget put aside for search engine submissions, you might want to list with both directory search engines and crawler search engines, such as Google™. When you first launch your Web site, you may want it to show up immediately in search engines, rather than waiting the allotted time for your listing to appear. If this is the case, you might want to consider using what is called a "paid placement" program. Remember that your pay-per-click advertising campaigns will show up with the top search engine rankings, based on your keyword bidding.

Submitting to Crawler Search Engines

Submitting to search engines that are crawlers means that you will likely have several Web pages listed within the search engine. One of the top Internet crawler search engines is, of course, Google™. Google™ is extremely popular because it is not only a search engine; it also is the main source of power and information behind many other search engines, such as AOL. The best thing that you can do when getting your Web site listed at Google™ is to make sure that you have links within your Web site. When you have accurate links on your Web site, you ensure that crawler search engines are able to find you, drill down through your site, and index your pages accordingly.

Using Search Engine Submission Software

There are dozens of software applications that can submit your Web site automatically to search engines. After reviewing most of these products, Dynamic Submission, at **www.dynamicsubmis-sion.com**, is recommended, although the success of these submission applications has been degraded over time as search engines reject these "autobot" submissions in favor of human submissions or paid submissions. Dynamic Submission was developed to offer Web site owners the ability to promote their Web sites to the ever-increasing number of search engines on the Internet without any hassles or complications. Their software helps you submit your Web site to hundreds of major search engines with just a few clicks and drive traffic to your Web site. To use Dynamic Submission, you simply enter your Web site details into the application as you follow a wizard-based system, which culminates in the automatic submission to hundreds of search engines.

Since nearly 85 percent of Internet traffic is generated by search engines, submitting your Web site to all the major search engines and getting them to be seen on the search engine list is extremely important, especially in concert with your pay-per-click advertising campaign. It is essential to regularly submit your Web site details to these Web directories and engines. Some search engines de-list you over time, while others automatically re-spider your site. Dynamic Submission is available in four editions (including a trial edition, which we highly encourage you to try) to fit every need and budget. Here are the major features of Dynamic Submission 7:

- Automatic search engine submission

- Supports pay-per-click (PPC) and pay-per-inclusion (PPI) engines

- Support for manual submission

- Keyword library and keyword builder

- Link popularity check

- Meta tag generator

- Web site optimizer

- Incorporated site statistics service

It is important to recognize that Google™ does not recommend the use of products such as WebPosition Gold or Dynamic Submission, which send automatic or programmatic queries to Google™. It is in violation of their terms of use and quality guidelines.

DMOZ

Be sure to manually submit your site to the Open Directory, at **www.dmoz.org**, which is free.

Search Engine Optimization Checklist

There are many aspects to SEO that you need to consider to make sure that it works. We have covered each of these in depth earlier in this chapter, but the following checklist can serve as a helpful reminder to ensure that you have not forgotten any important details along the way.

- **Title tag**. Make sure that your title tag includes keywords and key phrases relevant to your product or service.

- **Meta tags**. Make sure that your tags are optimized to ensure a high ranking in search engine lists. This includes meta description tags and meta keyword tags. Your meta description tag should have an accurate description so that people browsing the Internet are interested enough to visit your Web site. Do not forget to use misspelled and plural words in your meta tags.

- **ALT tags**. Add ALT tags to all the images that you use on your Web pages.

- **Web content**. Use accurate, rich keywords and key phrases throughout the Web content of all your Web pages.

- **Density of keywords**. Use a high ratio of keywords and key phrases throughout your Web pages.

- **Links and affiliates**. Make sure that you have used links and affiliates effectively for your Web site.

- **Web design**. Make sure that your Web site is fast to load and easy to navigate for visitors. You want to encourage people to stay and read your Web site by making sure that it is clean and looks good.

- **Avoid spamming**. Double check to make sure that you are not using any spamming offenses on your Web site. Some spamming offenses include cloaking, hidden text, doorway pages, obvious repeated keywords and key phrases, link farms, or mirror pages.

- **ALT Tags**. All images need ALT tags on your Web site.

Always be prepared to update and change the look, feel, and design of your Web pages to make sure that you are using SEO techniques wherever and whenever possible.

Free Web Site Search Engine Submission Sites

http://dmoz.org

http://tools.addme.com/servlet/s0new

www.submitcorner.com/Tools/Submit

www.quickregister.net

www.scrubtheweb.com

www.submitawebsite.com/free_submission_top_engines.
htm

www.nexcomp.com/weblaunch/urlsubmission.html

www.buildtraffic.com/submit_url.shtml

www.addpro.com/submit30.htm

www.website-submission.com/select.htm

Note: There are many other free services available online, and we make no guarantee as to the quality of any of these free services. We do recommend you create and use a new e-mail account just for search engine submissions (e.g., search@yourWeb site.com) to avoid spam, which is prevalent when doing bulk submissions.

Free Web Site Optimization Tools

www.websiteoptimization.com/services/analyze/ contains a free Web site speed test to improve your Web site performance. This site will calculate page size, composition, and download time. The script calculates the size of individual elements and sums up each type of Web page component. On the basis of these page characteristics, the site then offers advice on how to improve page load time. Slow load time is the #1 reason potential customers do not access Web sites.

www.sitesolutions.com/analysis.asp?F=Form is a free Web site that analyzes your page content to determine whether you are effectively using meta tags.

www.mikes-marketing-tools.com This Web site offers instant, online reports of Web site rankings in seven top search engines, including Google™, Yahoo! Search, MSN®, AOL®, Teoma ℠ (Ask Jeeves), AltaVista ℠, AllTheWeb ℠, and the top three Web directories — Yahoo! Directory, Open Directory (Dmoz), and LookSmart — all for free.

www.keyworddensity.com Free, fast, and accurate keyword density analyzer.

www.wordtracker.com/ The leading keyword research tool. It is not free, although there is a limited free trial.

adWords.Google.co.uk/select/KeywordToolExternal Gives ideas for new keywords associated with your target phrase, but does not indicate relevance or give details about the number or the frequency of searches.

Web Site Design and Optimization Tools

www.webmastertoolscentral.com/ A large variety of tools, guides, and other services for Web design and optimization.

www.htmlbasix.com/meta.shtml Free site that automatically creates properly formatted HTML meta tags for insertion into your Web pages.

Google's Webmaster Tools

Google™'s own Webmaster Tools are powerful applications that help you achieve better and higher rankings in the Google™ Search Engine. These tools provide you with a free, easy way to make your site more Google™-friendly. The tools show your site from the perspective of Google™ and let you identify problems, increase visibility, and optimize your site.

To increase your Web site's visibility on Google™, you need to learn how their robots crawl and index your site. Google™'s Webmaster tools show you exactly how to do this. Everything you need is available at **www.Google.com/webmasters/tools**.

You can see when your site was last crawled and indexed, view the URLs that Google™ had problems crawling, and then take corrective action to ensure all of your pages are indexed. You can view your Web site and see what key words Google™ is validating and which sites link to your site.

You can see what queries have been performed that are driving traffic to your site and where your site is in the search engine result for those queries. You can review how your site is indexed and whether you have any violations that Google™ is penalizing you for.

Take a closer look at each of these amazing Google™ tools. The first step is to sign up with Google™ and log into your account.

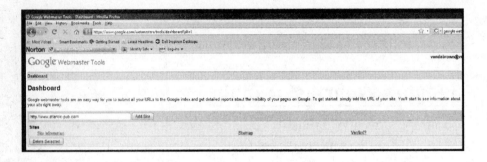

Google™ screenshots © Google™ Inc. Used with permission.

Add your URL into the "Add Site" box and click the button.

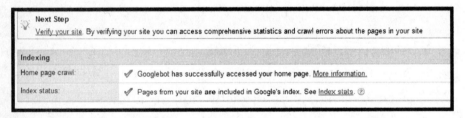

Google™ screenshots © Google™ Inc. Used with permission.

Google™ requires proof that you are the site owner to prevent you from using the same tools as your competition's site. You can do this by adding a meta tag to your Web site, which Google™ provides, or by uploading an HTML file. Add the meta tag to the HTML code in our index.asp Web page. Once you add the code, simply click on the VERIFY button to continue.

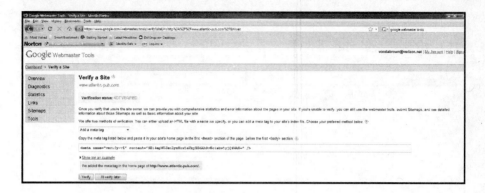

Google™ screenshots © Google™ Inc. Used with permission.

Once the site is verified, you can review the status of indexing and Web crawls. As we can see in the following screen shot, our site has been verified, and has been included in Google™'s Index. We can look at our index statistics, and we can also submit a site map, which we will create shortly. As we look at Web crawl errors, we see that we have 14 URLs not followed.

Google™ screenshots © Google™ Inc. Used with permission.

Detailed statistics about the Web crawls are available to us, as is PageRank™ information. As we can see, we are ranked "low" in Google™ PageRank™, so we have some work to do.

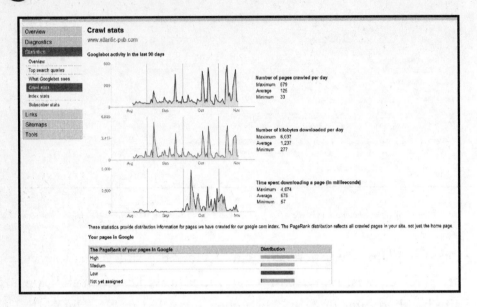

Google™ screenshots © Google™ Inc. Used with permission.

You can review your Top Search Queries and the relative position in which your results were ranked on the Google™ Search Engine.

Google™ screenshots © Google™ Inc. Used with permission.

Spend some quality time with the Google™ Webmaster Tools. They are all simple enough to use and understand as you analyze your site to improve overall rankings in the Google™ Search Engine. You can even set up Google™'s Webmaster Tools to monitor your site from your desktop, providing you with constant information flow about the performance of your site in relation to the Google™ Search Engine. The following is a screen shot of just some of the many tools available to analyze your Web site:

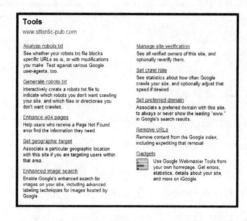

Google™ screenshots © Google™ Inc. Used with permission.

Remember those 14 URLs that Google™ reported that they could not follow? Often, they are caused by a problem with the HTML coding of a page or by a link to a page that does not exist, which is the case with the site we are looking at blow. Simply go into the site and fix the URLs to clear up this problem:

Web crawl

www.atlantic-pub.com ▾

Googlebot crawls sites by following links from page to page. We had problems crawling the pages listed here, and as a result they won't be added to our index and will not appear in search results.

Review the errors below and check any affected page for problems. For example, URLs not followed errors can be a clue that some of your pages contain content (such as rich media files or images) that Googlebot can't easily crawl, or structure is not Google-friendly.

Learn more about crawl errors

Note: Not all errors may be actual problems. For example, you may have chosen to deliberately block crawlers from some pages. If that's the case, there's no need to fix the error

Errors for URLs in Sitemaps (0) | HTTP errors (0) | Not found (0) | URLs not followed (14) | URLs restricted by robots.txt (0) | URLs timed out (0) | Unreachable URLs (0)

URLs not followed

URL	Detail	Problem Detected On
http://www.atlantic-pub.com/TOC/BuyBellbook.pdf	Redirect error	Nov 5, 2008
http://www.atlantic-pub.com/TOC/Cateringbook.pdf	Redirect error	Nov 5, 2008
http://www.atlantic-pub.com/TOC/FoodCostsbook.pdf	Redirect error	Nov 16, 2008
http://www.atlantic-pub.com/TOC/Menubook.pdf	Redirect error	Nov 10, 2008
http://www.atlantic-pub.com/TOC/OpCostsbook.pdf	Redirect error	Nov 5, 2008
http://www.atlantic-pub.com/TOC/Publicitybook.pdf	Redirect error	Nov 18, 2008
http://www.atlantic-pub.com/TOC/beveragecosts.pdf	Redirect error	Nov 18, 2008
http://www.atlantic-pub.com/catalogs/2007RealEstate.pdf	Redirect error	Nov 17, 2008
http://www.atlantic-pub.com/catalogs/2008%20Library%20Distributor%20Catalog.pdf	Redirect error	Nov 14, 2008
http://www.atlantic-pub.com/catalogs/Bakery%20cover.pdf	Redirect error	Nov 18, 2008
http://www.atlantic-pub.com/catalogs/Coffeecover.pdf	Redirect error	Nov 15, 2008
http://www.atlantic-pub.com/http://www.chiquilin.com	Redirect error	Nov 9, 2008
http://www.atlantic-pub.com/recffam/	Redirect error	Nov 19, 2008
http://www.atlantic-pub.com/www.atlantic-pub.com/http://www.chiquilin.com	Redirect error	Nov 10, 2008

Google™ screenshots © Google™ Inc. Used with permission.

Site Maps & Google

Submitting a site map to Google™ is a critical step toward achieving top rankings in the Google™ Search Engine. If you do nothing else with Google™'s Webmaster Tools and submit a site map. To create a site map, log back into Google™'s Webmaster Tools, select the URL you want to work with, which you have already verified, and click on the link "site maps." A site map is an HTML page listing of all the pages in your site — it tends to be designed to help users navigate your site, and it is especially beneficial if your site is large. In the case of Google™, create an XML site map, which provides Google™ with information about the site and improves our rankings with Google™.

Essentially, a site map is an organized list of every page in your Web site. It helps Google™ know which pages are in your site and ensures all your pages are discovered and indexed.

According to Google™, site maps are particularly helpful if:

- Your site has dynamic content

- Your site has pages that are not easily discovered by Googlebot during the crawl process

- Your site is new and has few links to it

- Your site has a large archive of content pages that are not well-linked to each other, or are not linked at all

Your site map can include additional information about your site, such as of how often it is updated, when each page was last modified, and the relative importance of each page. You must create your site map and submit it (or a URL to the site map) to Google™. There are a variety of ways to create a site map. Take a look at a few and go ahead and create and submit a site map to Google™. You can create a site map in the following three ways:

1. Manually creating it based on the site map protocol.

2. Using the site map Generator. If you have access to your Web server, and it has Python installed, you can use a Google™ provided script to create a site map that uses the site map protocol.

3. Using a third-party tool.

The easiest way to create an XML site map is to use the free tool at **www.xml-sitemaps.com/** (donations are accepted). This is an easy site to use; simply type in the URL, and it does the rest for you. You upload the XML file to your Web site and in the Google™ site map tool, you simply add the URL for the new file you placed on your Web server. Simply add your site map URL into the form, as shown in Google™'s Webmaster Tools in the next screenshot, and click the "Add General Web site map" button.

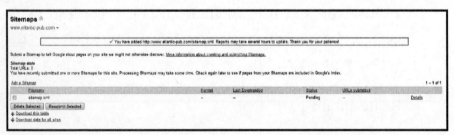

Google™ screenshots © Google™ Inc. Used with permission.

Google™ confirms that your site map was added, and updates in several hours. It is important to check back to ensure your site map is processed with no errors. Another feature of **www.xml-sitemaps.com/** is that it creates an HTML site map you can place on your site. It also creates the feed format to submit to Yahoo!, and a generic XML format for other major search engines.

Google™ screenshots © Google™ Inc. Used with permission.

Creating a site map with Google™ is a *must*, and it is one of the most important things you can do to improve site rankings. Google™'s Webmaster Toolset ensures your site is optimized, error-free, and properly indexed by the Google™ Search Engine.

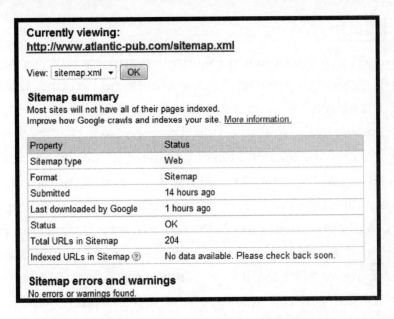

Google™ screenshots © Google™ Inc. Used with permission.

You can view your site map results at any time. In the preceding image, you can see that our 204 URLs in the site map were indexed properly, and there are no errors or warnings. With Google™'s Webmaster Tools, you can view a wide variety of analytics, statistics, and more. One useful report is Top Search Queries, which shows you what your potential customers have been typing in the Google™ Search Engine to find your Web site. Content Analysis can be used to show you meta and title tag issues, such as missing tags or duplicate tags. Each page should have its own unique title and description tags, customized to the content on that page. It is a common mistake to use generic tags throughout the site. A site map is a page which displays the structure of your Web site and allows users to quickly navigate to any particular age. An XML site map, which you submit through Google™'s Webmaster Tools, makes it easier for Google™ to discover all the pages on your Web site.

Snippets

A snippet is simply the text excerpt that appears below a page's title in the Google™ Search Engine results and describes the content of the page. Words contained in the snippet are bolded when they appear in the query results. The premise is that these snippets will give the user an idea of whether the content of the page matches what they may be looking for. The description snippet is taken directly from the description meta tag. If no description meta tag is provided, Google™ may extract a description from the page content. One source Google™ uses for snippets is the Open Directory Project. It is possible to tell Google™ to not use the ODP for generating snippets by using a piece of meta tag code. To direct the Google™ Search Engines not to use ODP information for the page's description, use the following on any Web page you want this rule to apply to:

```
<META NAME="Google™BOT" CONTENT="NOODP">
```

The Problem with Navigation Bars and Spiders

You need to have excellent navigation menus on your site to ensure that your customers can easily find your products and services, and for any Web site you develop, you must apply the same principles. One particular problem is that your Web site navigation menu, which is commonly on the top or the left-hand side of each page, is indexed by the search engine and can hurt you in search engine rankings when it indexes words from your menu, rather than from your page content. You need to get the search engines to index your content, not your navigation menus. Some advice is to put the navigation menu to the right of each page, which can be effective, although I would argue it is non-standard navigation and will turn site visitors off. There are a few options you can use to overcome this challenge if you want to keep your top or left navigation menus. One option is to use Cascading Style Sheets, in which you can place your navigation menu later in the code, or you can also use some Web accessibility settings to have the search engine "skip" over the navigation menu and go right to your Web content.

Breadcrumbs

Breadcrumb navigation is good for user-friendly site navigation and SEO. Essentially, Breadcrumbs are text-based navigation that shows where in the site hierarchy the current Web page you are viewing is located. It contains shortcuts to the next higher level of a Web site and lets you jump multiple layers at one time. An example of Breadcrumb navigation may be: "Home > Real Estate > Home Inspections > Books." Microsoft Expression Blend features a Breadcrumb trail tool, which allows designers to quickly and easily create Breadcrumb trails.

Inbound and Outbound Links

Since Google™ values quality Web links, part of the Google™ Webmaster's Tools include the ability to search for "relevant" sites. You can also do this at any time by typing *http://yourdomain-name.com* into the Google™ Search Engine. To get links, you often must give out links. Reciprocal links are fine, as long as you link to quality, relevant sites. Create outbound links as text-based, and use keywords in the text. In other words, do not just link to **www.gizwebs.com**; instead, use an embedded hyperlink on the text "Web Design and Search Engine Optimization."

Google TrustRank

Google™ uses a concept known as TrustRank to give higher search engine rankings to "trusted" sites and lower rankings to sites that are not trusted. Exactly how this works remains a bit of a mystery, so use the advice provided here as you strive to optimize your site for Google™.

Here are some factors that may affect your TrustRank ratings:

- **Performing Routing Updates to your site**. Adding content shows your site is maintained and current

- **Inbound Links**. Ensure your site is stacked with quality links from Web sites that are relevant to your site

- **Domain Name Age**. Having an established domain name for several years shows credibility and should give you a benefit over newly established domain names

- **Use site maps**. Use XML site maps to ensure that search engine spiders can easily index your Web site

- **Avoid Spam**. This means Spam e-mail as well as other techniques designed to "trick" search engines into giving you higher rankings, such as doorways, landing pages, hidden text, and stuffed keywords

Submitting Your Site to Other Search Engines

While this book is all about using Google™ to increase Web site traffic and increase income, do not count out the other major search engines. Most have mechanisms for you to add your Web site to their indexing — for free. Go to **www.Google.com** and type in "submit url," then start going down the list of links. You will find hundreds of excellent links to add your Web site to search engines. Here are a few to get you started:

- **www.dmoz.org/add.html**

- **www.scrubtheweb.com/addurl.html**

- **http://siteexplorer.search.yahoo.com/submit**

- **http://addurl.altavista.com/addurl/default**

- **www.homerweb.com/submit_site.html**

404 Pages & Search Engine Optimization

Even the best Web designers inevitably leave a link to a page that no longer exists. This is known as a 404 Error (Page Does not Exist). Make sure you have a custom 404 page to redirect users back to a page from which they can navigate your site. Often, 404 pages will redirect you to the home page. You may also wish to have links to your most popular pages. Using auto-redirect, which gives them a few seconds to click on a link, and if they take no action, brings them to the Web site home page.

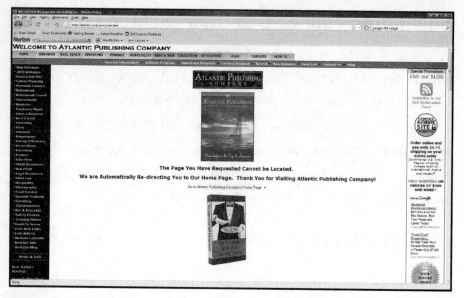

Sample 404 Error Page — Reprinted with Permission Atlantic Publishing Company

Google™ simplifies the process of creating 404 pages by providing a Google™ 404 Widget in Google™'s Webmaster's Tools. You can also use the widget to identify which page has the links to the nonexistent page so you can take corrective action.

Other Ways to Generate Traffic & Inbound Links

Become an expert in your specialty. Post entries into blogs, forums, discussion groups, and other Web sites. Establish yourself as an industry expert by writing and submitting articles to the dozens of free article distribution sites on the Web. You can get started at **www.articlealley.net**. Include your name, URL, and contact information, and you will be amazed at the viral distribution of "royalty free" articles throughout the Web. Press releases are another way to publish information about your company with links and other contact information to drive traffic to your site. Strive to get quality inbound links from .EDU, .ORG or other public, non-profit organizations. These quality links tend to weigh heavier than commercial ones in the Google™ Search Engine.

Section 508 and Web Site Accessibility

In 1998, Congress amended the Rehabilitation Act to require Federal agencies to make electronic and information technology accessible to people with disabilities. Inaccessible technology interferes with an individual's ability to obtain and use information quickly and easily. Section 508 was enacted to eliminate barriers in information technology, to make new opportunities available for people with disabilities, and to encourage development of technologies that will help achieve these goals. The law applies to all Federal agencies when they develop, procure, maintain, or use electronic and information technology. Under Section 508 (29 U.S.C. 794d), agencies must give disabled employees and members of the public access to information that is comparable to the access of others. You should design Web pages with accessibility in mind, as there are benefits for everyone. While the Section 508 rules are quite involved, and apply to much more than Web pages, here are the essential requirements for Web site design:

§ 1194.22 Web-based intranet and Internet information and applications.

- A text equivalent for every non-text element shall be provided

- Equivalent alternatives for any multimedia presentation shall be synchronized with the presentation

- Web pages shall be designed so that all information conveyed with color is also available without color; for example, from context or markup

- Documents shall be organized so they are readable without requiring an associated style sheet

- Redundant text links shall be provided for each active region of a server-side image map

- Client-side image maps shall be provided instead of server-side image maps except where the regions cannot be defined with an available geometric shape

- Row and column headers shall be identified for data tables

- Markup shall be used to associate data cells and header cells for data tables that have two or more logical levels of row or column headers

- Frames shall be titled with text that facilitates frame identification and navigation

- Pages shall be designed to avoid causing the screen to flicker with a frequency greater than 2 Hz and lower than 55 Hz

- A text-only page, with equivalent information or functionality, shall be provided to make a Web site comply with the provisions of this part, when compliance cannot be accomplished in any other way; the content of the text-only page shall be updated whenever the primary page changes

- When pages use scripting languages to display content, or to create interface elements, the information provided by the script shall be identified with functional text that can be read by assistive technology

- When a Web page requires that an applet, plug-in, or other application be present on the client system to interpret page content, the page must provide a link to a plug-in or applet that complies with §1194.21(a) through (l)

- When electronic forms are designed to be completed online, the form shall allow people using assistive technology to access the information, field elements, and functionality required for completion and submission of the form, including all directions and cues

- A method shall be provided that permits users to skip repetitive navigation links

- When a timed response is required, the user shall be alerted and given sufficient time to indicate that more time is required

A good place to check out your site for Section 508 compliance is at **www.contentquality.com**.

Google's Quality Guidelines

Google™ provides you with some good advice, which you should follow. Google™'s quality guidelines address most of the common techniques employed to overcome and "trick" search engines in order to achieve higher rankings. This list is not all-inclusive. Use your valuable time and energy toward implementing proven Web site design techniques and SEO standards to improve your site in Google™'s rankings. If you believe another Web site is abusing Google™'s quality guidelines, you may report it at **www.Google.com/webmasters/tools/spamreport**.

Here are Google™'s Basic Quality Guidelines:

- Make pages primarily for users, not for search engines

- Avoid tricks intended to improve search engine rankings

- Do not participate in link schemes designed to increase your site's ranking or PageRank™

- Do not use unauthorized computer programs to submit pages, check rankings, or perform other functions.

- Avoid hidden text or hidden links

- Do not use cloaking

- Do not load pages with irrelevant keywords

- Do not create multiple pages, sub-domains, or domains with duplicate content

- Do not create pages with malicious behavior, such as phishing or installing viruses or Trojans.

- Avoid "doorway" pages created just for search engines

- If your site participates in an affiliate program, make sure that it adds value and has content a person would want to view, regardless of whether it has an affiliate program

Generating Web Site Traffic

Google™ is king in the search engine world, and your goal should be to obtain the highest site rankings possible. Web site traffic is determined by the number of visitors and the number of pages they visit. Web sites monitor incoming and outgoing traffic to see which pages of their site are popular and whether there are any apparent trends, such as one specific page being viewed mostly by people in a particular country. Web traffic is measured to see the popularity of Web sites and individual pages or sections within a site. Most quality Web hosting companies provide you with detailed Web statistical analysis and monitoring tools as part of a basic Web hosting package.

Your Web site traffic can be analyzed by viewing the statistics found in the Web server log file, or using Web site traffic analysis programs. Any quality Web hosting company will provide free, detailed statistics for Web site traffic. A hit is generated when any file is served. The page itself is considered a file, but images are also files; thus, a page with five images could generate six hits (the five images and the page itself). A page view is generated when a visitor requests any page within the Web site — a visitor will always generate at least one page view (the home or main page) but could generate many more as they travel through your Web site. There are many ways to increase your Web site traffic — all leading to greater sales and profit potentials. We will discuss a variety of options that will lead to increased Web site traffic.

Web Site Design Essentials

You must have a Web site that is effectively designed and meets the needs of your site visitors. A poorly designed Web site, or one that is not functionally efficient, will drive away customers quickly. Make sure that your Web site is professional and has a good design. You want your Web site to have a clean, tight look so that customers are compelled to return. Professional site design means having a Web site that

- Is easy to navigate

- Has appropriate logos

- Has up-to-date information

- Answers customer questions

- Does not look amateur

- Implements a sound SEO plan

Never hide anything from your customers. Give them all the data they need to make an informed decision about your product or services. Follow through on what you say you offer at your Web site to maintain credibility and trust. You do not want to be identified in the media as a poor company, scam site, or rip-off artist. Bad news travels fast, especially on the Internet.

Using Press Releases to Generate Traffic

An online press release is part of the online medium of communication, and online communication is all about timing. Your press release, whether printed and faxed or online, is one method of communicating with your customers and your industry. It is up to you to make the most of a press release so that it has as much impact as possible.

Most companies use press releases to alert the public about a new product or service they offer. These press releases, while informative, tend to be somewhat dry, and consumers typically skim over them, sometimes missing the key points. The bottom line is that if it is not newsworthy, then you will not be selected by the media for coverage. That said, a press release promoting specific events, specials, or newsworthy items can be quite effective.

As an alternative to a written press release, you could try a multimedia approach. If you are giving a live press release, you can incorporate the audio or video files onto your Web site, either to complement a written press release or replace it altogether. It is highly recommended that you have a media section on your Web site to serve reporters, columnists, producers, and editors with your latest press release information. Many people find listening to an audio clip or, better yet, watching a video clip preferable to reading a written press release. There is so much written on the Internet that trying another medium to get your message across could be just the boost your company needs. You should also think of other Web site owners as another form of media channel, since everyone is looking for fresh content and expert advice.

Consider using an online press release service, such as **www. PRweb.com**, to generate successful media exposure for your online business. This free service is another tool to distribute your press release information to thousands of potential new customers or clients. Keep in mind the value of using highly relevant keywords often within the content of your online press release in order to use the benefits of SEO. Including live links within your online press release is another way to ensure increased media coverage. Linking to relevant Web sites increases the credibility and functionality of your online business.

Make sure that you give your customers a reason to visit your site, spend time browsing it, interact with it, and most importantly, return to it. Offer incentives by showcasing featured products or promotions, and use creative and new Internet tools, such as video and audio, to create an interactive experience. You can also import video clips from promotional products, CDs/DVDs, or create your own video clips and add them to your Web site.

Publish Customer Testimonials on Your Site

Using customer testimonials is a good way to promote the quality and reliability of your Web site and, more importantly, promote your products or services. This is an amazingly effective tactic. The media you create and the coverage that you get is a subtle, third-party referral to you. However, the strongest, most effective sales assistance comes from direct customer testimonials. Try using audio and video testimonials, as well as printed quotes, on your Web site. You should include your customer's name, e-mail address, and Web address with each unsolicited testimonial to increase believability.

Of course, no matter how flashy or impressive your Web site may look, it is customer service, satisfaction, and reliability that keep customers coming back.

Proven Techniques for Generating Traffic

The following techniques may be employed to increase Web site traffic. These proven methods *will* increase your Web site traffic.

- Create a "What's New" or "New Products" page. Site visitors like to see what is new, trendy, or just released. Make it easy for them.

- Establish a promotion program. The sky is the limit for promotions. Offer free products, trial samples, or discount coupons. Everyone loves a bargain, so give it to them.

- Establish a contest. Create an online contest to promote anything. Be creative, you don't have to market you products in a contest. Atlantic Publishing Company's Top 50 Restaurants contest drew tens of thousands of site visitors ranking the top restaurants Web sites their site visitors submitted. Winners got a free "Award Winner" image to place on their Web site, which also linked back to Atlantic Publishing Companies Web site. Similar contests cost nothing to create, are simple to manage, and draw visitors.

- Add content-relevant professional articles, news events, press releases, or other topics of interest on a daily basis to draw back visitors to your site.

- Establish a viral marketing campaign or embed viral marketing techniques into your current advertising programs or e-zines. Viral marketing is when you incorporate such things as a "forward to a friend" link within the advertisement. In theory, if many people forward to more friends, it will spread like a virus (hence the name) and eventually go to many potential customers.

- Use signature files with all e-mail accounts. Signature files are basically business cards through e-mail, so send your business card to all your e-mail recipients. Signature files are sent with every e-mail you send out and can contain all contact information, including business name and Web site URL. Signature files can be created in Microsoft® Outlook or Outlook Express.

- Start an affiliate program and market it. Include your affiliate information in e-mails, newsletters, e-zines, and on Web sites to promote your program. A successful affiliate program will generate a significant increase in Web site traffic. For an example of a highly effective affiliate campaign, visit **www.atlantic-pub.com/affiliate.htm**.

- Include your Web site URL on *everything*, such as business cards, letterhead, promotional items, and e-mails.

- Win some awards for your Web site. There are quite a few award sites that are nothing more than link exchange factories, but there are some reputable award sites, such as **www.webbyawards.com** and **www.100hot.com**

- Everyone loves search engines, so put Google™ right on your Web site (more details on how to do this later). Simply visit Google™ to add a free search feature to your Web site. This is a good tool that site visitors will love.

- Implement Google™ AdSense on your Web site to increase revenue and traffic.

- Implement Google™ AdWords to increase Web site traffic and generate sales revenue.

- Put your URL into your e-mail signature so you are constantly advertising your Web site.

- Put your Web site URL on your business card.

- Register your site with relevant online directories.

- Write free articles and submit them to other newsletters.

- Post often on content-related forums and message boards, and post your Web site URL with each entry.

- Submit content often to content-relevant e-mail discussion groups on related content, and post your Web site URL with each entry.

- Establish links from other sites to yours (backlinks). Create a links page or directory on your Web site, and offer your visitors a reciprocal link to your site for adding a link to yours on theirs.

- Develop quality Web site content that is well-organized and captivating.

- Use eBay® to generate Web site traffic by registering your eBay® store with search engines.

- List your URL on all offline advertising and printed materials, such as stationary and print advertisements.

- Begin a business blog on your Web site. If it is well done and has relevant content, people will link to it, increasing your site's visibility and ranking in search engines.

Link Exchanges & Web Site Traffic

A link exchange is when two or more Web sites exchange links and point to each other. Be careful here — do not sign up with "link farms," which do nothing more than exchange links with thousands of Web sites. Link Exchanges can be effective when they are selective, relative, and used in moderation. It is not uncommon for sites to establish a "link with us" page, such as the one at **www.atlantic-pub.com/links.htm**. This is often done on a separate Web page on the site, and they are used by individuals and search engines to find the links and follow them to the destination Web site.

Link exchanges can be done manually or automatically, but the manual method ensures strict quality control over whom you link with. Be selective, and ensure that you get a quality reciprocal link. For example, if you sell books about how to become a home inspector, linking to the state regulations on Home Inspection, or Web sites with hurricane standards in the state of Florida is fine. Also, you may want to link with companies who provide related services and supplies, such as hurricane shutters, roofing, and more. If you linked to companies that sell flowers, Web hosting, or shoes, they are not relevant, and you may be penalized by search engines.

A quick search on the Internet reveals many companies you can use for paid link exchange programs, but I recommend you stay away from them all. Yes, manual links take some manual labor to create, and you may only add a link or two a week. It may also require you to initiate the link request with relevant companies you want to exchange links with, but the benefits are well worth the time investment.

When you initiate a link request, ask for the exchange in a natural-style e-mail. Do not use a template, which sounds like a robot is asking for the exchange; you will find few responses to it. Here is an automated link exchange format that has been used for years, and I consider as a red flag to delete:

From: Axel Rhaidshu [mailto:axel@gmailaxel.ru]

Sent: Wednesday, November 26, 2008 6:52 AM

Subject: link exchange request

While looking for the potential link partners, I came across your Web site and found it relevant with our industry and I feel that exchanging links would be beneficial for both of us in order to get better rankings in SERP and traffic as well.

In return I will publish your link on my Web site at www. mysite.com. If you are interested, you can add our link with the following info:

Title: Search Engine Optimization Services

URL: www.gmailaxel.us

Desc: Guaranteed #1 ranking in all major search engines when you use our services.

Thanks for creating a great site. I assure you that this would be a long-term business relationship. I appreciate your attention and wish you great online business.

Looking forward to hearing from you.

Publishing Articles to Generate Site Traffic

Writing articles is amazingly effective for generating Web site traffic and increasing your ranking in search engines because you embed links to your site into articles. These articles may be published and re-published on several Web sites, and the viral effect of this generates quality inbound links, promotes awareness of your Web site, and increases your reputation as an expert in your specialty because you are publishing articles on the subject. Embed keywords into your article, as well as links to your Web site. Keep your articles fairly short (no more than 750 words). If your article is longer, break it up into a series (i.e., part I, part II). Draw readers to your Web site by giving them enough information to at least instill an interest in them to want more information from your Web site.

For all articles, ensure that you include a biography that includes contact information and information about your experience, education, company, and products, as well as links to your Web site. Establish yourself as an industry expert, and you will be recognized as one by your peers. Below are the most popular free article listing Web sites you can submit to. When you do submit your article, send it to each of the following:

- **www.articlealley.com**

- **www.ezinearticles.com**

- **www.articlecity.com**

- **www.earticlesonline.com**

- **www.articlecache.com**

- **www.goarticles.com**

You must first visit these sites and sign up as an author, which gives you an account login and simple instructions to publish your articles. Note that most of these sites have an approval process to ensure that your article meets their content standards.

Using Web Directories to Generate Site Traffic

A Web directory is simply an organized cataloging of Web sites by subject. The best examples of this are **http://dmoz.org** and **http://dir.yahoo.com**, which is also the largest Web directory maintained by humans. You should absolutely submit your Web site to Web Directories. Most provide you with a simple "add url" link.

While Web directories are often free, some, such as Yahoo, will charge you for the listing. The following Web site provides you with links to all of the top ranked Web directories and also provides you with cost information and the Google™ PageRank™ information. Use **www.seocompany.ca/directory/top-web-directories.html** as your guide for adding yourself to Web directories.When adding your Web site to directories, embed key words or key phrases into your title and description. There are programs that can automate this process for you, such as SubmitEaze, which is available for about $78 and even has a free trial you can download.

Google Analytics

Google™ provides you with a free tool to analyze your Web site traffic. This tool, Google™ Analytics, shows you how people searched for and found your site, what pages they visited, and how to enhance and improve your site. By employing Google™ Analytics, you may realize increased Web site traffic and increased revenue and sales.

Google™ Analytics consists of more than 80 reports that track visitors through your site and monitor performance of AdWords campaigns, e-mail marketing campaigns, and other advertising programs. You can monitor and evaluate keyword performance, conversions, lost conversions, and much more. The best part of the package is that Google™ Analytics is absolutely free. All that is required is a Google™ account.

To sign up, visit **www.Google.com/analytics**. You must place a code snippet on your Web page and then you will start gathering data to analyze. You just add your Web site to the list of domains you are monitoring:

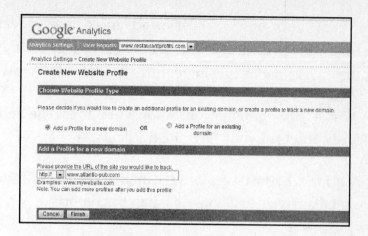

Google™ screenshots © Google™ Inc. Used with permission.

The tracking code is generated, and Google™ immediately starts looking for the tracking code snippet on your Web site. Note that you must insert this Javascript™ code into every page on the site you wish to analyze, just prior to the </body> tag.

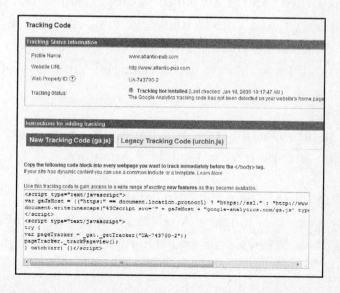

Google™ screenshots © Google™ Inc. Used with permission.

Google™ Analytics offers a host of advanced, useful features, which have proven critical to the overall success of online businesses. Below is a list of current features in Google™ Analytics:

- **Advanced Segmentation**: Allows you to isolate and analyze subsets of your Web site traffic.

- **Motion Charts**: Gives you the ability to add multi-dimensional analysis to Google™ Analytics reports.

- **Custom Reports**: You have the flexibility to create, save, and edit custom reports analyzing the data that you want, in the format you want it presented.

- **Fast Implementation**: It takes moments to set up and establish a fully-functional Google™ Analytics account.

- **Keyword and Campaign Comparison**: You can use Google™ Analytics to track and compare ads, e-mail marketing campaigns, affiliate marketing campaigns, referrals, paid links, and keywords on Google™ and most other major search engines.

- **Custom Dashboards**: You have full control over the design and interface of Google™ Analytics.

- **AdWords Integration**: One of the most powerful features. You can use Google™ Analytics to monitor your Google™ AdWords keywords and determine which are profitable and which are not.

- **Internal Site Search**: Use this to determine how visitors search your site, what words they are searching on, and how they navigate your Web site.

- **Benchmarking, Trend, and Data Slider**: Benchmark performance periods with yourself and others.

- **E-commerce Tracking**: Allows you to track searched keywords from search through transaction completion.

- **Funnel Visualization**: Find out why customers are being converted into buying customers, as well as see what pages they were on. Critical to improving your Web site perceptions and functionality.

- **Site Overlay**: Lets you view traffic and conversion information for every link as you browse your site.

- **E-mail reports**: You have full control over standardized or ad hoc reports, which you can share with others.

- **Geographic Targeting**: Determine where your Web site visitors come from and which geographic areas are most profitable for you.

In summary, Google™ Analytics will do the following, and much more:

- Track, measure, and record every click on each page of your Web site (that the tracking code in installed on)

- Track when a visitor arrives on your Web site

- Track how they came, what keywords they used, what search engine they used, what links they followed, and where they came from

- Track the last time they visited your Web site

- Track what they downloaded from your Web site

- Track conversion data

Google Website Optimizer

The Google™ Website Optimizer (**www.Google.com/websiteoptimizer**) is another incredible tool from Google™; it lets you test different versions of your site content and landing page elements to determine which work best to attract users to your Web site. Website Optimizer can help improve conversion rates and increase your overall return on investment. You can test different versions of the content on your live site to see what will lead to the highest conversion rates for both sales and with Google™ AdWords. For purposes of Website Optimizer, a conversion or landing page does not necessarily have to be a product sale. Whatever page you are driving individuals to is your conversion or landing page; if you get them there, you have succeeded. Website Optimizer lets you test a variety of page elements, evaluate success of users reaching your conversion or landing page, and compare results as you modify your Web page — driving you to the most optimized Web page to achieve the best results of conversions. Google™ will generate "tags" which you add to the test page and the landing or conversion page. That is the extent of the technical knowledge required to use Website Optimizer. With Web site Optimizer, you can test keywords, headlines, images, and other elements of your Web page. Website Optimizer, like all Google™ tools, has an online guide to getting started and a help center, which is available at **www.Google.com/support/websiteoptimizer**.

Expert Advice: Google Analytics & Google Website Optimizer – By Chris Hickman

Google™ analytics can be one of the most powerful, confusing, and time-consuming tools you can use to improve your Web site. This program allows you to see in detail information about where people are coming from and their behavior patterns on your Web site. It can also be used to track conversions so you can see whether different Web sites or traffic sources are generating conversions. For example, suppose you have ads on Google™ AdWords, Yahoo search markets, and banner ads on three different Web sites. By using Google™ Analytics, you can see the amount of people each traffic source delivered and the number that converted.

There are hundreds of different reports to look at on Google™ Analytics, but there are only a few that you need to look at to know what is going on with your site and how to increase your conversions: bounce rate, referring URLs, most-viewed content, top exit pages, conversions, browsers, and geographical areas.

Bounce rate means the number of people who enter your site and leave on the same page they enter. They essentially bounce off your site. If the bounce rate is high, this could be an indication that wherever people are coming from to get to this page, the people are not interested and leave right away. You might want to consider not sending traffic from that page, or changing your landing page to be more relevant. The typical bounce rate varies by industry, but on average, if it is over 30 percent, it should draw attention, and you should look at it and make a decision about changing the landing page or traffic sources.

Looking at the referring URLs to see where all your traffic comes from can help you identify which advertising sources are profitable. When you identify the profitable traffic sources, you can pull your money out of the ones that are not working and place it in those that are.

By looking at the most-viewed content, you can see what pages are getting the most attention by your potential customers. In most cases, you will see the greatest improvement by making changes to the pages with the most traffic. This also is a valuable tool because most businesses have limited resources in making changes to their Web site, and this can be used as a guide to determine whether changes should be made. The more people that come to that page, the higher the priority it should have for having changes and updates made to it.

Exit rate is similar to bounce rate, but the main difference is that with exit rate, someone has to look through at least two pages on your site and leave to be counted as an exit, if they only look at one page and leave, that is considered a bounce. Exit rate can be quite useful in determining where people are leaving on your site. It is like having a pool with holes in it and being able to see which holes are the biggest. This would be an advantage of using Google™ Analytics on your Web page, so you can see which holes you would want to fix first to keep the visitors you already paid for on your site.

Tracking conversions through Google™ Analytics will allow you to quickly determine which advertising sources are working. Conversion tracking on Google™ Analytics Is similar to

Google™ AdWords, except analytics can track traffic from every source and can give you much more in depth details of the visitors. AdWords can just track conversions (the overall percentage of site visitors who perform an action on the Web site which may be a purchase, sales lead or other specific action) from Google™ and can tell you whether there was a conversion or not. Google™ AdWords conversion tracking is a "yes" or "no." Google™ Analytics is a "yes" or "no," but also gives you more details on what happened.

There are many different browsers that people use to view your Web site. It is important to know which browsers your potential customers are using because Web sites can look different in different browsers. When you identify which browsers people are using to look at your site, you can then test those sites in those browsers, and if anything does not look right, then you can have your Web designer fix it for you. Most good Web designers will test your site in almost all the popular browsers.

When you advertise your Web site nationally, you are going to get traffic from all over the country, and Google™ analytics has a geographic report so you can see cities, states, and regions that your traffic is coming from. If you are using the Google™ Analytics conversion counter "goals," then you will be able to see which cities and states are producing traffic.

If you have never used Google™ Analytics before, it will take some time to get familiar with. If you do not have a Web designer, you will have to learn how to install it, which, depending on your HTML knowledge, can be an easy or complex task. Installing it involves putting an HTML code at the bottom of every page. To set up "goals" in the admin panel of the account, you specify the pages you want to set as your goals. If you stick to the previous reports, that will help you use your time wisely, and you can look at many reports. The last thing to keep in mind about Google™ Analytics is this is a tool for you to use to identify your best traffic sources and customize your site to the needs and wants of your consumers.

Split Testing with Google Website Optimizer

Split testing is when you can take multiple items and compare them to each other in relation to how many conversions each one brings in. Split testing can be used to compare pictures, headlines, forms, or anything else on a Web page. If you have multiple ideas, it is easy to see which one is going to have the best performance. An example of this would be testing two different headlines on a landing page. If you have a hundred visitors come to the page, then 50 would see the first headline, then the other 50 will see the other headline while the page stays the same. Then you would be able to see which headline holds the most conversions. It is important to make sure everything else stays the same while split testing so another factor will not have an effect on the split testing results.

Google™ AdWords offers a free service for split testing called Google™ Website Optimizer, which will allow you to split test any element on any Web page and find out the best combination for converting visitors. To set up Google™ Website Optimizer, you need to have an understanding of HTML. Some of the best things to test are headlines, pictures, and forms to pages that receive considerable traffic. You should always be testing something on your landing page to improve it.

Chris Hickman is the founder and Co-Owner of Silver Scope Promotion, LLC., one of the world's leading search engine marketing firms. Silver Scope Promotion has helped thousands of clients worldwide have an effective, profitable online presence. A small number of firms worldwide have the status that Silver Scope Promotion has, being a Google™ Qualified Company and Yahoo Search Marketing Ambassador. Chris provides search engine marketing and consulting services in pay-per-click advertising, SEO, Web site analytics, split testing, consumer behavior improvement, landing page development, and copy writing. Starting the company while in college, Chris graduated from the University of Missouri St. Louis with a Bachelors degree in Management Information Systems and a minor in Math. Chris has almost eight years of search engine marketing experience.

Company e-mail: info@SilverScopePromotion.com

Chris Hickman's e-mail: Chris@SilverScopepromotion.com

Introduction to Pay-Per-Click Advertising

The key concept to understand regarding pay-per-click advertising is that unlike other paid advertising campaigns where you pay for the campaign in hopes of generating customers and revenues, you are not paying for any guarantees or promises of sales, Web site traffic, or increased revenues. You are no longer paying out money in print advertising or other online marketing techniques hoping for a return on your significant investment. Google™ makes pay-per-click advertising easy, effective, and profitable with Google™ AdWords.

Banner advertising was the largest type of advertising on the Internet, and it still holds a small market share, but the main disadvantage of banner advertising is that the ads are embedded within pages. You have to rely on a Web designer to put your banner ad on a page that has similar or complementary content and, of course, it is useless unless someone clicks on it. With pay-per-click advertising, you do not pay to have your advertisement loaded on a Web page or to have your advertisement listed at the top of search engines, you only pay for results. In other words, pay-per-click advertising has entirely no cost (minus potential setup costs), even if your advertisement is viewed by millions of Web site visitors. You pay when your ad is clicked, thus the term pay-per-click.

When someone clicks on your AdWords advertisement, Google™ charges your account, based on a formula price. Bear in mind that the "click" in no way guarantees sales; it merely means that someone has clicked on your advertisement and will be routed in the browser to the pre-determined Web page you specified when you created your advertisement. Do not underestimate the importance of having a user-friendly, information-rich Web site to capture the attention of the site visitor and close the deal. Not all pay-per-click campaigns must result in a purchase — many advertisers use pay-per-click advertising to sell products, but many more use them to sell services, promotional material, news releases, and other media, all intended to build business or disseminate information.

Pay-per-click advertising began in 1998 by a company called **Goto.com**, which was then purchased by Yahoo.com. The original concept was that anyone with a brick-and-mortar or online business could manage and determine their own search engine ranking based on pre-selected keywords and how much money they were willing to pay for the resultant "click" on their advertisement.

Pay-per-click advertising is the fastest growing form of online marketing today. Google™ is the industry leader in terms of market share and offers advertisers a feature-rich application called Google™ AdWords.

You will likely admire the simplicity and functionality of pay-per-click advertising, which allows you to have significant control over your campaign. Before you forge the path toward implementing a Google™ AdWords pay-per-click marketing plan, it is critical to understand pay-per-click advertising and develop strategies to design an effective campaign, optimize and monitor overall ad performance, and employ sound business principles in the overall management and financial investment of your campaign. One of the success factors in creating and managing a Google™ AdWords pay-per-click campaign is the effective selection and use of keywords, key phrases in the creation of an effective ad using advanced statistical reporting tools from Google™, as well as your Web hosting company. To ensure the potential for success of a Google™ AdWords pay-per-click campaign, you must choose the most effective keywords, design an effective and captivating advertisement, and, as we mentioned earlier, have a well-designed, information-rich Web site with easy navigation.

Pay-Per-Click Advertising Walkthrough

You pay a rate which you specify for every visitor who clicks through from the search engine site to your Web site. Every keyword has a "bid" price, depending on the popularity of the keyword in search engines. You set your own budget and financial limitations, and you are done. Here is a step by step walkthrough:

- You join Google™ AdWords, and, with a credit card, put money on your account to get started

- You create your ad as you want it to appear with your own selected keywords you wish to target

- Based on the keyword value, you set how much you are willing to spend on each keyword; more popular keywords are more costly per click than others

- Upon completion, your ad is ready to appear in the Google™ Search Engine

- When someone searches through Google™, by using one of your keywords, the advertisement is matched to the keyword query, and the ad is displayed in the Google™ Search Engine results

- If the person "clicks" on your advertisement, they are navigated to your site, and you are "charged" for the click

The search engine will return a rank-ordered list of the most popular Web sites matching your search criteria, and may display your advertisement if it also matches the search criteria and keyword. One of the benefits of Google™ AdWords pay-per-click advertising is that your advertisement will be placed right up there with the top-ranked Web sites in your search category.

The rules for most pay-per-click search engine applications operate on the same principles: the advertiser with the highest bidder gets top billing in the search engine return. It is a combination of experience, knowledge of the market, and some trial and error which lets you balance keywords and phrases with optimal delivery results. Tools provided by Google™ AdWords help you achieve that goal.

Google AdWords Pay-Per-Click Benefits

- It is easy to implement

- The results are clearly measurable

- It is cost-effective in comparison to other types of traditional and online advertising programs

- It is for both large and small businesses

- It is ideal for testing out market response to new products or services

- It gives you full control over your budget — you can set systematic budgetary limits to minimize your overall financial risk and investment

- It is more effective than banner advertising

- It delivers a higher click-through rate than banner advertising

- Ads are ideally placed with top search engine results on the world's most popular search engine

- It is only delivered to your potential customers when they are searching on keywords related to your products or services contained in your pay-per-click ad

- Ads are delivered based on keyword searches, and delivered immediately — meaning the chances of turning one of those potential customers into an actual customer is dramatically increased

- It allows you to design your ad, which is strategically placed in a prominent location on the Web site

- Ads can be delivered in search engine results or within the content of a Web page

This is an example of a Google™ AdWords pay-per-click advertisement in a Google™ Search Results page. The ads are located at the top of the search results, known as "sponsored links," as well as in the column along the right side of the page:

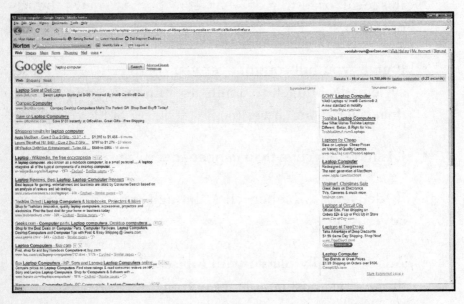

Google™ screenshots © Google™ Inc. Used with permission.

In the "Sponsored Links" section on the top, right-hand side of the page, you will see the pay-per-click results based on the query "laptop computer." As you can see, Sony® is top shelf, with Toshiba® second. Notice TigerDirect has "Google™ Checkout," which will be discussed in a later chapter of the book. There is no cost to any of these advertisers to have their sponsored links shown in your search engine results. If you click on one of those links, say the link for Sony®, you would be taken to their site, and they would be charged a pre-determined amount for that click.

Google™ screenshots © Google™ Inc. Used with permission.

Another primary benefit of a Google™ AdWords pay-per-click campaign is that you have fully customizable advertising solutions in your toolbox. You can create dozens of separate pay-per-click ads, with different wording, and based on different keywords, all within a single advertising campaign. This gives you tremendous flexibility to target a wide array of potential customer segments. Having a wide variety of advertisements available is a critical component of Google™ AdWords, where you are delivered pay-per-click advertisements based on a variety of keywords.

Google AdWords Common Terms

Keyword: The keywords you choose for a given ad group are used to target your ads to potential customers.

Campaign: A campaign consists of one or more ad groups. The ads in a given campaign share the same daily budget, language and location targeting, end dates, and distribution options.

Ad Group: An ad group contains one or more ads targeting one set of keywords. You set the maximum price you want to pay for an ad group keyword list or for individual keywords within the ad group.

Impression: The number of impressions is the number of times an ad is displayed on Google™ or the Google™ Network.

Keyword Matching Options: There are four types of keyword matching — broad matching, exact matching, phrase matching, and negative keywords. These options help you refine your ad targeting on Google™ search pages.

Maximum cost-per-click (CPC): With keyword-targeted ad campaigns, you choose the maximum cost-per-click (Max CPC) you are willing to pay. AdWords Discounter automatically reduces this amount so that the actual CPC you are charged is just one cent more than the minimum necessary to keep your position on the page.

Maximum cost-per-impression (CPM): With site-targeted ad campaigns, you choose the maximum cost per thousand impressions (Max CPM) you are willing to pay. As with Max CPC, the

AdWords Discounter automatically reduces this amount so that the actual CPM you are charged is the minimum necessary to keep your position on the page.

Cost of AdWords Pay-Per-Click Advertising

Google™ AdWords pay-per-click advertising is, of course, limited by the size of your advertising budget. You will know in advance how much you will pay-per-click, and most start out with a minimum price per click, such as 10 cents, and can quickly escalate to significantly more money, even as much as $100 per click, depending on the keyword. Essentially, you "bid" with your competitors with the amount you are willing to pay for each click on your advertisement based on the keywords you choose. It may be cost-prohibitive to be the top bidder, as your advertising budget will be consumed much quicker than if you were a #2 or #3 bidder, but there are also times when it is more critical to be the #1 bidder, regardless of the financial impact. Your bid is the maximum amount you are willing to pay for the Web site visitor to click on your advertisement, so be careful what amount you are willing to bid per click, as you may have to pay it.

Tips for AdWords Pay-Per-Click Advertising

- Design Google™ AdWords ads so they target potential customers who are ready to buy.

- Ensure your Google™ AdWords ad is specific in nature.

- Target one product for each Google™ AdWords ad, instead of a generic ad that targets a large market segment.

- Link the ad directly to the product page with a link to buy the product on that page, instead of a generic page or the Web site home page.

- If your Google™ AdWords ad targets a specific product, you may see a reduction in clicks (because your advertising segment is narrow), but those clicks are most likely extremely profitable, since you are only getting clicks from individuals seeking information on your specific product.

- Be willing to bid for a good position.

- Bid enough to gain the exposure you need, but balance exposure to stretch your advertising budget (It is typically not worth the cost to have the #1 bid, and it is often significantly less costly if you are in positions 2-10).

- The top listing is the one that is clicked the most often, but it also has the worst percentage of converting clicks into sales. Many "click happy" people click on the top listing without ever converting a sale. Those "clicks" will quickly eat up your advertising budget. You may have better luck by being below the #1 listing, since the potential for better qualified clicks exists as potential customers screen all the advertisements, instead of just clicking on the first one.

- Use Google™ AdWords Tools to monitor performance and adjust keywords/bidding as necessary.

- Choose specific keyword phrases, and you will lower your overall costs.

- Do not serve your advertisement to countries where you will not do business. Save your money and concentrate in your primary market areas.

- Use capital letters for each word in the Title and Description fields of your pay-per-click ad.

- Use Google™ AdWords Ad Targeting if you are trying to reach a specific geographic area.

- Use the Google™ Keyword Suggestion Tool to help determine which keywords are most effective for your campaign.

- Keep an eye out for fraud.

- Check the spelling in your Google™ AdWords ad to ensure it is correct.

- Embed keywords within your actual Google™ AdWords pay-per-click advertisement.

This chapter was to provide you with an in-depth introduction to Google™ AdWords pay-per-click advertising, how it works, and what it looks like, and to arm you with the most effective tips, tricks, and secrets to get the most out of your campaign. Over the next couple of chapters, we will concentrate on creating a Google™ AdWords campaign and choosing effective keywords.

Expert Advice: Pay-Per-Click Management Software – By Chris Hickman

If you manage multiple or large accounts, finding the *right* pay-per-click management software can save you considerable time and make you more efficient. Many of the daily tasks, such as increasing or decreasing bids, identifying low performing ads, and having the account overviewed can be automated.

When the software is used on a Google™ AdWords account, look at the "change history" and make sure you agree with the changes the software is making. It is crucial for you to know what changes the software is making. Fully relying on the software to make all the decisions about your pay-per-click account could be a costly mistake.

How to Pick the Right Pay-Per-Click Software for You

To find the best software to make you more productive and profitable, you must be clear on two things. One, how much are you able to spend on pay-per-click (PPC) management software? The amount you spend on PPC software should be a small percentage of what you spend on Google™. There are PPC software services available that cost as little as $50 per month and go all the way up to thousands per month. The second thing you must know is what exactly you need the software to do for you. Knowing what you want will help you to ask the right questions and find the software to meet your needs faster. Most PPC software companies will let you take a demo so you can see the interface and the features.

Pay-Per-Click Software Features to Look For

1. The software should be able to understand your goals. Most of the time, there is one main goal. Sometimes, it is to maintain a position in the search results for branding purposes, but for the most part, it is to make the account profitable. The software must be able to make or suggest changes to the account based on a cost per conversion that you specify. If it cannot do this, then you should strongly consider not using this software. It will most likely not save enough time to be worth the money. You will have to look thought the account for the cost per conversion for ads, keywords, and ad groups.

2. The second feature is automation of the changes or suggested changes that need to be made to keep the account profitable. This is similar to playing darts blind folded. It is going to be hard to hit your target if you do not know where to aim. For the pay-per-click software to be effective, it must be able to identify keywords, ads, and ad groups that are over the cost per conversion you are willing to pay. For example, if your target cost per conversion is $10, and the cost for an ad, keyword, or ad group on the content network is over $10, the software should be able to bring this to your attention. Bid updates for keywords and ad groups on the content network should be automated based on cost per conversion, and for ads, this should be brought to your attention. The bids on keywords and ad groups on the content network should be able to be automated because this a process that can be put into a mathematical equation based on the profitable or not profitable performance.

If a keyword is doing well and making money, raise the bids, and if the keyword is doing badly, then lower the bids. The amount the bid is raised or lowered would depend on how close or far away the keyword or ad group on the content network is from the desired cost per conversion. The reason the ad changes should not be automated is that all you can do with an ad is turn it off or change it, so if the software automatically pauses the ad, then you might not have anything running on Google™. Having the software write ads for you would be a big mistake, because there is no computer that can compete with a skilled human mind for ad writing. This is why is better to bring the underperforming ads to your attention rather than pause them or rewrite them.

Multiple Account Overview for Google and Yahoo

If you are managing multiple accounts, you will want to have some type of overview where you can see all your accounts at a glance. If you do not have this, then you will have to log in to each account just like you normally would, and the software will not be saving you any time when looking at multiple accounts. Some numbers that will be important are cost, clicks, impressions, click-through rate, conversions, and conversion rate.

Interface for Each Account

Does the software allow you to do everything from the interface that you can from the account, or do you have to log in to the account to perform account management tasks? Some of the less expensive software will not have a full interface where you can do everything that you can do in the account. This means you will have to still log in to the account to make updates. Try the software and see whether you are happy having to still log in to your Google™ or Yahoo account to make changes.

Alerts

Does the software allow a feature to send you alerts when a change you have specified has happened? If there is a major change in the account — for example, the spend or clicks dramatically increase or decrease — is there an alert to let you know? You may or may not need alerts to be more productive with the software, but it is a feature that is available on some pay-per-click software, and you should know about it.

Reports

What are the different types of reports available through the software? Can they be automated and e-mail out when you specify? The reports are nice to have, but if the account overview screen and the account interface are well designed, you will not need to look at the reports too often. If you are working for someone and sending them reports, this feature could save you time. Make sure they allow for private branding, because you do not want to send a report to a client with another company's logo on it.

Make the Company Prove They're Worth Your Money

If you go to the home page of any pay-per-click software company, they will all look like they are able to perform miracles on your account and quickly increase your profits, but this is not the case. The software will do exactly what it has been programmed to do, and that may not always make your account more profitable. The more you understand about how the software works and what exactly it does, the more efficient you will be. Have the representative from the software company explain the main features to you, and tell them the goals for your account and see how much help and information they give you.

Also, look at the "change history" in your Google™ AdWords account, and make sure you agree with all the changes the software is making.

Whichever software you decide to use, it is a tool to help you automate the tasks you normally do. It is not going to think for you, and it will make mistakes. Ultimately, you are responsible for the account. The right software will help you be more successful in a shorter amount of time.

Chris Hickman is the founder and Co-Owner of Silver Scope Promotion, LLC., one of the world's leading search engine marketing firms. Silver Scope Promotion has help thousands of clients worldwide to have an effective and profitable online presence. A very small number of firms worldwide have the status the Silver Scope Promotion has, being a Google™ Qualified Company and Yahoo Search Marketing Ambassador. Chris provides search engine marketing and consulting services in pay-per-click advertising, search engine optimization, Web site analytics, split testing, consumer behavior improvement, landing page development and copy writing. Starting the company while in college, Chris graduated from the University of Missouri St. Louis with a Bachelors degree in Management Information Systems and a minor in Math. Chris has almost eight years of search engine marketing experience.

Company E-mail: info@SilverScopePromotion.com

Chris Hickman's E-mail: Chris@SilverScopepromotion.com

Using Google AdWords

In addition to being the most popular search engine in the world today, Google™ also boasts the #1 pay-per-click advertising program, Google™ AdWords. To work with Google™ AdWords, you perform these three simple steps:

1. **Create your ads**: Create ads based on your keywords and key phrases, which are words that are relevant to your product or business.

2. **Ads are displayed on Google™**: When users search using matching keywords or key phrases, your ad may be displayed in the search results. Since the user selected the keyword, your advertisement is a match for the products they are looking for.

3. **Grow customers**: Users click on the ad and are taken to the landing page you established for your campaign. You just increased Web site traffic and found a new customer.

What is Google AdWords?

Google™ AdWords is a user-friendly, quick, and simple way to purchase highly targeted cost-per-click (CPC) or cost-per-impression (CPM) advertising. AdWords ads are displayed along with search results on Google™, as well as on search and content sites in the growing Google™ Network, including AOL®, EarthLink ℠, **Ask.com** ℠, and Blogger. When you create an AdWords keyword-targeted ad (pay-per-click advertisement), you choose keywords for which your ad will appear and specify the maximum amount you are willing to pay for each click, and you only pay when someone clicks on your ad.

When you create an AdWords site-targeted ad, you choose the exact Google™ Network content sites where your ad will run and specify the maximum amount you are willing to pay for each thousand page views on that site. You pay whenever someone views your ad, whether the viewer clicks or not. Start out with a Google™ AdWords keyword targeted ad, and do not allow content matching. There is no minimum monthly charge with Google™ AdWords, but there is a one-time activation fee for your account. Although your campaign can start in minutes, you may want to invest the time to identify the best keywords possible. Google™ has hundreds of thousands of high-quality Web sites, news pages, and blogs that partner with them to display AdWords ads. The Google™ content network reaches across the entire Web, and you can even use text, image, and video formats for your ads.

Using the keywords you specify when you create your ad, Google™'s contextual targeting technology automatically matches your ads to Web sites that are most relevant in content to your business — this means your ads are displayed only on relevant content sites in relevant content searches. For example, an ad for a laptop hard drive may show up next to an article reviewing the latest notebook computers.

By using the Google™ Placement Performance Report, you can monitor where all your ads appear, as well as their performance based on impression, click, cost, and conversion data. You can use this in-depth analysis tool to adjust your campaigns, change content, and remove underperforming ads from your campaign. There is no minimum spending threshold, and you can set your maximum monthly budget for each ad. Google™ provides you with a wealth of tools and information, which will help you choose keywords and stretch your budget to its fullest potential.

Google™ lets you specify country, state, city, or regions as you create your ads, so they are only served in the markets you choose. This will save your budget from clicks in markets where you have no presence. Thanks to Google™ Maps, your business location will show up on maps along with contact information. Google™ Maps will be discussed in detail later.

How Google AdWords Ranks Ads

Ads are positioned in both search and content pages based on their Ad Rank. Simply put, the ad with the highest Ad Rank appears in the first position, and so on down the page. If your ad achieves the fourth highest Ad Rank, your ad will be positioned number four in search engine results.

Here is where it starts to get confusing. While the Ad Rank determines where an ad is placed, the criteria Google™ uses to determine Ad Rank differs for keyword-targeted ads, depending on whether they appear on Google™ and the search network or just on the content network.

How Ad Rank is Determined on Google and the Search Network

A keyword-based ad is ranked on a corresponding search engine result page based on the matched keyword's cost-per-click (CPC) bid and Quality Score.

Ad Rank = CPC bid × Quality Score

The Quality Score for Ad Rank on Google™ and the search network is determined by a number of factors, including:

- Historical click-through rate (CTR) of the keyword and the matched ad on Google™

- Account history, measured by the CTR of all the ads and keywords in your Google™ AdWords account

- Historical CTR of the display URLs in the ad group

- Relevance of the keyword to the ads in its ad group

- Relevance of the keyword and the matched ad to the search query

- Your account's performance in the geographic region where the ad will be shown

- Other relevance factors, as determined by Google™

Google™ allows up to three AdWords ads to appear above the search results, as opposed to on the side. It is important to note that **only** ads that exceed a certain Quality Score and CPC bid threshold may appear in these positions. If the three highest-ranked ads all surpass these thresholds, then they will appear in order above the search results.

The CPC bid threshold is determined by the matched keyword's Quality Score; the higher Quality Score, and the lower the CPC threshold.

How Ad Rank is Determined on the Content Network

Your keyword-based ad is positioned on a content page based on the ad group's content bid and Quality Score.

Ad Rank = content bid × Quality Score

The Quality Score related to Ad Rank is determined by:

- The ad's past performance on the site and other similar sites

- Relevance of the ads and keywords to the site

- Landing page quality

- Other relevance factors, as determined by Google™

How Ad Rank is Determined for Placement-Targeted Ads on the Content Network

If a placement-targeted ad wins a position on a content page, it uses up all the ad space so no other ads can show. To determine whether your placement-targeted ad will show, Google™ considers the bid you have made for that ad group or for the individual placement, along with the ad group's Quality Score.

Ad Rank = bid × Quality Score

Google™ states that the Quality Score for determining whether a placement-targeted ad will appear on a particular site depends on the campaign's bidding option. If the campaign uses cost-per-thousand-impressions (CPM) bidding, Quality Score is based on:

- The quality of your landing page

If the campaign uses cost-per-click (CPC) bidding, Quality Score is based on:

- The historical CTR of the ad on this and similar sites

- The quality of your landing page

How to Improve Your Ranking

The bottom line is that relevant keywords, relevant text within your ads, a good click-through rate on Google™, and a high keyword cost-per-click bid all result in a higher position for your ad. The theory is that this system, which is not based entirely on the price you are willing to pay-per-click, uses well-targeted, relevant ads to ensure that the quality of your ads is factored into the placement and helps ensure that your ads can get placed, despite not being the top keyword bidder. The AdWords Discounter monitors other ads and will automatically reduce the CPC for your ads, so that you pay the lowest possible price for your ad's position on the search engine results page. One of the main advantages of this system is that you cannot be locked out of the top position, as you would be in a ranking system, based solely on price.

When you have completed the account setup process, you will be required to activate your account through an opt-in e-mail, which is sent to your specified e-mail account. Once this is confirmed, your account is activated and you can log into your new Google™ AdWords account. At this point, you will be required to enter your billing information. Upon completion of your billing information, your ad often appears within minutes. Google™ AdWords is set up to operate with three distinct levels — Account, Campaign, and Ad Group. In summary:

- Your account is associated with a unique e-mail address, password, and billing information.

- At the Campaign level, you choose your daily budget, geographic and language targeting, distribution preferences, and end dates.

- At the Ad Group level, you create ads and choose keywords. You can also select a maximum CPC for the Ad Group or for individual keywords.

- Within each Ad Group, you create one or more ads and select a set of keywords to trigger those ads. Each Ad Group runs on one set of keywords. If you create multiple ads in an Ad Group, the ads will rotate for those keywords.

- When you log in to your account, you can see your ads' click-through rates (CTRs) listed below each of the ads. If a particular ad is not performing as well as the others, you can delete or refine it to improve the overall performance of your Ad Group.

How Much Will Google AdWords Cost?

There are two versions of Google™ AdWords, the Starter Edition and the Standard Edition. Starter Edition is for those who want to advertise a single product or service and for those who are new to Internet advertising. You can upgrade from the Starter Edition to the Standard Edition at any time. You may pay a small set-up fee (currently $5) to set up your Google™ AdWords account. Each keyword has a minimum bid that is based on the quality of the keyword specific to your account. If your keyword or Ad Group's maximum CPC meets the minimum bid, and based on the other quality guidelines for ad placement we already outlined, your ad will be displayed in response to search queries. Remember, it is no longer based only on your keyword bids. Use the tips you will learn here regarding how to successfully bid on keywords. Following are some key cost factors to remember:

- The position of an ad is based on maxCPC and quality

- The higher the Quality Score, the lower the CPC require to trigger ads, and vice versa

- There is no minimum spending requirement

- You set the daily limit on how much you are willing to spend

- You set how much you are willing to pay-per-click or per impression

- You only pay for clicks on your keyword-targeted advertisement

The Google™ Keyword Tool generates potential keywords for your pay-per-click campaign and tells you their statistics, including search performance and seasonal trends. We will cover keywords in depth, as well as how to use this tool, in the next chapter.

Your cost per click will drive your total cost for AdWords, so knowing how much a keyword "costs," is critical to estimating your total monthly costs. Google™ provides a wide variety of tools to help you establish your account, choose keywords, and manage your budget and your account.

Establishing and Managing Your Account

Let us check out the starter edition, which is a good place to start a new campaign.

The first step you must complete is to create a new Google™ AdWords campaign. To create a new campaign, click on the Create a New Campaign link on the Google™ AdWords Campaign Management Screen.

Simply answer the questions and follow the steps to walk through the process of creating your account and first ad. Note that if you do not have a Web site, Google™ will help create one for you. Make sure you select whether you currently have a Web site now. Assume there is already a Web site:

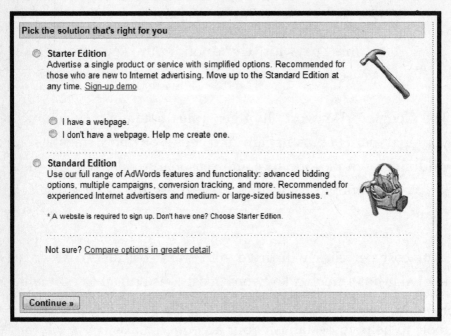

Google™ screenshots © Google™ Inc. Used with permission.

In the AdWords Starter Edition, you choose your customer base, language, and the Web site your ad will direct them to (the URL they will go to when they click on your ad; it can be your home page, or a page just for the advertisement or products).

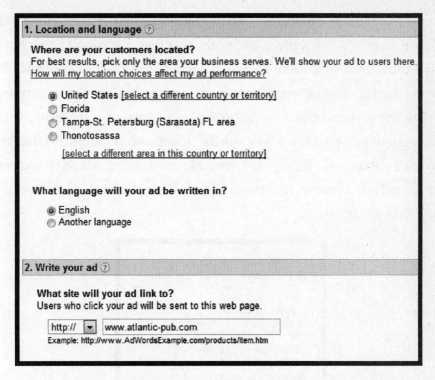

Google™ screenshots © Google™ Inc. Used with permission.

Next you will create the actual advertisement that will be displayed in the search engine results page. Google™ AdWords formats it for you as you type your advertisement.

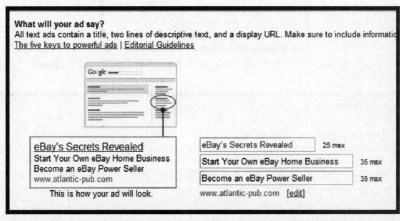

Google™ screenshots © Google™ Inc. Used with permission.

The next step is to choose your keywords. Although the next chapter covers keywords in depth, I will recommend now that you choose your keywords in advance, using the Google™ Keyword Tool to ensure your keywords are optimal for your advertising campaign. Simply enter your keywords, one at a time, and then click the "check my keywords" to see what Google™ thinks of your choices. Google™ also makes recommendations based on keywords or phrases it scans on your Web page as other recommended alternatives.

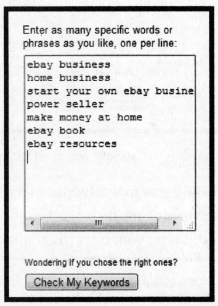

Google™ screenshots © Google™ Inc. Used with permission.

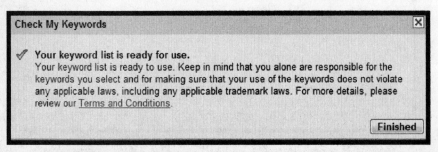

Google™ screenshots © Google™ Inc. Used with permission.

Next, you choose your currency, set your monthly budget, and sign up for tips, newsletters, and other ideas from Google™ to improve your AdWords campaign. You can set any monthly budget you want, and your ad will be served until you reach this dollar amount, until it resets the following month or billing cycle.

Google™ screenshots © Google™ Inc. Used with permission.

At this point, you follow the screen prompts to create your actual account and log into your newly created Google™ AdWords account. Keep in mind that your ad is not yet running, and will not be until you enter your billing information and activate your ad. At this point, you are set. You can activate your ad; monitor your performance through impressions, clicks, or total cost; delete, edit, or add keywords or phrases; and manage your account.

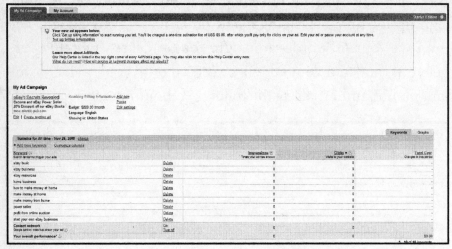

Google™ screenshots © Google™ Inc. Used with permission.

How to Graduate to Standard Edition AdWords

You can easily move from the Starter Edition to the Standard Edition. It does not cost anything to upgrade, and your account settings and ads will transfer over.

Below is a side-by-side comparison of Starter and Standard editions:

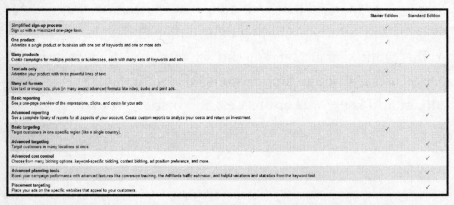

Google™ screenshots © Google™ Inc. Used with permission.

Standard Edition offers significantly more features over the Starter Edition, including:

- Multiple ad campaigns

- Advanced location targeting

- Access to the complete Google™ Network and the ability to pick the sites where your ad will show

- Powerful campaign planning and reporting tools

Creating a Standard Edition AdWords Account

The process for creating a standard account is quite similar to the Starter Edition, except that you do not create your single add as you create you account. Instead, establish your account, and then all the tools and resources are available to you to create ads and manage your campaigns.

Google™ screenshots © Google™ Inc. Used with permission.

Within the Campaign Management module, you can create, edit, and monitor your campaigns and advertisements, as well as run reports, perform analysis, use the tools and the conversion tracking module, optimize your Web site, and more. This is your command center for Google™ AdWords. The screenshot above is a real, active Google™ AdWords account which will modify and improve with each of the under-performing ads.

Google Bidding Strategies

Google™ now offers a variety of bidding strategies to help you maximize your budget and maintain flexibility in how your ads are placed. The options you may choose are:

- **Manual Bidding:** This option sets the highest price you are willing to pay for each click. Use this option if you need maximum control of each bid.

- **Conversion Optimizer:** This option sets the highest price you are willing to pay for each conversion. Google™ will optimize your performance to aim for the best possible return on investment. To use this feature, you must use Google™ Conversion Tracking.

- **Budget Optimizer:** No bids needed; your budget is set on a 30-day budget, and Google™ will manage your bids, trying to earn you the most possible clicks within that budget. This is the best option for simplified bidding and is the best choice for new users.

- **Preferred Cost Bidding:** This option sets the average price you want to pay for each click and lets Google™ manage your bids to give you a predictable average cost per click.

Google AdWords Tools

Google™ provides you with a variety of tools to manage and op-timize your campaigns with. They include:

- **Campaign Optimizer**: Automatically creates a customized proposal for your campaign.

- **Keyword Tool**: Builds a list of new keywords for your ad groups and reviews detailed keyword performance statistics, like advertiser competition and search volume.

- **Edit Campaign Negative Keywords:** Manages your negative keywords and reduces wasted clicks.

- **Site and Category Exclusion**: Prevents individual Web sites or categories of Web pages from showing your ads.

- **IP Exclusion**: Prevents specific Internet Protocol (IP) addresses from seeing your ads.

- **Traffic Estimator**: Estimates how well a keyword might perform.

- **Ad Creation Marketplace**: Finds specialists to help you create multi-media ads.

- **Ads Diagnostic Tool**: Shows how and if your ads are showing up as a result of a search.

- **Ads Preview Tool**: Allows you to see your ad on Google™ without accruing impressions.

- **Disapproved Ads**: Lets you review ads that have been disapproved.

- **Conversion Tracking**: See which ads are your best performers.

- **Web site Optimizer**: Helps you to discover the best content for boosting your business.

- **Download AdWords Editor**: Enables you to make changes offline, then upload your revised campaigns.

Creating a New Campaign in Google AdWords

At this point, you have created your Standard Google™ AdWords account, and are ready to create a new campaign. From your Campaign Summary screen, click on "New Online Campaign," then choose "Start with Keywords."

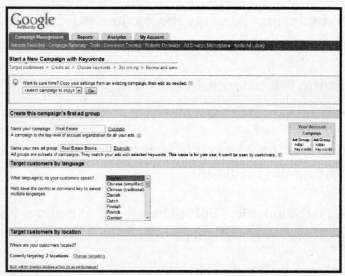

Google™ screenshots © Google™ Inc. Used with permission.

The first steps are to name your campaign, name your ad group, choose your target language, and target your location. The next steps are to create you actual ad. You do this in the same format as you did in the Starter Google™ AdWords application.

Create an ad

Create ad: Text ad | Image ad | Local business ad | Mobile ad | Click-to-play video ad | Display ad builder New!

Example:

Make Money in Real Estate
Avoid Foreclosure Problems
Books For Success in Real Estate
www.Atlantic-pub.com

Headline:	Make Money in Real Estate	Max 25 characters
Description line 1:	Avoid Foreclosure Problems	Max 35 characters
Description line 2:	Books For Success in Real Estate	Max 35 characters
Display URL:	http:// www.Atlantic-pub.com	Max 35 characters
Destination URL:	http:// ▼ www.atlantic-pub.com/real_estate.htm	Max 1024 characters

« Back   Reset Ad   Continue »

Google™ screenshots © Google™ Inc. Used with permission.

Once you complete your add and click the continue button, your advertisement is validated and checked by Google™.

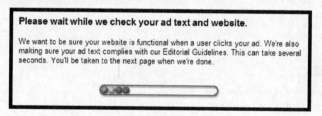

Please wait while we check your ad text and website.

We want to be sure your website is functional when a user clicks your ad. We're also making sure your ad text complies with our Editorial Guidelines. This can take several seconds. You'll be taken to the next page when we're done.

Google™ screenshots © Google™ Inc. Used with permission.

Once complete, you enter your keywords and use the keyword checker to validate them. It will recommend removal of under-performing keywords or those that are too general in nature. Google™ will also scan your Web site and make recommendations for additional keywords to add.

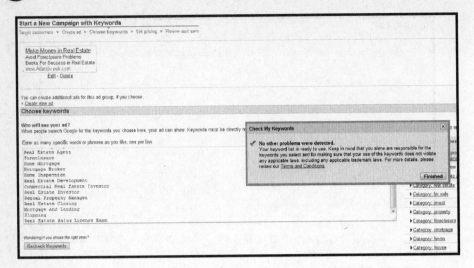

Google™ screenshots © Google™ Inc. Used with permission.

Now you must set your daily budget and bidding strategy.

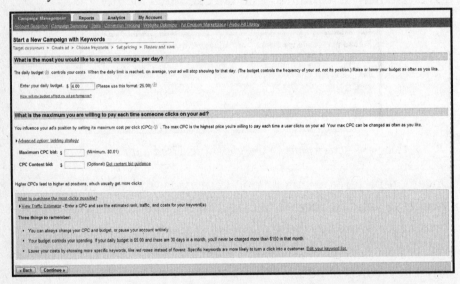

Google™ screenshots © Google™ Inc. Used with permission.

Google™ provides you with help each step of the way. There are always options for help, more information, and guides to improve your campaign. One excellent tool is the Traffic Estimator, which you can use to enter a CPC and see the estimated rank,

Traffic Estimates

View the ad performance estimates for your selected keywords on the Google Search Network below. Estimates are provided only as a guideline; your actual costs and ad positions for your keywords may vary. Learn more

Your keyword and CPC changes have not been saved.
You may continue making changes and re-calculating estimates below.
When satisfied, please save your changes.

Without budget limitations:
At an average CPC of $2.69 - $1.00 these keywords could potentially generate 8,341 - 12,439 clicks per day (which would cost you $6,680 - $12,400)
► Show total potential clicks in the table below

Keywords ▾ Search Network Total	Max CPC	Search Volume	Estimated Avg. CPC	Estimated Ad Position
			$0.69 - $1.00	1 - 3
mortgage books (to be added)	$1.00		$0.69 - $0.88	1 - 3
Commercial Real Estate Investor	$1.00			
Overlaps with: commercial real estate, Real Estate Investor			$0.00	
Flipping	$1.00		$0.66 - $0.82	1 - 3
Foreclosure	$1.00		$0.68 - $1.00	4 - 6
Home Inspection	$1.00		$0.65 - $0.98	4 - 6
Home Mortgage	$1.00		$0.66 - $0.96	7 - 10
Mortgage Broker	$1.00		$0.84 - $0.96	4 - 6
Mortgage and Lending	$1.00		$0.60 - $0.75	1 - 3
Real Estate Agent	$1.00		Not enough data to give estimates.	
Overlaps with: real estate agent				
Real Estate Closing	$1.00		$0.63 - $0.94	1 - 3
Real Estate Development	$1.00		$0.66 - $0.96	1 - 3
Real Estate Investor	$1.00		$0.87 - $1.00	4 - 6
Real Estate Sales License Exam	$1.00		Not enough data to give estimates.	
Rental Property	$1.00		$0.67 - $1.00	1 - 3
Rental Property Manager	$1.00		$0.60 - $0.57	1 - 3
Overlaps with: Rental Property				
commercial real estate	$1.00		$0.68 - $1.00	1 - 3
commercial real estate investing	$1.00		$0.00	
Overlaps with: commercial real estate, real estate investing				
investing books	$1.00		$0.55 - $0.84	1 - 3
investment property	$1.00		$0.73 - $1.00	1 - 3
private mortgage investing	$1.00		$0.66 - $0.97	11 - 16
real estate agent	$1.00		$0.73 - $1.00	1 - 3
real estate books	$1.00		$0.67 - $1.00	1 - 3
real estate broker	$1.00		$0.56 - $0.99	1 - 3
real estate closing	$1.00		Not enough data to give estimates.	
Overlaps with: Real Estate Closing				
real estate financing	$1.00		$0.81 - $0.92	4 - 6
real estate investing	$1.00		$0.69 - $1.00	4 - 6
real estate investments	$1.00		$0.65 - $0.99	4 - 6
real estate listings	$1.00		$0.65 - $0.97	1 - 3
reverse mortgage	$1.00		$0.49 - $0.72	4 - 6
second mortgage	$1.00		$0.44 - $0.66	4 - 6

Google™ screenshots © Google™ Inc. Used with permission.

Google™ features multiple advertisement options, which include:

- Text Ad

> **Luxury Cruise to Mars**
> Visit the Red Planet in style.
> Low-gravity fun for everyone!
> www.example.com

Google™ screenshots © Google™ Inc. Used with permission.

- Image Ad

Google™ screenshots © Google™ Inc. Used with permission.

- **Local Business Ad**: Local business ads are AdWords ads associated with a specific Google™ Maps business listing. They show on Google™ Maps with an enhanced location marker. They also show in a text-only format on Google™ and other sites in our search network.

- **Mobile Business Text Ad**: Your ads will appear when someone uses Google™ Mobile Search on a mobile device.

Google™ screenshots © Google™ Inc. Used with permission.

- **Video Ad**: A video ad is an ad format that appears on the Google™ content network. Your video ad will appear as a static image until a user clicks on it, playing your video.

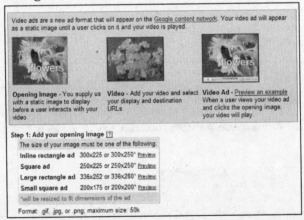

Google™ screenshots © Google™ Inc. Used with permission.

- **Display Ad Builder**: This new feature lets you create your own display ad as easily as building text ads. When you are done creating your new ad, it will run on Google™ partner sites based on the target settings you choose.

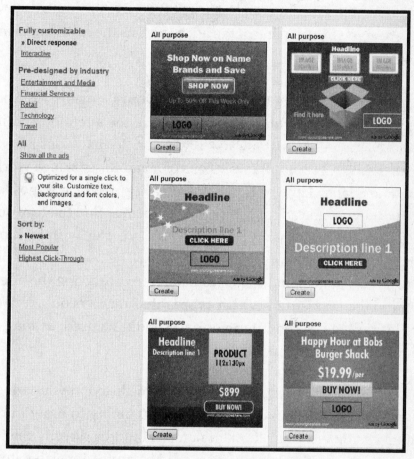

Google™ screenshots © Google™ Inc. Used with permission.

Start out your campaigns with the Text Advertisement. Google™ AdWords provides you with a simple form to create your text advertisement. As you enter data into the form, the example is updated with your data. In the following screenshot, notice that we have capitalized each keyword in each line, in addition to providing the display URL and the actual destination URL, which may be different, depending on your campaign.

You will need to give some extra time and attention to the wording of your ad. Wording can be tricky because of the limited space you are given on each line of the ad, as well as the restrictions imposed by Google™.

It is critical to load the title (first line of your Google™ AdWord ad) with keywords. Your goal is to capture the attention and interest of a potential customer — if you can do that, your ad will be successful. Test multiple versions of an ad to see which works best, and change keywords to help you analyze which is most effective. Review the ads of competitors; you may find they are outperforming you simply because their ad is better written, more captivating, or has more customer appeal. The use of words like free, rebate, bonus, and cash, are perfect for attracting the attention of Web site surfers. Other words that may encourage Web site visitors to click through your ad should be used, as long as your ad message is concise and clear.

You should also consider the domain name listed in your advertisement, as it may have an effect on your ability to draw in potential customers. Your domain name should be directly related to your products or services and should be professional in nature. You will find an abundance of companies that offer search engine copywriting services, which is a good option if you are having problems developing successful ad campaigns.

Some recommended sources for copywriting include:

- **www.searchenginewriting.com/**

- **www.grantasticdesigns.com/copywriting.html**

- www.roncastle.com/web_copywriting.htm

- www.futurenettechnologies.com/creative-copywriting.htm

- www.tinawrites.com

- www.brandidentityguru.com/optimized-copywriting.html

Search engine copywriting is critical to a successful pay-per-click advertising campaign. While professional services are recommneded for this task, it is not overly difficult to achieve if you apply some basic discipline and rules. Simply cramming keyword after keyword into your pay-per-click advertisements may be counter-productive, and is not search engine copywriting. Successful SEO copywriting takes planning, discipline, analysis, and some degree of trial and error. Below are some guidelines for successful SEO copywriting:

- Use no more than four keywords per ad. Four keywords provide a wide keyword variety without saturating the ad with keywords and losing the meaning of the ad.

- Use all your allowed characters in each line of the advertisement. There is no incentive for white space.

- Write in natural language. "Natural language" is a popular term used extensively with copywriting. It simply means that the reader should not be able to — or should barely be able to — detect what keywords the ad is targeting. The best ads are written for an individual to read and understand, embedded with subtle keywords, and project a clear message; thus, they read "naturally." The opposite of this is a keyword-crammed ad that is just a collection of keywords, and is therefore entirely "unnatural" to read.

- Use keywords in the Title and Description lines, but use common sense so you do not overload them.

- Test your ad and analyze your reports and results. Your ad may need tweaking or improvements, or it may be entirely ineffective and may need to be replaced.

Google™ screenshots © Google™ Inc. Used with permission.

You may discover that the costs can escalate quickly if you do not set daily and monthly budget limitations. Keep in mind that limits on your daily/monthly budgets will also affect your ad performance, since your ad will not be displayed once you hit your budget limits. Google™ recognizes when your advertisement is bumping against its budget constraints and may suggest you increase your budget amount to increase visibility of your advertisement, as well as subsequent potential customers visiting your Web site, as shown on the next page:

> **Campaign Budget Alert**
> In the last 15 days, your ads missed 46% of impressions for which they were eligible. Increasing your budget could allow your ads to show more often and get more clicks.
> Tell me more | Remove this message

Google™ screenshots © Google™ Inc. Used with permission.

The Google Campaign Summary

The Campaign Summary screen is where you will control all your Google™ AdWords campaigns. At this screen, you will be presented with an overview of each campaign, including campaign name, status, budget, clicks, impressions, click-through ratio, average cost-per-click, and total cost.

To drill down into each campaign, simply click on the campaign name to view detailed status based on keywords and ad variation performance. This module will help you determine the effectiveness of each keyword and add/remove keywords. Your keywords may be marked "inactive for search" in the "status" column, and stop showing on search results if they do not have a high enough Quality Score and maximum cost-per-click (CPC). This is another way of saying that your keyword or Ad Group's maximum CPC does not meet the minimum bid required to trigger ads on Google™ or its search network partners. This typically occurs when keywords are not as targeted as they could be, and the ads they deliver are not relevant enough to what a user is searching for — which ultimately means you need to refine your keywords or your ad.

Keywords marked "inactive for search" may continue to trigger ads for content sites if you have the Google™ content network enabled for that campaign. Thus, a keyword marked as inactive for search may continue to generate clicks and charges on the content network. If your keyword is inactive for search, increase your keyword's Quality Score by optimizing for relevancy.

Optimization is a technique for improving the quality of your keywords, ad, and campaign to increase your keyword's performance without raising costs. Try to combine your keyword with two to three other words to create a more specific keyword phrase. This will result in better targeting, and potentially, better performance. You may also Increase your keyword's maximum CPC to the recommended minimum bid. Your keyword's minimum bid is the amount required to trigger ads on Google™ and is determined by your keyword's Quality Score. When your maximum CPC falls below the minimum bid, your keyword will be inactive for search. For this reason, you can simply increase your maximum CPC to the minimum bid to reactivate your keywords. You may also choose to delete all keywords that are inactive.

The Ad Variations links allows you to review performance for each ad within a selected campaign. It is common to have multiple ads created for the same (or different) keyword combinations within the same campaign. In the following screenshot, it is clear by the "% served" that the first ad is served considerably more than the second ad, which is rarely served. The reasons for this may vary, depending on the keywords chosen or campaign settings.

If you click on the Edit link, under the Actions column, you can tweak your campaign ads to improve your statistics.

Example short ad:

Restaurant Consulting
Cheftec Recipe Software Solutions
Discounts+ Free Technical Support
restaurantprofits.com

Headline:	Restaurant Consulting	Max 25 characters
Description line 1:	Cheftec Recipe Software Solutions	Max 35 characters
Description line 2:	Discounts+ Free Technical Support	Max 35 characters
Display URL: [?]	http:// restaurantprofits.com	Max 35 characters
Destination URL: [?]	http:// restaurantprofits.com	Max 1024 characters

Save Ad   Cancel

Restaurant Consulting
Cheftec Recipe Software Solutions
Discounts+ Free Technical Support
restaurantprofits.com
2 Clicks | 1.58% CTR | $0.85 CPC
Served - 0.7%

Restaurant Consulting
Increase Your Restaurant's Profit
Controls to Lower Food & Labor Cost
restaurantprofits.com
192 Clicks | 1.09% CTR | $0.78 CPC
Served - 99.3%

Google™ screenshots © Google™ Inc. Used with permission.

For each Ad Group, you can create up to 50 ad variations. The variations can be in any of the formats offered for AdWords, including text, image, and video ads. When you first sign up for an account, you will be offered the chance to create additional ad variations immediately after you create your first ad. You can also create ad variations later, after your account is running. Sign into your account and choose the Ad Group you want to work with. Click the Ad Variations tab, find the line reading "Create new ad," and then select the type of ad you want to create. All ad variations in a single Ad Group are triggered by the same set of keywords. You may choose to have ads optimized, which would show better-performing ads more often, or to rotate, which shows all ads equally. If you want different ads to appear for different keywords, you can create multiple Ad Groups or campaigns.

Editing Your Campaign Settings

In the "Edit Campaign Settings" menu, you have the ability to modify your campaign settings, including campaign name, budget options, ad scheduling, keyword bidding, network and bidding, and scheduling and serving.

Google™ screenshots © Google™ Inc. Used with permission.

Google™ AdWords will suggest the recommended budget amount for your campaign by clicking on the View Recommended Budget link in the Edit Campaign Settings screen, as shown in the following screenshot.

Based on your current keywords, your recommended budget is **$8.00 / day**.

If the recommended amount is too high, try raising your budget to a comfortable amount. Or, to make the most of your budget, try refining your ads and keywords.

Google™ screenshots © Google™ Inc. Used with permission.

Ad scheduling lets you control the days and times your AdWords campaigns appear. Your AdWords ads normally are available to run 24 hours each day. Ad scheduling allows you to set your campaigns to appear only during certain hours or days of each week. For example, you might set your ads to run only on Tuesdays, or from 3:00 until 6:00 p.m. daily. With ad scheduling, a campaign can run all day, every day, or as little as 15 minutes per week.

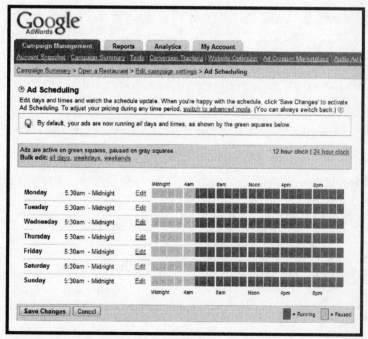

Google™ screenshots © Google™ Inc. Used with permission.

To determine when you want your ads to show, you may want to run an hourly report. Ad scheduling can be used with both keyword-targeted and site-targeted AdWords campaigns. If you select the advanced setting, the bid multiplier will apply to both CPC and cost-per-thousand-impressions CPM bids. Ad scheduling will not raise or lower your budget. The AdWords system will try to reach your usual daily budget in whatever number of hours your ad runs each day.

Position preference lets you tell Google™ where you would prefer your ad to show among all the AdWords ads on a given page. Whenever you run a keyword-targeted ad, your ad is assigned a position (or rank) based on your CPC bid, your keyword's Quality Score, and other relevant factors. There may be dozens of positions available for a given keyword, spread over several pages of search results. If you find that your ad gets the best results when it is ranked third or fourth among all AdWords ads, you can set a position preference for those spots. AdWords will then try to show your ad whenever it is ranked third or fourth, and avoid showing it when it is ranked higher or lower. If your ad is ranked higher than third for a given keyword, the system will automatically try to lower your bid to place your ad in your preferred position.

You can request that your ad be shown only when it is:

- Higher than a given position, such as above 7

- Lower than a given position, such as below 4

- Within a range of positions, such as from 2 to 8

- In a single exact position, such as position 2

Position preference does not mean that your ad will always appear in the position you specify. The usual AdWords ranking and relevance rules apply. If your ad does not qualify for position No. 1, setting a position preference of 1 will not move it there. Position preference simply means AdWords will try to show your ad whenever it is ranked in your preferred position, and to avoid showing it when it is not. Position preference also does not affect the overall placement of AdWords ad units on the left, right, top, or bottom of a given page. It only affects your ranking relative to other ads across those units.

Google™ AdWords allows you to track and measure conversions and ultimately, help you identify how effective your AdWords ads and keywords are for you. It works by placing a cookie on a user's computer when he/she clicks on one of your AdWords ads. Then, if the user reaches one of your conversion pages, the cookie is connected to your Web page. When a match is made, Google™ records a successful conversion for you. Please note that the cookie Google™ adds to a user's computer when he/she clicks on an ad expires in 30 days. This measure, and the fact that Google™ uses separate servers for conversion tracking and search results, protects the user's privacy.

Demographic Bidding

Demographic bidding is a way in which Google™ AdWords allows you to choose your audience by age and gender. Since some publishers on the Google™ content network know details about their users, such as social networking sites, they can serve ads based on age and gender. Google™ AdSense can display your AdWords ads to the demographic groups that you select, or block them from groups you do not want to reach.

Google AdWords Reports

Google™ provides full online statistical, conversion, and financial reporting for the Google™ AdWords program. You can view all your account reports online 24 hours a day, 7 days a week, and you can also have them set up to be e-mailed to you on a scheduled basis.

The AdWords Report Center allows you to easily create customized performance reports to help you track and manage multiple facets of your AdWords campaigns. There are dozens of highly customized options available for you to choose, all of which are simple and easy to generate.

Key features include:

- Quick report generation in categories such as Site/Keyword Performance, URL Performance, Campaign Performance, Ad Group Performance, and Account Performance

- The ability to select individual campaigns and/or ad groups for report

- Customizable report columns to focus only on the data you need

- Performance filters screen for the most relevant information in categories such as Cost, Impressions, Clicks, CTR, and other statistics

- Scheduling for automatic report generation and delivery

- E-mailing option for multiple recipients

- Saved templates for reusable reports

Impressions 2,026,900	Clicks 36,300	CTR 1.38%	Avg CPC $0.21	Cost $7,678.84

Google™ screenshots © Google™ Inc. Used with permission.

Impressions 2,626,900	Clicks 36,300	CTR 1.38%	Avg CPC $0.21	Cost $7,678.84	Avg Position 3.74

Google™ screenshots © Google™ Inc. Used with permission.

Google AdWords Ads Diagnostic Tool

One of the nicest features of Google™ AdWords is the Ads Diagnostic Tool, which helps you find out why your ads may not be showing on the first page of search results for a certain keyword

Ads Diagnostic Tool
Choose one of the two options below to find out why your ads may not be showing on the first page of search results for a certain keyword.

Option 1: Search Terms and Parameters
Use this option if you're concerned about all ads within your account that should be appearing for a specific search term. For example, you could check your ad status for the phrase-matched keyword "Hawaiian cruises," targeted to California users.

Keyword:	
Google domain:	www.google.com << ex: froogle.google.com, www.google.co.uk
Display language:	English
User location:	⊙ Geographic: United States
	All regions within this country
	○ IP address: Format: xxx.xxx.xxx.xxx

[Continue >>]

Option 2: Search Results Page URL
Use this option if you're concerned about a particular search results page that you believe should be showing one of your ads. Copy and paste the URL from the address bar on the search results page where your ad should be showing.

Search results page URL

[Continue >>]

Google™ screenshots © Google™ Inc. Used with permission.

Tips for AdWords Pay-Per-Click Advertising

This is a compilation of some tips and hints that will help you to develop and manage a highly effective Google™ AdWords Campaign, which in turn will generate higher click-through rates, lower your cost per click, and get conversions.

- Design Google™ AdWords ads so they target potential customers who are ready to buy — rarely will banner ads or pay-per-click ads draw in the curious Web site browser and result in a sale.

- Ensure your Google™ AdWords ad is specific in nature.

- Target one product for each Google™ AdWords ad, instead of using a generic ad that targets a large market segment.

- Make your ad link directly to the product page with a link to buy the product on that page, instead of to a generic page or the Web site home page.

- If your Google™ AdWords ad targets a specific product, you may see a reduction in clicks because your advertising segment is narrow, but those clicks are most likely extremely profitable since you are only getting clicks from individuals seeking information on your specific product — this means your advertising cost may actually be reduced, while your sales go up.

- Be willing to bid for a good position. If you do not want to spend much money or are willing to settle for the bottom of the bids, no one is going to see your ad.

- Bid enough to gain the exposure you need, but balance exposure to stretch your advertising budget. It rarely worth the cost to have the #1 bid, and it is often significantly less costly if you are in positions 2 through 10.

- Being the #1 listing on search engines may not be all it is cracked up to be. The top listing is the one that is clicked the most often, but is also has the worst percentage of converting clicks into actual sales. Many "click happy" people click on the top listing without ever converting a sale. Those clicks will quickly eat up your advertising budget. You may have better luck by being below the No. 1 listing, since you have the potential for better qualified clicks.

- Use the provided tracking tools to monitor performance and adjust keywords/bidding as necessary.

- Chose specific keyword phrases and you will lower your overall costs while increasing the potential conversion rate by choosing multiple highly targeted words or phrases instead of generic terms.

- Use capital letters for each word in the Title and in the Description fields of your pay-per-click ad.

- Use demographic and geographic targeting with your Google™ AdWords ad.

- Use the Google™ Keyword Suggestion Tool to determine which keywords are most effective for your campaign.

- Keep an eye out for fraud. Although Google™ has fraud detection and prevention, if you suspect your competition is clicking on your ads, you may want to invest in additional protection Try it at: **www.whosclickingwho.com**.

- Check the spelling in your Google™ AdWords ad to ensure it is correct.

- Embed keywords within your actual Google™ AdWords pay-per-click ad.

- Define your target audience and narrow the scope of your ad to potential customers.

- Develop multiple advertisements for each campaign, and run them at the same time. You will quickly determine which is effective, and which is not. Do not be afraid to tweak or replace poorly performing advertisements.

- Monitor and use Google™ Reports by tracking your costs, return on investment (we showed you how to calculate that earlier), and the click-through ratios for each ad.

- Include targeted keywords in the Headline and Description lines of your ad. Keywords stand out in search engine results, help to attract the attention of potential customers, and increase your overall advertisement effectiveness. Be quite specific in your keywords.

- Include words that stand out and grab the attention of potential customers, such as "new" and "limited offer."

- Do not just link to the homepage of your Web site. Link directly to the relevant landing page for your specific product or service — this will help you convert the "visit" to a "sale."

- Free may not be good for you. If your advertisement says "free," then you can expect considerable traffic from folks who just want the "free" stuff, which will increase your costs. Consider limiting the use of "free" to cut back on traffic that will never culminate in a sale.

Expert Advice: Using Google AdWords: Before You Start – By Chris Hickman

Know the competition: Before you start advertising and spending money on Google™, it is crucial to know what you will be paying to go up against. Many people will look at a few Web sites and compare services and prices before deciding to buy or give their contact information.

Know the problem you are helping the consumer solve: Take Google™, for example; they are helping the world easily find whatever they want. How does your product or service help someone, and how easy it for someone else to do what you do?

Knowing the answer to this question can help you in selecting your keywords, writing your ads, and writing the copy for your landing page.

Starting a campaign: Before you start your campaign, it is important to realize the importance of what your Google™ AdWords account is doing, which is getting someone's attention. You are paying for 6 to 8 seconds (which is the average amount of time you have to convince someone to stay after they click on your Google™ ad) of someone's attention. It is also important to realize that everything you do on Google™ is meant to help connect with and solve the problems of the person doing the search. The ads you write and the landing page you send the traffic to should all be designed to connect with the user and help them solve the problem they have.

Setting a budget: When trying to decide how much to start your budget with, you want to start with an amount that you are comfortable spending. Google™ allows you to set a daily budget, so if you are spending ten dollars a day or ten thousand dollars a day, Google™ can stay within your budget. When you advertise, there is no guarantee that you will make your money back. The only guarantee is that Google™ will charge your credit card for the traffic that they deliver to your Web site. A common mistake most people make is spending more than they can afford. Having the mindset that simply advertising on Google™ will make you a profit can get you into trouble. Pick a budget that you are comfortable spending, then, with the proper testing and optimization, you can use the profits to gradually increase your budget.

Finding the Right Keywords: There are many keyword tools out there to give you suggestions and variations for your base keywords. A base keyword is the main keyword you are going to use and the variations of it. An example of this would be having cars as a base keyword and the variations would include new cars, used cars, buy a car, red car, and sports car. Some of these keyword tools cost money, and others are free. A common difference between paid and free keyword tools is that paid tools offer you more keyword variations off of your base keyword and will save the results for you. The free versions will give you fewer results, and they will not save those results for you. Two good free key word tools to use are Google™ AdWords key word tool and the one provided by Word Tracker, at **http://freekeywords. wordtracker.com**. Having more key words is like having a larger net on the Web to catch more people and bring them to your Web site.

How to Write Good Ads: An ad should be like a window to your Web site. A person searching can look at the ad and have a good idea of what is going to be on the site. This is crucial because you are not paying for someone to see your ad, only for someone to click on your ad. When you include the keyword in the ad, and someone does a search for that keyword, it will appear in bold, which will draw more attention and get more clicks. A common mistake most people make is putting the company name in the ad. The company name might not mean anything to the searcher, and listing a benefit in place of the company name would better describe what is on the Web site. The ad should focus on the benefits and advantages you have to offer. This would be an example of a dentist's advertising on Google™ that could use improvement:

Jaber Orthodontics
Quality Orthodontics for Miami;
Invisalign and traditional braces
www.dentistwebsite.com

This ad could be changed to an ad like this:
Don't Want Braces?
Try Invisalign & Straighten Your
Teeth. Come See Dr. Jaber Today
www.dentistwebsite.com

The second ad is starting off with identifying a problem someone has and offering a solution. While the first ad is just stating the doctors last name and type of practice. The second ad also had a call to action. The more qualifying your ad is, the more likely the person searching will be taking the action you want by either giving you their information or buying something. I normally recommend writing three to five ads for each ad group and having Google™ set to turn off the ad optimizer and rotate them evenly. This means if you have five ads, each ad will display 20 percent of the time. The reason to do this is that Google™ will automatically show the ad with the highest click-through rate, and the highest click-through rate ad does not always have the highest conversion rate. Do not let Google™ think for you in terms of which ads to display, it is your Web site, your ad, and your advertising dollars. Make sure you agree with what ads are being displayed.

Setting up conversion counter: One of the most important features on Google™ AdWords is the conversion counter because it allows sales and/or leads to be tracked down to the specific keyword and ad. This will allow you to quickly identify where your profits are coming from and how to eliminate wasted money. It is easy to set up. All you do is place an HTML code that is given to you by Google™ on the page someone goes to after they give you their name and e-mail address or buy something, which is normally called a thank-you page or is a page that says "thank you for submitting your order." Google™ also has a feature that allows e-mail instructions to be sent to your Web designer if you are not knowledgeable in HTML. Do whatever it takes to get the Google™ conversion counter installed. Not tracking where conversions are coming from can be one of the most expensive mistakes you can make.

Chris Hickman is the founder and Co-Owner of Silver Scope Promotion, LLC., one of the world's leading search engine marketing firms. Silver Scope Promotion has help thousands of clients worldwide to have an effective and profitable online presence. A very small number of firms worldwide have the status the Silver Scope Promotion has, being a Google™ Qualified Company and Yahoo Search Marketing Ambassador. Chris provides search engine marketing and consulting services in pay-per-click advertising, search engine optimization, Web site analytics, split testing, consumer behavior improvement, landing page development and copy writing. Starting the company while in college, Chris graduated from the University of Missouri St. Louis with a Bachelors degree in Management Information Systems and a minor in Math. Chris has almost eight years of search engine marketing experience.

Company E-mail: info@SilverScopePromotion.com

Chris Hickman's E-mail: Chris@SilverScopepromotion.com

Expert Advice: Managing a Google AdWord Account – By Chris Hickman

How to dramatically reduce wasted money on Google™ by following the money: Think of your Google™ account as a pool that is leaking water. The water would represent your budget. You would want to quickly identify the biggest holes in the pools first, which, in the Google™ account, would be where the most spend is. To do this when you are logged into your Google™ account, looking at the campaign overview screen, click on the "cost sort" tab and sort the campaigns from most to least expensive. Then click on the most expensive campaign and do the same for the ad groups to find the most expensive ad group. Then, when you are in the ad group, do the same to find the most expensive keyword(s) and ad(s). This will make you aware of the most expensive areas of your account so you know where your money is going, and this is where you should spend most of your attention. There is an 80/20 rule in business that means 80 percent of your business will come from 20 percent of your costumers. In many Google™ accounts, a small percentage of ads and keywords will account for a majority of the spend or sales. When you follow the most expensive campaigns, ad groups, keywords, and ads, this will let you see where your money is going. If the conversion counter is installed, you will be able to quickly identify whether this is profitable. This is how a Google™ AdWords account can be optimized, and the profits can be dramatically increased. Just like you would walk around the pool that is leaking water to find the biggest hole, this strategy is allowing you to find the biggest spending area in your account. To fix the leaking pool, you would first fix the biggest leak, then the second, third, then fourth.

Ads: Knowing when to delete or pause an ad: I never delete ads; I keep an ad that is under-performing paused so I can see the text in the ad, and since its paused, I know that it did not perform well. When writing new ads, I can have an idea of what has not worked in the past. I always write three to five ads with them rotating evenly. At least two ads are going to focus on the benefits that are being offered. One ad is going to be a "left field ad" that is going to be different and stand out to test and see how it performs. For the last two ads, I look for similarities between the top three sponsored results by doing a search on Google™ for the main key word associated with that ad. The reason I look for these similarities is because in most cases, the top ads have the highest click-through rate, which means that the competing advertiser has already tested those ads and is showing the best ads.

This will allow you to benefit from someone else's testing.

Sometimes, you will find a bid company with a large budget or an inexperienced advertiser who just continues to lose money with an ad that does not work, so be careful if you come across a competitor like that. I pause an ad when it has reached two to three times the desired cost per conversion, or 20 to 30 clicks — whichever comes first. For example, if the desired cost per conversion is $10, and an ad has received 30 clicks and is over $10 per conversion, then I would pause that ad. Now if the ad has received only ten clicks, but is at $30 in spend with no conversions, I would pause that ad as well. This sets a threshold on the amount of clicks and spend the ad can receive without getting a conversion, or getting a conversion by costing more than you are willing to pay for that conversion before its paused. There are exceptions to this rule, but this can be applied to most cases and used to know when to pause an ad.

Keywords: knowing when to delete, pause, increase bid, decrease bid, or pull it out and separate it from the other: I will only delete a key word if it is not relevant to the product or service, which normally happens when I take over someone's account. If the key word is relevant, I will never delete it, but I will lower the bid because the lower bid is a way to keep track of underperforming keywords. When a keyword has an extremely low bid, I know I lowered it for a reason and leave it lowered. When deciding on increasing a bid for a keyword, I look at the cost per conversion, impression, and number of clicks. If a keyword is under the desired cost per conversion, I will raise the key word bid by 10 to 20 percent to allow for higher placement and more clicks. If a keyword is receiving very few clicks or impressions in relation to the other keywords, then I will raise the bid to give that keyword the chance to perform. When deciding on lowering a key word bid, I look at the cost per conversion of the keyword. If the cost per conversion of that key word is higher than the cost of conversion for the account to be profitable, then I will lower the bid.

For example, if an advertiser can pay $10 per conversion, and the cost per conversion for that keyword if $15, then it is time to lower the bid. The amount I lower the bid by is determined by how big the gap is between profitability of the cost per conversion and the actual cost per conversion for the keyword. For example, if the desired cost per conversion is $10, and the cost per conversion for the keyword is $12, then I would lower the bid by 10 to 20 percent. Now if the cost per conversion of the keyword was $30, then I would lower the cost per click of the keyword by 50 to 75 percent. The worse the keyword is performing, the larger the reduction in the cost per click will be.

Example:

Desired cost per conversion to be profitable: $15
Keyword 1 -> Buy Ecommerce Books Online
Current bid: $0.80
Cost per conversion: $17
New lowered bid: $0.65
Keyword 2 -> Ecommerce Books
Current bid: $0.80
Cost per conversion: $35
New lowered bid: $0.30

How to improve quality score: Quality score is one of the major ways Google™ determines how much you have to pay-per-click to be on the first page. Google™ gives words a quality ranking such as poor, OK, and great. In most cases, if your keyword quality score is poor, you will have to bid a considerable amount more compared to someone whose keyword is OK or great. Quality score is Google™'s way of determining the relevancy of your keyword, ad, and landing page. Google™'s purpose when assigning a quality score is letting you know how relevant they think your page is, and they will also give suggestions on what to do to improve your quality score to make your keyword, ad, and landing page more relevant for the user experience.

A common way to improve a quality score is to write ads that have the keyword in them and to select a landing page that has that keyword and information about that keyword on that landing page. On the landing page, if you collect someone's personal information, you should clearly state your privacy policy, and you should have three to five links to external Web sites with similar content. The links can be very small and at the bottom of the page so as not to draw attention from the user and Google™ can still see them when they scan your landing page as they assign a quality score. Mastering quality score can be one of the harder things to do on Google™ AdWords, but is worth the time and effort because of the large role it plays in cost per click and minimum bid to be on the first page.

Search and content: Break up campaigns by search and content. You can have the same keywords in each category. The reason for this is to quickly see the difference in performance for ads and keywords in the search and content networks. Since you cannot see the individual keyword performance on the content network like you can on search, you can still see the ad group performance and the click-through rate of the different ads.

There are multiple dimensions of banner ads that can be put on the network, but many advertisers use only text ads and no banners, and the ones that do use banners normally use the standard banner size of 468x60 and neglect to use the other banner sizes.

This is a consistency I have noticed in the hundreds of accounts I have looked at and worked on. Adding banners can increase impression and clicks from 25 to 50 percent. This number will vary from industry to industry.

Chris Hickman is the founder and Co-Owner of Silver Scope Promotion, LLC., one of the world's leading search engine marketing firms. Silver Scope Promotion has help thousands of clients worldwide to have an effective and profitable online presence. A very small number of firms worldwide have the status the Silver Scope Promotion has, being a Google™ Qualified Company and Yahoo Search Marketing Ambassador. Chris provides search engine marketing and consulting services in pay-per-click advertising, search engine optimization, Web site analytics, split testing, consumer behavior improvement, landing page development and copy writing. Starting the company while in college, Chris graduated from the University of Missouri St. Louis with a Bachelors degree in Management Information Systems and a minor in Math. Chris has almost eight years of search engine marketing experience.

Company E-mail: info@SilverScopePromotion.com

Chris Hickman's E-mail: Chris@SilverScopepromotion.com

CHAPTER 6

Creating an Effective Google Pay-Per-Click Advertising Campaign: Keywords, Key Phrases, & Your Google AdWords Budget

In addition to the techniques we have discussed so far, to increase Web site traffic, you must develop an effective Google™ Ad-Words campaign. One major step is determining what keywords or key phrases your potential customers may use when seeking out your company, products, or services.

In the use of Google™ AdWords, a keyword is a word or phrase that people (consumers or businesses) would employ to locate information on the products or services or topic that they are interested learning more about or purchasing. When choosing the keywords you will eventually bid on and embed within your advertising campaign, you need to think like a potential customer, not as the seller or advertiser. You must determine which search terms a potential customer might use to find you through Google™. High rankings in both a search engine and achieving high visibility of your Google™ AdWords advertisement, success is directly related to how "competitive" your keywords are in relation to terms used by individuals searching the Google™ Search Engine.

You do not own any keywords or have exclusive rights to them, and chances are, your competitors are targeting the exact same keywords. The cost to buy a keyword in a Google™ AdWords pay-per-click advertising campaign is primarily determined by how many other Web sites are competing for the same keyword or key phrases. A key component in a Web site or Google™ AdWords campaign is the keywords you choose. Keywords are critical to achieving success in the Google™ Search Engine and in your Google™ AdWords advertising campaigns. The Google™ Traffic Estimator tool provides a wealth of data relevant to your chosen keywords and assists you with determining expected traffic, daily budget, costs per keyword, and overall campaign success.

Keep your keywords focused and specific to your products or services. Extremely general keywords, such as "real estate" are typically more expensive, since many people search on them. For these same reasons, they are not as productive as specific keywords or phrases, such as "real estate foreclosure Miami." Using specific keywords to narrow the amount of times your ads are served will ensure that your advertisement is seen, and potentially clicked by those most interested, reducing your overall cost and avoiding paying for clicks that do not convert into sales.

Google™'s Exact Match is a good feature that serves your advertisement only when the search phrase is an "exact match," instead of a close match or matching on one or more keywords in the search parameters. If your advertisement is on "private mortgage financing," Exact Match will eliminate your ad being served when someone searches on "mortgage financing." If your keywords are not popular, generic terms, then Exact Match may not be the best option. For example, if you are selling ChefTec software, which is Recipe Costing Software, the searcher may not know the brand name "ChefTec," and may be searching for "Recipe Costing Software" with Exact Match, in which case they would never see your ad.

Google™ offers some sound advice for developing your keywords at **http://adWords.Google.com/support/bin/static. py?page=tips.html**. Essentially, Google™ recommends that you choose your keywords carefully by including specific keywords that are directly related to your ad group or landing page. You should include relevant keyword variations, along with singular and plural versions. The goal is to have your ad served often (impressions), but drive your click rate up. Using keyword matching options enables you to drill down to your specific audience by ensuring that your ad is served to the most likely audience to click on it. Using negative keywords will reduce your ad impressions and increase your quality score with Google™, and will ultimately save you money by avoiding clicks.

If the user is searching for a specific product or information, take them directly to it so they have the information they are seeking instantly. Sending them to the home page to search for information will drive customers away from your Web site. Incorporate your keywords into your ad text, and especially into the title of the ad. Provide insightful, unique, or captivating information in your ad and landing pages that will draw in customers.

To use the Google™ Keyword Tool and Google™ Keyword Cost Calculator to help you determine what keywords to use and how much they may cost, enter keywords into the appropriate fields — along with some optional entries, such as maximum cost per click, daily budget limits, and targeted languages and locations — and click continue to see the results. The results provide you with an average cost per click, volume, estimated ad position, estimated number of clicks per day, and estimated cost per day.

Average CPC: **$8.19** (at a maximum CPC of $17.32)
Estimated clicks per day: **17 - 20** (at a daily budget of $160.00)

Estimates are based on your bid amount and geographical targeting selections. Because the Traffic Estimator does not consider your daily budget, your ad may receive fewer clicks than estimated

Maximum CPC:	Daily budget:	Get New Estimates			
Keywords ▼	Search Volume	Estimated Avg. CPC	Estimated Ad Positions	Estimated Clicks / Day	Estimated Cost / Day
Search Total		$6.54 - $9.87	1 - 3	17 - 20	$80 - $150
cheflec		$0.71 - $0.89	1 - 3	0	$1
recipe software		$10.06 - $15.09	1 - 3	1	$6 - $20
restaurant consulting		$1.69 - $2.53	1 - 3	6	$10 - $20
restaurant management		$5.93 - $8.90	1 - 3	10 - 13	$70 - $120

Estimates for these keywords are based on clickthrough rates for current advertisers. Some of the keywords above are subject to review by Google and may not trigger your ads until they are approved. Please note that your traffic estimates assume your keywords are approved.

Google™ screenshots © Google™ Inc. Used with permission.

The primary factor in determining cost is the relationship of the keyword to top 10 rankings within a search engine. If your keywords are not competitive (meaning that not many companies are trying to use the same keywords in their campaign) then the cost of the keyword is relatively low, and they will yield high search engine rankings if used in a keyword search. If you are competing with hundreds or thousands of other companies for the same keywords, the cost of those keywords will escalate dramatically. Google™ AdWords' minimum cost-per-click base rates depend on your location and currency settings. Your minimum CPC rates can fluctuate for each keyword based on its relevance (or Quality Score). The quality is the most important factor in determining the cost you will pay when someone clicks on your ad.

Your Quality Score sets the minimum bid you will need to pay in order for your keyword to trigger ads. If your maximum CPC is less than the minimum bid assigned to your keyword, you will need to either raise the CPC to the minimum bid listed or optimize your campaign for quality.

A key principle in selecting keywords is in the determination of how often someone will search the Web using that keyword or phrase. Logically, keywords that are less competitive will typically bring you less traffic simply because the keyword is not used often during a search. Conversely, you can expect more traffic with highly competitive keywords, but this may not always be the case, as the field of competitors often grows directly in proportion to the keyword competitiveness. When you begin your pay-per-click campaign, you should be provided with in-depth analysis on a regular basis to help you monitor, adjust, and evaluate the performance of your marketing campaign. These reports should tell you exactly what keywords are being used by people who are using search engines with your campaign, which helps you determine whether your chosen keywords are effective.

Keyword Research Tools

Another method to determine what keywords you should use is to use one of many keyword research tools provided on the Internet (please note that not all these tools are free). Some of the keyword research tools are:

- **Wordtracker (www.wordtracker.com)**: Promises to find the best keywords for your Web site. "Restaurant consulting" was entered into the generation tool, and the application returned the following generated keyword suggestions:

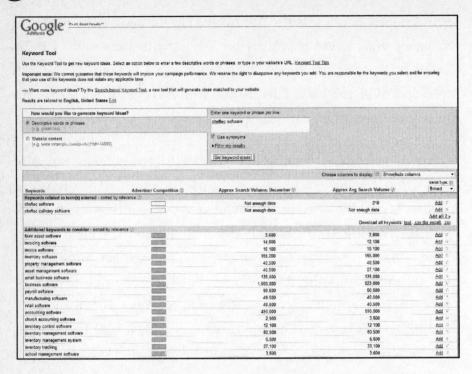

Google™ screenshots © Google™ Inc. Used with permission.

You choose the keywords you want to use and the application returns "count" and "prediction" reports. Count is the number of times a particular keyword has appeared in the Wordtracker database, while prediction is the maximum total predicted traffic for all of the major search engines/pay per bids and directories today.

- Google™: The Google™ Keyword Tool generates potential keywords for your ad campaign and reports their Google™ statistics, including search performance and seasonal trends.

The Google™ Keyword Tool can generate a variety of data, including keywords, key phrases, keyword popularity, cost and ad position estimates, global search, positive trends, and negative keywords. Of the tools listed, Google™ is by far the most user-friendly and comprehensive. There are also dozens of other keyword generation tools available on the Internet. The Google™ Search-based Keyword Tool provides keyword ideas based on actual Google™ search queries, matched to specific pages of your Web site with your ad. The Google™ Search-based Keyword tool is available at **www.Google.com/sktool/**.

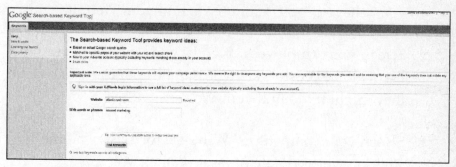

Google™ screenshots © Google™ Inc. Used with permission.

Google™ screenshots © Google™ Inc. Used with permission.

How to Develop Keywords

One of the biggest challenges when establishing your Web site and Google™ AdWords pay-per-click campaign is developing your initial list of keywords and key phrases. You must develop a list of "potential" keywords or key phrases. Here are some tips on how to develop your initial keywords and key phrases:

- Develop a list of all the possible keywords or key phrases you believe people might try to find your Web site with.

- Screen your employees, friends, and customer base for a list of all the possible keywords or key phrases you believe they might try to find your Web site with.

- Screen your competitors' Web sites for a list of all the possible keywords or key phrases on their Web site.

- Take your entire list of keywords and key phrases and use the tools we have provided to refine your list and identify the most competitive, cost-effective keywords.

Tips When Developing Keywords or Phrases

The following is a compilation of the tips, tricks, and best practices you can employ to assist you with the process of creating your keywords and key phrases for your Google™ AdWords campaign.

- Brainstorm a list of any relevant keyword or key phrase you can think of. Take some time away from the list, and over a period of seven to ten days, keep adding more potential keywords and key phrases to the list. It is not uncommon to have thousands of keywords initially for your pay-per-click campaign.

- Incorporate your company name, catch-phrases, slogans, or other recognizable marketing material into keywords.

- Add both the singular and the plural spellings of your keywords.

- Add your domain names to your list of keywords. Many people search for a company by the URL instead of the company name (i.e., searching for **http://atlantic-pub.com** instead of Atlantic Publishing Company).

- Take a peak at the meta tags on competitors' Web sites, in particular, the "keywords" tag, review this list and add them to your keywords list.

- Avoid trademark issues and disputes. Although there is some degree of latitude in regard to trademarks, it is best to avoid using other companies' trademarks unless you are an authorized distributor or reseller of their products.

- Put keywords in the title of your pay-per-click advertisement to generate a much higher click-through rate.

- Use bold face font in the title of your pay-per-click advertisement.

- Find your target audience.

- Incorporate words that add to your pay-per-click advertisement, such as amazing, authentic, fascinating, powerful, revolutionary, or unconditional.

- End your ads with words that promote an action on the part of the reader, such as Be the First, Click Here for all the Details, Limited Time Offer, or Free Today.

Design your Web page and Google™ AdWords ads to provide the information people are looking for with simple navigation and usability. Embed your keywords or key phrases into your Web site content. Key phrases are simply keywords that are joined together. They refine the search and narrow down generalized searches into very specific result sets. Key phrases are often overlooked as people create keyword lists, but they are vitally important to your AdWords campaign and to the optimization of your Web site. Use your Web server logs to research what keywords or key phrases people are using to find your Web site, as this will likely help you refine your keyword and key phrase lists. If people are searching on words that drive them to your site, it makes sense to use these words and phrases in your ads and Web site content to increase your overall visibility. Keyword density is important in Web site design. You need to feature keywords in your Web site content, but ensure that the page content still reads properly. The number of keywords embedded into page content in comparison to your other text determines the "density" of a keyword. Five to 10 percent is often considered to be the proper density for a Web page. Ensure your pages have the proper number and amount of keywords to ensure smooth readability and clarity for the Web site visitor.

Ensuring that you have a well designed, up-to-date, and optimized Web page with a proper balance of keywords or key phrases will ultimately help you to reach thousands of potential customers and dramatically increase your potential earnings. Maintaining the correct keywords and keyword density is one of the most important things to achieve when creating landing pages or designing your Web site. Google™ Page Rank is an important, useful tool when developing your Web page content.

You should constantly analyze your keyword or key phrase performance through Web logs and other tools. Optimize your Web site content by increasing frequency of productive keywords to increase visibility and traffic. Do not discount spending a proportionate amount of time on your Web site home page. Although landing pages are ideal for individual Google™ AdWord campaigns, more than half of all Web site traffic and searches land on your home page. This is where you should spend a significant time to analyze your Web content, embed your key words and phrases, and optimize it for the Google™ Search Engine.

The basic premise with Google™ AdWords is that it simply uses your keywords to ensure that your ads are served up based on relevant searches by keyword and on relevant pages based on keyword. The ultimate goal with keywords or key phrases is to choose those that deliver results, and results tend to be measured in revenue conversions or sales. Growing the number of clicks will only increase your Google™ AdWord costs, and if you are not converting these clicks into sales, your need to modify your AdWords campaign. Refining your keywords and key phrases lets you target buyers within your primary market audience.

How to Establish a Budget for Your Campaign

Google™ AdWords advertising allows you to quickly pay to have your ad listed on Google™ and Google™ partners. Since they are considered "sponsored links," they are significantly different than standard search engine results you might see when you perform a search, since these links will ultimately impact your advertising budget as pay for each "click." Sponsored links, or pay-per-click ads, usually appear at the top, bottom, or right side of the results page following a search with any search engine.

You may see Google™ AdWords ads called Sponsored Links. Pay-per-click advertising allows you to have your ad listed on search engines with the agreement that you will pay for each "click" on your ad based on bids you have placed on your chosen keywords. When your ad is clicked, depending on the keyword used to perform the search and the value of that keyword, you pay a fee to Google™ for that click.

You need to give some considerable thought and planning to determining a manageable budget before starting your pay-per-click campaign. Establishing a monthly budget for a Google™ AdWords campaign is difficult because pricing is based on keyword bids, which change in value often, and may fluctuate over time. Most businesses tend to shift advertising funding from traditional marketing programs, such as print media and radio, toward pay-per-click advertising. An alternative method is to estimate your increased revenue based on your pay-per-click campaign and establishing a percentage-based budget (percent of anticipated or realized increased revenue due to the pay-per-click campaign). The advantage of this type of budget is that you can scale the percentage up or down based on your actual sales derived from the pay-per-click campaign. Google™ provides you with a Budget Optimizer for AdWords, which helps you to receive the highest number of clicks possible within your specified budget.

Measuring Return on Investment

You can measure the return on investment (ROI) for your Google™ AdWords campaign, plus, if you exceed your budget, a pay-per-click campaign can be cancelled at any time. To determine what your starting budget should be, you will need to decide how much a pay-per-click conversion (this is when someone clicks on your advertisement and subsequently placed an order) is worth in profit to your business, how many additional sales leads your company is ready to handle, your conversion rate (provided by your PPC company), and your conversion goal. The formulas below will help you to establish your pay-per-click budget:

- Number of conversions = sales leads per day x % of conversion x 20 work days in month

- PPC budget maximum = $ in profits per conversion x number of conversions

- PPC profit = total profit from pay-per-click campaign - total budget for PPC

Increase Profits by Combating Fraud with Google AdWords

Google™ AdWords Pay-per-click advertising can be extraordinarily profitable and, if managed correctly, will dramatically increase your customer base and potential revenue by driving targeted visitors to your site. Once you master the techniques of pay-per-click advertising, in addition to managing and optimizing your campaigns, one of your biggest challenges will be recognizing and combating fraud.

Pay-per-click fraud refers to a well-thought-out, targeted, technologically advanced, and highly destructive automated process of creating applications, scripts, robots, or even sometimes humans, which will continue to generate thousands of clicks using ingenious techniques to disguise their identify with IP spoofing (and many others). This is all designed to cost you thousands of dollars in fraudulent clicks while hiding behind a false identity.

You need to recognize and understand that you will not sell a product with every click on your advertisement. If you have ten clicks today on your advertisement and sell two products as a direct result of those clicks, your conversion rate is 20 percent. Most PPC providers provide you with free tools to automate the tracking of your conversion rates. Not everyone who clicks on your pay-per-click ad will buy your products, some of these reasons may include:

- Lack of interest in your products

- Being turned off by your Web page or Web site

- Inability to find enough information about your product on your site

- Price

- Brand

- Availability

- Competition

- Technical problems, such as a malfunctioning shopping cart

Fraud in Relation to Pay-Per-Click Marketing

As much as 70 percent of annual online advertising spending is wasted because of click fraud. Corrupt affiliates of ad networks, such as Google™ and Yahoo, account for 85 percent of all click fraud.

The site **http://clickfraud.com** is one of a growing number of companies that can assist you in combating pay-per-click fraud. Click-risk offers "Click Verification Service," a full-service 12-month engagement that helps detect click fraud, guard against it in the future, and obtain refunds on your pay-per-click ad spending.

Pay-per-click fraud is typically the result of:

- Unscrupulous pay-per-click traffic and content partners of pay-per-click search engines (PPCs) and directories. These companies gain financially based upon the volume of referral traffic to their partner, and may resort to fraudulent methods to obtain it.

- Competitors who attempt to break your budget by "clicking" away on your ad, quickly consuming your budget with no sales conversion.

- Webbots, spiders, and crawlers designed to maliciously generate fraudulent clicks and consume your budget with no sales conversion.

You should know the following facts about pay-per-click fraud:

- Search engine companies, PPC providers, and advertisers agree that click fraud exists.

- Search engine companies & PPC providers agree that pay-per-click advertisers should not be billed for fraudulent click activity.

- Search engine companies have stated they have effective "click fraud" protection built into major search engines.

How does Google Detect Invalid Clicks?

The following link provides the detailed explanation of how Google™ detects invalid clicks on Google™ AdWords ads: **http://adWords.Google™.com/support/bin/answer. py?hl=en&answer=6114**.

Tips & Suggestions to Combat Fraud

Here are some tips and suggestions on how you can combat click fraud without breaking your budget:

- Keep current with published anti-click-fraud tips and suggestions.

- Do your research when selecting a pay-per-click provider. While there are many reputable providers, review their policies and tools for combating fraud before you sign up.

- Do not sign up with PPC companies that allow "incentive sites." An incentive site is one that offers free products, free competitions, or "junk" promotions (this applies to AdSense-type campaigns where you are allowing advertisement on your Web site).

- Monitor click-through rates.

- Review your Web site traffic reports.

- Place daily click limits in your campaign.

- Establish a daily budget to limit your total costs per day.

- Limit your ad to your target geographic audience.

- Review your IP referral logs (usually provided by your Web site hosting company or the PPC provider). If you have multiple clicks from the same IP address, you are likely the victim of fraud.

- Report potential fraud to your PPC provider.

- Consider an advanced fraud-detection or tracking tool.

White Paper - How to Defend your Web site Against Click Fraud

By Dmitri Eroshenko and Michael Bloch

Click fraud is a problem that can seriously undermine your PPC advertising efforts. This white paper expands on what we know about click fraud and outlines the steps you can take to protect your investment:

- What do you really need to know about PPC advertising
- Who's behind the different types of click fraud
- Using scoring algorithm to detect and document click fraud
- Measuring your traffic quality with Click Inflation Index (CII)

PPC Advertising in a Nutshell

Pay-per-click is a paid inclusion model used by some search engine companies that usually requires you to bid on words (keywords) or phrases (key phrases) that your target market might use when performing searches. The highest bidder gets the top ranking in the search results, with the next highest bid below and so on. Each time a listing is clicked on, the bid amount is subtracted from the advertisers' deposit.

Some companies charge a flat rate per click, so there's no actual bidding. In this model, ranking is determined by the perceived quality of the page as calculated by a ranking algorithm. When this model is used, it then becomes particularly important to ensure that landing pages are optimized for search engines. In fact, regardless of the PPC model, considering the investment you are making, you should ensure your site is as close to perfect as possible in every aspect in order to achieve maximum conversions.

Pay-per-click is an excellent marketing strategy as it can send very targeted clients to your site; but it can also be a budget black hole. Before you launch a PPC campaign, you'll first need to perform some calculations for projected ROI (Return On Investment).

Calculating the Cost

You should first calculate your current visitors/sales ratio. If one Web site visitor out of a hundred currently purchases your product, then bidding 10 cents per click will cost you an estimated $10.00 per sale. If your profit margin is $15 per sale, then it may be viable. If it's $9, then it's just not worth it. This is just a rough guide, but a good rule of thumb to work by.

Be Cautious of PPC Bidding Wars

Some PPC advertisers, through either aggressive marketing strategies, ignorance or "auction fever," engage in a bidding wars for the No. 1 spot – keep well clear of these scenarios. In very competitive markets, it's not unusual to see a difference of many dollars between the No. 1 and No. 2 rank bids. Given that not everyone who clicks on a listing will purchase, it can become a very expensive marketing exercise to be No. 1. Positions 2 - 5 may still perform well in terms of sending converting traffic to you.

Keyword Targeting

You may also find it more economical to bid on more targeted keywords and phrases that aren't quite as popular. For example, a search on "freeBSD Web hosting" on a leading PPC search engine showed that the top bidder only pays 10 cents for each click; a difference of over $8.30 on the term "Web hosting." Using this strategy will cut down your advertising costs and the more refined targeting may generate improved conversion rates. Searchers who are clear on what they wish to buy tend to be specific in their search criteria. The novice searcher and "tire-kickers" tend to be more generalized in the search terms they use. If you bid on generic terms; you'll be paying the bill while they are learning to refine their queries. Using a tool such as Clicklab will help you in refining your keyword lists by identifying the words and phrases that actually result in conversions.

Choosing a PPC Search Engine

Hundreds of pay-per-click search engines have sprung up in recent years; but very few of them will actually deliver traffic, regardless of what their promotion states. A few companies, such as Overture and Google™, account for the vast majority of PPC traffic. PPC search engines extend network coverage by offering other site owners search boxes/feeds under a revenue share (affiliate) arrangement. The site owner is paid for each search carried out via their site, or for each click a search generates. The better pay-per-click engines have networks consisting of thousands of good quality sites where your listings can appear.

Things to Look for in a PPC Company

- Tools. Does the company offer keyword suggestion features and extensive reporting?

- Coverage. Who uses their data feeds?

- Cost. Are there setup fees or minimum balances? What is the minimum bid?

- Support. Try out their e-mail support - ask a few questions before signing up. If they are slow in responding during the pre-sales process, you can practically guarantee that after sales support will be shocking.

- Click fraud. This costs advertisers millions of dollars each year. Ask what type of anti-click fraud strategies the company has implemented. Will the company investigate fraud aggressively and compensate you where click fraud is proven? It's also wise to invest in an external monitoring system such as Clicklab. Clicklab's advanced analytics engine will flag instances of click fraud that occur in your campaigns. There's no doubt that PPC advertising can be very profitable, but click fraud is probably the most ignored, yet potentially most expensive and damaging aspect of PPC that advertisers need to be very familiar with.

What is click fraud?

Online advertising fraud has been around from the early days of the Internet. To justify the expensive rates and create additional inventory, shady publishers devised the means of artificial inflation of impressions and click-throughs to advertisers' Web sites.

Today, click fraud refers to the premeditated practice of clicking on pay-per-click ads without the intent to buy advertisers' products or services or take other actions. Essentially, click fraud is the practice where a person or persons systematically click on links, or use software to do so, to either garner a profit for themselves through click commissions or to purposefully deplete the PPC funds of a competitor.

Who Engages in Click Fraud?

Click fraud can be as minor as an affiliate who clicks on an ad once a day to bump up his revenues, or a competitor who occasionally clicks on an ad out of spite. Major click fraud is very well organized, fleecing millions of dollars from advertisers each year. Some fraudsters create complex robots (software) to generate thousands of clicks, while spoofing IP addresses in order to avoid detection.

There are also ready-made software products, freely available on the market, for generating false clicks. For example, SwitchProxy, a third party extension for Mozilla Firefox® browser, allows anyone to click on the same paid links repeatedly from a different IP address (that of a proxy server) without ever switching an Internet connection. Still too much work? There are commercial tools you can download.

Other fraudsters employ teams of people in developing countries to click on ads. This may sound a little extreme but with some click bids as high as $10 - $20 each, and if you only have to pay someone $5 a day to click on links, this strategy can be very profitable for the fraudster. In March of this year a 32-year-old California man was arrested and charged with extortion and wire fraud in connection with the software he developed called

Google™ Clique. Google™ Clique was designed to automatically click on paid ads, while remaining virtually undetectable by the search engine.

Michael Anthony Bradley allegedly contacted Google™ and demanded a payoff, threatening to release it to the "top 100 spammers" otherwise. Bradley claimed that Google™ Clique could defraud Google™ of 5 million dollars in half a year's time. Bradley (or someone pretending to be him) posing under the nickname CountScubula, posted on alt.Internet.search-engines newsgroup: "Google™ even called me to their office, I flew up, met with them, and lets' just say, they are scared and don't want this software to get out, bottom line, I don't care anymore." Google™ wrote in its S-1 registration statement filed with the Security and Exchange Commission on April 29, 2004: "We are exposed to the risk of fraudulent clicks on our ads. We have regularly paid refunds related to fraudulent clicks and expect to do so in the future. If we are unable to stop this fraudulent activity, these refunds may increase. If we find new evidence of past fraudulent clicks we may have to issue refunds retroactively of amounts previously paid to our Google™ Network members."

On May 3, 2004, the India Times published a widely read article, "India's secret army of online ad clickers." An excerpt from that article: "A growing number of housewives, college graduates, and even working professionals across metropolitan cities are rushing to click paid Internet ads to make $100 to $200 per month..."

Why Do People Steal?

"People shoplift to get something for nothing," says Terrence Shulman, an attorney, therapist, corporate consultant, book author, and founder of Cleptomaniacs And Shoplifters Anonymous (CASA), a self-help support group. Shulman estimates that the addictive-compulsive shoplifters represent 85 percent of total shoplifting population of 23 million (that's one in every 11 Americans). "This group emotionally has a lot of repressed anger and often exhibits signs of other compulsive addictions, such as overeating, shopping, drug use, or gambling," says Shulman. "When caught and confronted, they will often break down and cry." The remaining 15 percent is shared between the professionals who steal for profit; impoverished stealing out of economic need; thrill seekers getting their fix; drug addicts; and kleptomaniacs, those who steal for no reason at all. Bradley "does not appear to be typical of most of the persons I have worked with," says Shulman. "His plotting and planning and brazen 'extortive' pressures on Google™ are different from the shy, passive-aggressive kinds of thefts I and most of my clients have engaged in."Shulman hypothesizes that Bradley could have "rationalized that he was not hurting anybody – that Google™ is a rich company, not a particular person, and that they could afford it. There can also be a sense of inferiority in people who feel the need to outsmart others or 'beat the system'."

How Widespread Is the Problem?

Instances of advertisers who have had thousands of dollars drained from their accounts in just a few hours are not isolated. Over time, even on a small scale, click fraud can add up to significant amounts of money, dramatically affecting advertisers small and large. Click fraud can also inflate cost of each click for all advertisers as some PPC companies adjust the minimum price of each click based on the popularity of the category or keyword.

Some of Clicklab clients estimate that up to 50 percent of PPC traffic in certain competitive categories is illegitimate. While that figure may be somewhat of an exaggeration as a general average, it does occur in that range in some sectors, perhaps at even higher percentages. As PPC technology has evolved, so too have the built-in anti-fraud mechanisms that search companies implement.

The major companies recognize click fraud as a problem that seriously threatens their businesses. The situation is somewhat similar to the battle against viruses - as a "cure" for a virus is released, a new virus appears. Given the nature of the battlefield, it's of crucial importance that PPC advertisers have solid anti-fraud strategies in place and not to rely solely on the search company to provide protection.

Anti-Click Fraud Strategies

Fraud can be simple to minimize initially, only requiring you to choose a pay-per-click company wisely and then monitoring results on a daily basis. The increasing incidences of more organized fraudsters will require you to use special tools to monitor activity for you. The following strategies will assist you in minimizing the amount you lose to click fraud.

Avoid PPC Networks That Allow Incentive Sites

Before opening an account, always ask the company if they allow incentivized sites into their network as feed partners or affiliates. An incentives site usually offers something to its' visitors in exchange for clicking on links or performing some other action. Given this model, the clicks that you'll receive from these sites will more than likely not convert as the focus of the click isn't based on interest in your product. Incentive driven sites aren't fraudulent, but it's important to gain this clarification.

Frequency Caps on Clicks

Ask the PPC company if they utilize frequency caps and what the cap is. A frequency cap is a method that will prevent duplicate clicks originating from the same IP from being deducted from your balance.

Limit Daily Spend

Start your campaign with a reasonably low daily spend limit, then increase it slowly while monitoring results regularly. As an example, say you set a limit of $50 a day and during the first week you average $40 worth of clicks for a 24 hour period. Then the following week, that $40 is chewed through in the first 6 hours, without an appreciable increase in sales or leads - this could be due to click fraud. By using this strategy, your losses would have been minimized.

Country Filtering

What is your target market - do you really need coverage, for example, in Romania? Also keep in mind that the majority of all types of online fraud originates in Eastern Europe, Africa and some Asian countries.

Server Log Analysis

Study your server logs daily and check for multiple clicks originating from the same IP or range of IP addresses.

Display Warning Message

For dealing with the rotten apples among your competition, have your programmers write a script that will display a nice warning message after several repeated clicks to your Web site from a paid listing on a PPC search engine.

Greetings!

Thank you for your interest in our product and services.

We noticed that you visited our site more than once recently by following a paid link from one or more of the pay-per-click search engines. Please bookmark our site for future reference so you can save a step and visit us directly. Enjoy your visit!

IP address: 123.45.67.89

This technique can dramatically reduce your click fraud rate.

Use Specialized Click Fraud Tools

Manual fraud monitoring can be very laborious - your valuable time is probably better spent in doing what you do best - marketing, following up on leads, refining products or developing new content. Modern third party analytical tools, unlike their predecessors, have become increasingly affordable, accurate and easy to use. One such product is Clicklab managed click fraud detection service.

Statistical Scoring System to Combat PPC Click Fraud

Larger PPC networks have a working mechanism for detecting fraudulent clicks. Otherwise, we suspect that they wouldn't be able to stay in business. Today's PPCs are likely to be able to weed out non-malicious bots and amateur perpetrators. But do these systems have the capacity to stop the professionals? We're not so certain. If the history of spam-fighting is any indicator, the click inflation problem is here to stay. Define them. Score them. Own them.

In order to remain undetected, professional inflators need to closely simulate real visitor behavior and visit parameters. They know the number of page views their clicks generate is among the first things to be evaluated. The good news is if you use statistical methods, you will be able to beat the perpetrators at their own game. Whether it's for your internal use or for negotiating a refund from a PPC provider, what's needed is a system for statistically defining and documenting fraudulent click activity. Enter the Click Inflation Index system. This system performs a variety of tests to detect fraudulent user session signatures, assigning penalty points to each offense. If the cumulative score - we call it Click Inflation Index (CII) - exceeds the threshold, the user's session is tagged as fraudulent. This chapter explains the basic principles and tests you can use when developing your own Click Inflation Index algorithm. You will need a competent technical team armed with an adequate Web analytics solution. The process is fun and the results are well worth the effort. Words of caution before you begin to implement a wide-scale click fraud fighting campaign: make sure your keyword bidding strategy is up to date. Top expensive keywords remain a high-profile target for con-artists. Unless your marketing strategy calls for you to engage in a bidding war – and provides the budget for it -- it's a good idea to diversify and bid on the largest possible number of well-researched, lower-cost keywords.

The click-fraud detecting tests you can use include:

Test 1. Visit depth. How many page views did this particular user session generate? If it's just one, it's a good reason to lift a red flag a notch or two – but not more. Keep in mind that there could be a variety of reasons behind the single-page visits. Perhaps your ad copy isn't clear and misleads the visitors, or maybe the network connection was too slow and user decided not to wait for the other pages to load.

Test 2. Visitors per IP. Because of the proxy servers and networks of users sharing one Internet connection, there will always be unique visitors with the same IP address. It's normal. You just need to calculate the norm for your Web site's unique mix of traffic sources. IP addresses whose visitor counts exceed the control group by a certain percentage are added to the blacklist and trigger a penalty.

Test 2a. Paid clicks per IP. Works the same way as Test 2, except it counts only user sessions that resulted from clicking on one of your paid links. Typically, you will track these by the unique destination URLs used in pay-per-click listings.

Test 3. No cookie - no play? Many marketers will tell you that because most bots and scripts are not capable of supporting the cookie mechanism, a user session without a cookie is a good cause for alarm. Others will say that it can't be an accurate indicator because some privacy devotees do not accept cookies and thus look indistinguishable from bots. So, penalize or not? We think you should.

Test 3. Pageview frequency. Most bots travel through your site and request pages from the server much faster than humans. If a particular user session has generated a few pageviews in a matter of seconds, it's a good enough reason to penalize it. On the other hand, you have to be careful not to go overboard when defining your threshold. Humans can surf through your site pretty fast too!

Test 4. Anonymous proxy servers. Click thieves know that the IP address is the primary means for identifying the user session. Therefore they need to launch their attacks from many different IP addresses. The more, the merrier. Fortunately, IP address spoofing is not a trivial task. For this reason, click inflators often channel their activity through anonymous proxy servers. Your solution is to develop and maintain an up-to-date list of anonymous proxy servers and penalize user sessions originating from them. Most legitimate visitors have no reasons to use anonymous proxies.

Test 5. Geographic origin. Now on to the politically incorrect part. You get to blacklist any country in the world you'd like! Just think of the countries from which you never have and likely never will receive a viable lead. Remember, you are not about to ban visitors from these countries to access your Web site. You are just going about your regular business of assigning points.

Test 6 and beyond. Finesse and customize. You can devise your own triggers and assign points to them. For example, if 98% of your business activity occurs during normal business hours, you may want to penalize visitor sessions originated at all other times.

Or you may track visits from a set of suspicious IP addresses for a period of time, and plot their activity vs. time of the day. Does it follow your site's average activity patterns? It better! Now you need to sit down with your technical, design, sales, and marketing teams. The agenda for the meeting is to: 1) decide on which tests to use, 2) come up with the scoring system for the selected tests, and 3) pick the right threshold.

To test and adjust your selections, run through the possible actions of a dozen or so hypothetical real user personas, and calculate their scores. They shouldn't trip the alarm. Now do the same exercise using personas of click-inflating robots and humans. Visits made for the sole purpose of depleting of your PPC account should trip the wire every time.

Remember, to make sure your scoring system works precisely as intended, always compare your results against a control group of unbiased traffic sources, such as Google™'s and other major engines' organic search results. Click fraud is a contact sport with no rules. Click Inflation Index is a defense system you can use to protect yourself and fight back.

About Clicklab Click Fraud Detection Service

Clicklab Click Fraud Detection Service is the most advanced click fraud detection technology on the market today. It is the result of over two years of research and development work performed by mathematicians, programmers, and SEM and PPC specialists.

Clicklab Click Fraud Detection Service monitors your Web site traffic for suspicious activity and applies a series of statistical tests to detect fraudulent click signatures. Each failed test is assigned a weighed penalty score. If cumulative score exceeds the threshold, Clicklab declares the visitor session fraudulent and flags it for analysis and further action.

Click Inflation Index (CII) is then calculated for each PPC search engine and keyword, allowing you to adjust your bidding strategy and generate detailed actionable reports to negotiate a refund with PPC providers. Clicklab click fraud reports serve as a form of documentation from a third party service that has no vested interest in your PPC campaigns.

Available Fraud Protection Options

This list of recommended fraud protection providers will help you in your fight to combat fraud and protect your financial investment in your pay-per-click marketing campaign. All major pay-per-click providers have active fraud protection measures in place, but their degree of effectiveness is difficult for you to determine. If you want to provide an additional layer of protection for your investment, you may want to consider one of these companies:

- AdWatcher (**www.adwatcher.com**);

- ClickDetective (**www.clickdetective.com**);

- ClickForensics (**www.clickforensics.com**);

Increase Profits & Generate Income with Google AdSense

Google™ AdSense lets you place Google™ advertisements on your Web pages, earning money for each click by site visitors. While it is similar in concept to AdWords, you do not pay for it; instead, you give up some real estate on your Web site to "host" advertisements (relevant content to your Web site), which Google™ places onto this space. Instead of paying per click, you actually earn revenue per click, just for hosting the advertisements on your Web site. The bottom line is that AdSense is simple to use, costs nothing, and can generate significant amounts of residual monthly income for you. Google™ lets you generate revenue from advertisements you allow on your Web pages. The cost is free, and there is minimal effort to implement, you simply sign up and place a small bit of code on your Web page.

The concept of Google™ AdSense is simple. You earn revenue potential by displaying Google™ ads on your Web site. Essentially, you become the host site for someone else's pay-per-click advertising. Since Google™ puts relevant CPC and CPM ads through the same auction and lets them compete against one another, the auction for the advertisement takes place instantaneously, and

Google™ AdSense subsequently displays a text or image ad(s) that will generate the maximum revenue for you.

There are three basic types of AdSense products you can use.

1. **AdSense for Content**: Crawls the content of your Web pages and delivers text and image ads that are relevant to your audience and your site content

2. **AdSense for Search**: Enables Web site owners to provide Google™ Web and site search to their visitors and to earn money from clicks on Google™ ads on the search results pages

3. **AdSense for Mobile Content**: Earn money from your content with a simple, integrated solution for mobile-device-compatible Web sites

Becoming an AdSense publisher is simple. You must fill out a brief application form online at **https://Google.com/AdSense/**, which requires your Web site to be reviewed before your application is approved. Once approved, Google™ will e-mail you HTML code for you to place on your Web pages. Once the HTML code is saved onto your Web page, it activates, and targeted ads will be displayed on your Web site.

You must choose an advertisement category to ensure only relevant, targeted advertisements are portrayed on your Web site. Google™ has ads for all categories of businesses and for practically all types of content, no matter how broad or specialized. The AdSense program represents advertisers ranging from large global brands to small, local companies. Ads are also targeted by geography, so global businesses can display local advertising with no additional effort. Google™ AdSense also supports multiple languages.

You can also earn revenue for your business by placing a Google™ search box on your Web site — literally paying you for search results. This service may help keep traffic on your site longer since site visitors can search directly from your site; it is also available to you at no cost and is simple to implement.

Google™ states that their "ad review process ensures that the ads you serve are not only family-friendly, but also comply with our strict editorial guidelines. We combine sensitive language filters, your input, and a team of linguists with good hard common sense to automatically filter out ads that may be inappropriate for your content." Additionally, you can customize the appearance of your ads, choosing from a wide range of colors and templates. This is also the case with Google™'s search results page. To track your revenue, Google™ provides you with an arsenal of tools to track your advertising campaign and revenue.

How to Set Up Your Google AdSense Campaign

The first step is to complete the simple application form, which is on the Web at **https://Google.com/AdSense/g-app-single-1**. It is critical that you carefully review the terms of service. In particular, you must agree that you will:

- Not click on the Google™ ads you are serving through AdSense

- Not place ads on sites that include incentives to click on ads

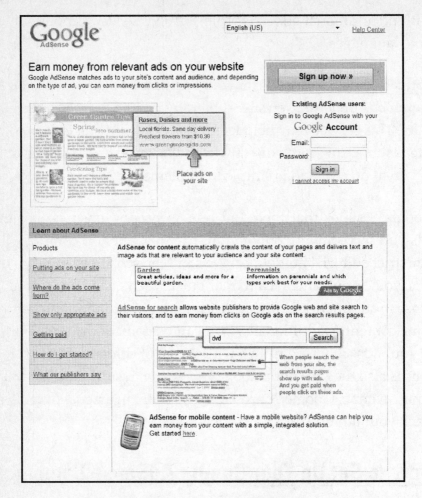

Google™ screenshots © Google™ Inc. Used with permission.

You cannot click on your ads, have others click on your ads, or place text on your Web site asking anyone to click on your advertisements. The reason for this is simple — you cannot click on (or have anyone else) click on your own advertisements to generate revenue.

Google™
AdSense

Welcome to AdSense What is AdSense? | Already have an account?
Please complete the application form below.

Website Information

Website URL:

• Please list your primary URL only.
• Example: www.example.com

Website language: Select a language:

• Tell us your website's primary language to help our review process.

☐ I will not place ads on sites that include incentives to click on ads.

☐ I will not place ads on sites that include pornographic content.

Contact Information

Account type: ⓘ   Select an account type:

Country or territory: Select a country or territory:

⚠ **Important** - Your payment will be sent to the address below. Please complete all fields that apply to your address, such as a full name, full street name and house or apartment number, and accurate country, ZIP code, and city. Example.

Payee name (full name):

• Your Payee name needs to match the name on your bank account.
• Payee must be at least 18 years of age to participate in AdSense.

Street Address:

City/Town:

State: Select state

ZIP: [?]

UNITED STATES

• To change your country or territory, please change your selection at the top of this form.

☐ I agree that I can receive checks made out to the payee name I have listed above.

Telephone Numbers
Phone:

Email preference: We'll send you service announcements that relate to your agreement with Google.
☐ In addition, send me periodic newsletters with tips and best practices and occasional surveys to help Google improve AdSense.

Google™ screenshots © Google™ Inc. Used with permission.

When your Web site is reviewed, and your account is approved, which tends to take a day or two, you will receive an e-mail similar to the following:

"Your Google AdSense application has been approved. You can now activate your account and start displaying Google ads and AdSense for search on your site in minutes.

To quickly set up your account, follow the steps below. Or, for a detailed video walkthrough, view our Getting Started tutorial:

http://www.google.com/AdSensewelcome_getstarteddemo.

STEP 1: Log in to your account.

Visit https://www.google.com/AdSense?hl=en_US and log in using the 'Existing Customer Login' box at the top right. If you've forgotten your password, visit https://www.google.com/AdSense/assistlogin for assistance.

STEP 2: Generate and implement the AdSense code.

Click on the 'AdSense Setup' tab, then follow the guided steps to customize your code. When you've reached the final step, copy the code from the 'Your AdSense code' box and paste it into the HTML source of your site. If you don't have access to edit the HTML source of your pages, contact your webmaster or hosting company.

Not sure how to add the code to the HTML source of your page? Our Help with Ad Code video tutorial can guide you through the process - find the tutorial at http://www.google.com/AdSensewelcome_implementingadcode.

Once the code is implemented on your site, Google ads and AdSense for search will typically begin running within minutes. However, if Google has not yet crawled your site, you may not notice relevant ads for up to 48 hours.

Step 3: See the results.

After your ads start running, you can see your earnings at anytime by checking the online reports on the Reports tab in your account. For a quick overview of your earnings reports and the 5 steps to getting paid, view our Payments Guide: https://www.google.com/AdSense/payments.

Have any questions? The AdSense Help Center is full of useful information and resources to help you familiarize yourself with

AdSense: https://www.google.com/support/AdSense?hl=en_US. You can also find the latest news and tips on the AdSense blog:

http://www.AdSense.blogspot.com.

IMPORTANT NOTES:

* Want to test your ads? Please don't click on them - clicking on your own ads is against the AdSense program policies (https://www.google.com/adsguide/policies). Instead, try the AdSense preview tool, which allows you to check the destination of ads on your page without the risk of invalid clicks. For additional information, or to download the AdSense preview tool, please visit https://www.google.com/support/AdSense/bin/topic.py?topic=160.

* You can add the code to a new page or site at any time. Please keep in mind, however, that we monitor all of the web pages that contain the AdSense code. If we find that a publisher's web pages violate our policies, we'll take appropriate actions, which may include the disabling of the account. For more information, please review the Google AdSense Terms and Conditions (www.google.com/adsguide/tnc).

Welcome to Google AdSense. We look forward to helping you unleash the full potential of your Web site.

Sincerely,

The Google AdSense Team

Google™ screenshots © Google™ Inc. Used with permission.

Google AdSense Program Policies

Publishers participating in the AdSense program are required to adhere to the following policies. If you fail to comply with these policies, Google™ may disable ad serving to your site and/or disable your AdSense account.

Invalid Clicks and Impressions

Clicks on Google™ ads must result from genuine user interest. Any method that artificially generates clicks or impressions on your Google™ ads is strictly prohibited. These prohibited methods include but are not limited to repeated manual clicks or impressions; using robots; automated click and impression generating tools; third-party services that generate clicks or impressions, such as paid-to-click, paid-to-surf, autosurf, and click-exchange programs; or any deceptive software. **Please note that clicking on your own ads for any reason is prohibited**.

Encouraging Clicks

In order to ensure a good experience for users and advertisers, publishers may not request that users click the ads on their sites or rely on deceptive implementation methods to obtain clicks. Publishers participating in the AdSense program:

- May not encourage users to click the Google™ ads by using phrases such as "click the ads," "support us," "visit these links," or other similar language

- May not direct user attention to the ads via arrows or other graphical gimmicks

- May not place misleading images alongside individual ads

- May not promote sites displaying ads through unsolicited mass e-mails or unwanted advertisements on third-party Web sites

- May not compensate users for viewing ads or performing searches, or promise compensation to a third party for such behavior

- May not place misleading labels above Google™ ad units — for instance, ads may be labeled "Sponsored Links" but not "Favorite Sites"

Site Content

While Google™ offers broad access to a variety of content in the search index, publishers in the AdSense program may only place Google™ ads on sites that adhere to our content guidelines, and ads must not be displayed on any page with content primarily in an unsupported language.

Sites displaying Google™ ads may not include:

- Violent content, racial intolerance, or advocacy against any individual, group, or organization

- Pornography, adult, or mature content

- Hacking/cracking content

- Illicit drugs and drug paraphernalia

- Excessive profanity

- Gambling or casino-related content

- Content regarding programs that compensate users for clicking on ads or offers, performing searches, surfing Web sites, or reading e-mails

- Excessive, repetitive, or irrelevant keywords in the content or code of Web pages

- Deceptive or manipulative content or construction to improve your site's search engine ranking (PageRank™)

- Sales or promotion of weapons or ammunition (e.g., firearms, fighting knives, or stun guns)

- Sales or promotion of beer or hard alcohol

- Sales or promotion of tobacco or tobacco-related products

- Sales or promotion of prescription drugs

- Sales or promotion of products that are replicas or imitations of designer goods

- Sales or distribution of term papers or student essays

- Any other content that is illegal, promotes illegal activity, or infringes on the legal rights of others

Copyrighted Material

Web site publishers may not display Google™ ads on Web pages with content protected by copyright law unless they have the necessary legal rights to display that content.

Webmaster Guidelines

AdSense publishers are required to adhere to the Webmaster quality guidelines posted at **www.Google.com/Webmasters/guidelines.html**.

Site and Ad Behavior

Sites showing Google™ ads should be easy for users to navigate and should not contain excessive pop-ups. AdSense code may not be altered, nor may standard ad behavior be manipulated in any way that is not explicitly permitted by Google™.

- Sites showing Google™ ads may not contain pop-ups or pop-unders that interfere with site navigation, change user preferences, or initiate downloads.

- Any AdSense code must be pasted directly into Web pages without modification. AdSense participants are not allowed to alter any portion of the code or change the behavior, targeting, or delivery of ads. For instance, clicks on Google™ ads may not result in a new browser window being launched.

- A site or third party cannot display your ads, search box, search results, or referral buttons as a result of the actions of any software application, such as a toolbar.

- No AdSense code may be integrated into a software application.

- Web pages containing AdSense code may not be loaded by any software that can trigger pop-ups, redirect users to unwanted Web sites, modify browser settings, or otherwise interfere with site navigation. It is your responsibility to ensure that no ad network uses such methods to direct traffic to pages that contain your AdSense code.

- Referral offerings must be made without any obligation or requirement to end-users. Publishers may not solicit e-mail addresses from users in conjunction with AdSense referral units.

- Publishers using online advertising to drive traffic to pages showing Google™ ads must comply with the spirit of Google™'s Landing Page Quality Guidelines. For instance, if you advertise for sites participating in the AdSense program, the advertising should not be deceptive to users.

Ad Placement

AdSense offers a number of ad formats and advertising products. Publishers have a wide variety of placements, provided the following policies are followed:

- Up to three ad units may be displayed on each page.

- A maximum of two Google™ AdSense search boxes may be placed on a page.

- Up to three link units may also be placed on each page.

- Up to three referral units may be displayed on a page, in addition to the ad units, search boxes, and link units specified above.

- AdSense for search results pages may show only a single ad link unit in addition to the ads Google™ serves with the search results. No other ads may be displayed on your search results page.

- No Google™ ad or Google™ search box may be displayed in a pop-up, pop-under, or e-mail.

- Elements on a page must not obscure any portion of the ads.

- No Google™ ad may be placed on any non-content-based pages.

- No Google™ ad may be placed on pages published specifically for the purpose of showing ads, regardless of whether the page content is relevant.

Competitive Ads and Services

In order to prevent user confusion, we do not permit Google™ ads or search boxes to be published on Web sites that also contain other ads or services formatted to use the same layout and colors as the Google™ ads or search boxes on that site. Although you may sell ads directly on your site, it is your responsibility to ensure these ads cannot be confused with Google™ ads.

Google Advertising Cookies

Google™ uses the DoubleClick DART cookie on publisher Web sites displaying AdSense for content ads. Subject to any applicable laws, rules, and regulations, you will have the sole and exclusive right to use all data derived from your use of the DoubleClick DART cookie for any purpose related to your business, provided that Google™ may use and disclose this data subject to the terms of Google™'s advertising privacy policies, and any applicable laws, rules, and regulations.

Landing Page and Site Quality Guidelines

The following Google™ site guidelines will help improve your landing page quality score. As a component of your keywords' overall quality scores, a high landing page quality score can affect your AdWords account in three ways:

1. By decreasing your keywords' CPCs

2. By increasing your keyword-targeted ads' positions on the content network

3. By improving the chances that your placement-targeted ads will win a position on your targeted placements

Relevant and Original Content

Relevance and originality are two characteristics that define high-quality site content. Here are some pointers on creating content that meets these standards:

Relevance

- Users should be able to easily find what your ad promises.

- Link to the page on your site that provides the most useful information about the product or service in your ad. For instance, direct users to the page where they can buy the advertised product, rather than to a page with a description of several products.

Originality

- Feature unique content that cannot be found on another site. This guideline is particularly applicable to affiliates that use the following types of pages:

  o Bridge pages: Pages that act as an intermediary, whose sole purpose is to link or redirect traffic to the parent company.

  o Mirror pages: Pages that replicate the look and feel of a parent site; your site should not mirror (be similar or nearly identical in appearance to) your parent company's or any other advertiser's site.

- Provide substantial information. If your ad does link to a page consisting mostly of ads or general search results, such as a directory or catalog page, provide additional, unique content.

Transparency

In order to build trust with users, your site should be explicit in three primary areas: the nature of your business; how your site interacts with a visitor's computer; and how you intend to use a visitor's personal information, if you request it. Here are tips on maximizing your site's transparency:

Regarding your business information:

- Openly share information about your business — clearly define what your business is or does

- Honor the deals and offers you promote in your ad

- Deliver products and services as promised

- Only charge users for the products and services that they order and successfully receive

- Distinguish sponsored links from the rest of your site content

Regarding your site's interaction with a visitor's computer:

- Avoid altering users' browser behavior or settings, such as back button functionality or browser window size, without first getting their permission

- If your site automatically installs software, be upfront about the installation, and allow for easy removal

Visitors' personal information:

- Unless necessary for the product or service that you are offering, do not request personal information

- If you do request personal information, provide a privacy policy that discloses how the information will be used

- Give options to limit the use of a user's personal information, such as the ability to opt out of receiving newsletters

- Allow users to access your site's content without requiring them to register, or provide a preview of what users will get by registering

Navigability

The key to turning visitors into customers is making it easy for users to find what they are looking for. Here is how:

- Provide a short, easy path for users to purchase or receive the product or offer in your ad

- Avoid excessive use of pop-ups, pop-unders, and other obtrusive elements throughout your site

- Make sure that your landing page loads quickly

Setting up Google AdSense on your Web Site

To set up your initial AdSense account, click on the "My Account" tab. Since Google™ will be paying you, you will be required to completed several steps before your account is activated, such as provide W-9 tax data and choose your form of payment (electronic transfer or check payment).

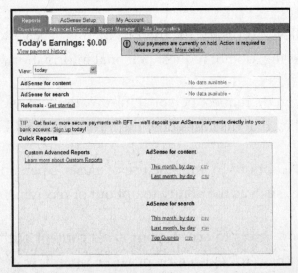

Google™ screenshots © Google™ Inc. Used with permission.

Click on the "Account Setup" to begin setting up your ads. The following screen will be displayed:

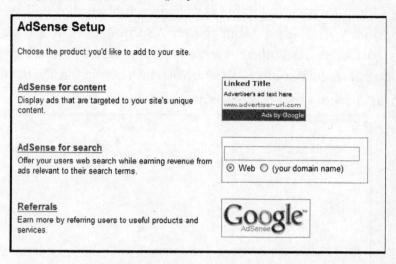

Google™ screenshots © Google™ Inc. Used with permission.

Choose which product you would like to add to your Web site. You may choose either AdSense for content, AdSense for search, or referrals. Set up a Google™ AdSense for content ad on our Web site. You will now choose your ad type. You may choose ad unit (use the drop down menu to choose text and image ads, text only, or image only ads). Ad unit with text and images is the default (and recommended) setting, or you may choose a link unit, which displays a list of topics relevant to your Web page. Click on ad unit to continue.

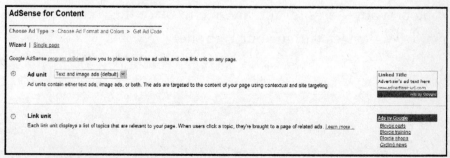

Google™ screenshots © Google™ Inc. Used with permission.

You will be presented with several options to choose from, including unit format and colors. Choose your desired options using the drop-down menus (note: this is not the actual ad that will be displayed on your Web site, but merely a sample of how it may appear). AdSense lets you customize the appearance of ads to match the look and feel of your Web site. You can also customize the style of your AdSense for search box and search results page.

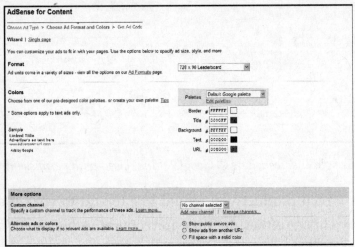

Google™ screenshots © Google™ Inc. Used with permission.

You may use "more options" to enable custom channels or elect to alternate ads or colors, including the option to show public service ads if there is no advertisement ready to be displayed on your Web site. After making your selections, you will be provided with HTML code, which simply needs to be placed in the HTML code on your Web site. You are free to place the code on one or many Web pages within your Web site.

AdSense for Content

Choose Ad Type > Choose Ad Format and Colors > Get Ad Code

Wizard | Single page

Click anywhere in this box to select all code.

You may paste this code into any web page or website that complies with our program policies.

For more help with implementing the AdSense code, please see our Code Implementation Guide. For tips on placing ads to maximize earnings, see our Optimization Tips.

Your AdSense code:

```
<script type="text/javascript"><!--
google_ad_client = "pub-2693250782343896";
google_ad_width = 120;
google_ad_height = 240;
google_ad_format = "120x240_as";
google_ad_type = "text_image";
google_ad_channel ="";
//--></script>
<script type="text/javascript"
  src="http://pagead2.googlesyndication.com/pagead/show_ads.js">
</script>
```

Google™ screenshots © Google™ Inc. Used with permission.

When you insert the HTML code into your Web site, your campaign is activated and advertisements are immediately served to your site. Since you cannot click on your advertisement at any time, even to "test" them, Google™ provides a preview mode for testing. Google™'s AdWords technology matches the most relevant, highest performing AdWords ads to your Web site. You can bid on ads on a per-click or per-impression basis. Depending on the type of ad appearing on your site, you will be paid for valid clicks and impressions. You also have the option of payment monthly via check or Electronic Fund Transfer (EFT). How much you earn depends on a number of factors, including how much an advertiser bids on your site, but you will receive a portion of what the advertiser pays.

The following ad was created and set up on our Web site in under five minutes:

Ads by Goooooogle

First Time Authors
Publish your book now.
Free Guide. 50 year
tradition of quality
books.
www.vantagepress.com

**Book Publishing
Company**
Become Your Own
Publisher Through a
Random House
Ventures Partner.
www.Xlibris.com

Google™ screenshots © Google™ Inc. Used with permission.

You can expand your AdSense account well beyond traditional Web pages. They can be implemented successfully into blogs and feeds. Last year, Google™ even implemented "AdSense for Feeds," which lets you place ads into RSS feeds, allowing you to increase the reach of your content while earning revenue.

How to Set Up Your Google Referrals

Google™ AdSense program policies allow you to place one referral per product, for a total of up to four referrals, on any page. You simply click on the referral link to choose your referrals, as shown on the next page.

Google™ screenshots © Google™ Inc. Used with permission.

Google™ AdSense will generate the HTML code for your Web site. Once the code is placed on your Web pages, your referral will be activated and displayed on your Web site, as shown in the following screenshot. You have a variety of options in size, color, and wording to choose from and are free to change your referral ads at any time.

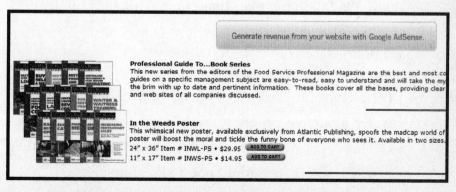

Google™ screenshots © Google™ Inc. Used with permission.

Google™ AdSense is simple to implement, uninstrusive to your Web site, and allows you to open channels to earning potential revenue for your business.

Tips for Maximizing AdSense on Your Web Site

Google™ AdSense is an outstanding way to generate Web site traffic, attract advertisers, and create a revenue stream for your business. Use these hints and tips to maximize your earning potential:

- Always follow the Google™ AdSense Guidelines.

- Do not modify or change the Google™ AdSense HTML code you place on your Web site.

- Do not use colored backgrounds on the Google™ AdSense ads. If you have a Web site with a colored background, modify the advertisement to match your background.

- Place your ads so they are visible. If someone needs to scroll down to see your ads, you may not get any clicks on them. Play with the placement to maximize visibility.

- Do not place ads in pop-up windows.

- Do not buy an "AdSense Template Web site," which is readily available on eBay® and other online marketplaces. These get-rich type "click" campaigns are against Google™'s policies and do not make money.

- Text ads tend to do better than Image ads. If you insist on image ads, keep them reasonable; use the 300x250 medium rectangle.

- You can modify the URL link color in the ad through the Google™ AdSense account panel to make it stand out among your ads and attract the eye of the site visitor.

- If you have a blog, use it to have others place ads in it. You will need to get Google™ approval for your blog.

- If your Web site has articles on it that you wish to embed ads in, use these guidelines:

  o   For short articles, place the ad above the article.

  o   For long articles, embed the ad within the content of the article.

- Wider-format ads are more successful. The paying ad format is the "large rectangle."

- Distribute ads on each Web page. Combine ads with referrals and search boxes so your Web site does not look like a giant billboard.

- Put the Google™ search box near the top right-hand corner of your Web page.

- If your ads are based on content, the first lines of the Web page determine your site content for ad serving purposes.

- Set the Google™ AdSense search box results window so that it opens in a new window, as this will keep your browser open and users will not navigate away from your Web site.

- Google™ AdSense allows Webmasters to customize their Google™ AdSense ads. You can actually customize the links, borders, and color themes of your ads. Borderless AdSense Web banners tend to produce more clicks.

Google Base & Google Product Search: Free Tools to Generate Income and Promote Your Products and Web Site

Google™ Base and Google™ Product Search are two separate, but inter-related, applications available from Google™. Google™ Product Search replaced Google™ Froogle (**www.froogle.com**), which is an online pricing comparison of products — essentially, Google™'s online shopping search engine. Google™ Product Search lets you search the Web for virtually any product and retrieve relevant results, specifically intended to compare pricing and vendors and let you shop for products. Google™ Base is a free service which simply lets you publish information or products online for inclusion into Google™ search results. Items in Google™ Base will appear in either Google™ Base or Google™ Product Search, depending on the type of submission. For your products to appear in Google™ Product

Search, you must submit your information to Google™ Base. The Google™ Base database will be incorporated into other Google™ tool results, such as the Google™ Search Engine and Google™ Maps. This is important because it means you can potentially load all your products into Google™ Base and make them available for free on the Google™ Search Engine and in other Google™ applications.

Google Base

Google™ Base is an online database offered by Google™ that allows you to add your products to it in a preset format, and then your products are featured on the Google™ Search Engine and through other Google™ searches, including Google™ Product Search and Google™ Base. Google™ Base has been called the Google™ version of Craig's List because you can use it to buy and sell products, post resumes, search for jobs, find vacation rentals, and buy and sell vehicles — even houses have appeared on Google™ Base.

Google™ Base is absolutely free. You can submit information about all types of online and offline content to Google™ Base, by either the standard Web form or, if you have more than ten items to submit, via Google™'s bulk upload options. When you submit information via the Web, you can attach up to 15 digital files in the following formats: PDF (.pdf), Microsoft Excel (.xls), Text (.txt), HTML (.html), Rich Text Format (.rtf), Word Perfect (.wpd), ASCII, Unicode, and XML. Google™ is available in English and German interfaces. Items submitted to Google™ base may be displayed on Google™, Froogle, and Google™ Maps.

Google™ screenshots © Google™ Inc. Used with permission.

Google™ screenshots © Google™ Inc. Used with permission.

By clicking on the "products" link, you can narrow your search to "product" listing only, where you are presented with a variety of sort options, including price, relevance, stores, brand, and links to view via Google™ Maps:

Google™ screenshots © Google™ Inc. Used with permission.

A unique feature of Google™ Base is called attributes, which allows you to describe an item's characteristics and qualities for any potential buyer. To publish your items to Google™ Base, first establish a free Google™ account. Google™ Base is not just about selling products, it lets you put anything online, for free. It can be products, inventory, books, resumes, jobs, letters, or a diary. You can submit items via a Web form, or use data-feed options for larger product databases. Many shopping carts, such as PDG Cart, automate the data export process for creating a Google™

Base data file based on your product inventory. All items are up-loaded must comply with Google™ Editorial and Program Policies (**http://base.Google.com/support/bin/answer.py?hl=en_US&answer=61118**).

How to Add Products to Google™ Base

To add products to Google™ Base, you must have a free Google™ Account, which gives you access to all Google™ services within your account management page. Visit **www.Google.com/accounts/NewAccount** to establish your Google™ account:

Google™ screenshots © Google™ Inc. Used with permission.

Google™ screenshots © Google™ Inc. Used with permission.

You can upload products one at a time or through a data feed or API. Detailed instructions for how to create your bulk upload file are located at **http://base.Google.com/base/products.html**. Google™ even provides you with sample bulk load files to help you ensure your file is properly formatted.

To submit an item using the Google™ Base standard form, simply click on "post your own item." On the Post an Item page, choose an item type from the drop-down menu or create your own item type in the text box below. Then click "next" to add details, edit, review, and publish your item. In about 15 minutes, your item will have a unique Web address and be visible to the world. If you have a Web site that you would like to lead searchers to, include an attribute as type "Web URL," which includes the page's full URL. If you would like to submit more than ten items, you will want to use a data feed. Following is a sample one-at-a-time entry form for adding products to Google™ Base:

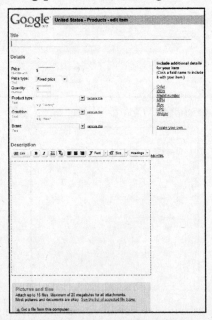

Google™ screenshots © Google™ Inc. Used with permission.

To establish and use "data feeds," simply choose the "data feed" option to set up your account options to register and load your data file or data feed into the Google™ Base database. Google™ will process and validate your file. After your file has been processed and approved, it will tell you the date and time it was uploaded, as well as the number of active items and when the listing will expire (they are good for 30 days), and then you must upload a new data file. Detailed instruction on how to create your data feed in .txt, XML, or other formats is available at **http://base. Google.com/support/bin/answer.py?hl=en&answer=59461**.

Google™ screenshots © Google™ Inc. Used with permission.

Following is a sample properly formatted Google™ Base bulk upload file in .TXT format:

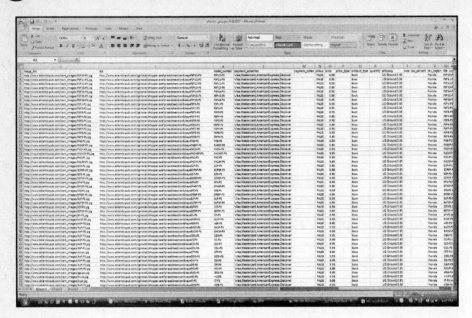

Google™ screenshots © Google™ Inc. Used with permission.

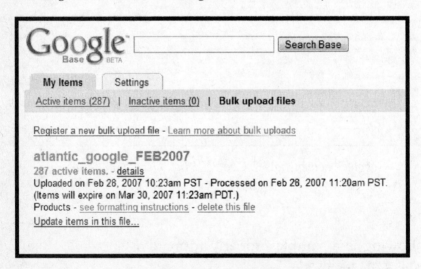

Google™ screenshots © Google™ Inc. Used with permission.

Google™ will perform edits and validations on your bulk upload file and notify you via your Base control panel if there are problems with your upload. You will also be notified via e-mail. Go to the "bulk upload" page to load your file into the Google™ Base database. Google™ will process and validate your file to ensure it passes all edits and controls. Initially, your upload will show as "pending approval," and then it will migrate to "approved" or "disapproved." Once your items are approved, they are visible in Google™ Base and Google™ searches. There are no commissions, fees, or other charges associated with Google™ Base, and it is simple to use. Once your bulk upload file is created (Google™ Base will accept feeds in TSV, RSS 1.0, RSS 2.0, Atom 0.3, and Atom 1.0 formats), content providers who already have RSS feeds can easily submit their content to Google™ Base. Google™ Base can essentially provide free promotion of your company, products, and services. A product spreadsheet, and the products, were searchable in Google™ Base within hours of creation.

Detailed instructions on how to create and upload your Google™ Base items are contained in the comprehensive Google™ Base Help Center, located at **http://base.Google.com/support**. Additional resources about Google™ Base can be found on the official Google™ Base blog, at **http://Googlebase.blogspot.com/**.

Google Product Search

Google™ Product Search is a price comparison program. You can use it to drive business to your Web site and promote your products for free. Google™ Product Search helps shoppers find and buy products across the Web and provides you with pricing and seller comparisons so you can find the best deal on products, and you can use it to provide the best deals to your potential customers and drive traffic to your Web site. You can easily submit your products to Google™ Product Search, allowing shoppers worldwide to find your products, as well as your Web site, quickly and easily. Google™ Product Search allows you to:

- **Increase Web Site Traffic and Generate Sales:** Google™ Product Search connects your products to the shoppers searching for them. Products submitted to Google™ Product Search appear in Product Search results, and may also appear on Google™.com.

- **Submit Your Products to Google™ for Free:** Inclusion of your products is completely free. There are no charges for uploading your items or for additional traffic you receive.

- **Find and Connect with Qualified Shoppers:** You will find potential buyers at the precise moment they are searching for your products.

Uploading products to Google™ Product Search is identical to the process used for Google™ Base, using the Google™ Base interface, Web forms, API, or data feeds exactly as you would for Google™ Base. Additionally, you may use the Store Connector, which is a free download that extracts and places products from your Yahoo, eBay®, and osCommerce stores directly into Google™ Base. Additionally, it automatically formats items to align with the Google™ Base requirements. You can access Google™ Product Search through your Google™.com account for adding products, establishing an account, and more. To access the user interface to search for products, go to **www.Google.com/products**.

Google™ screenshots © Google™ Inc. Used with permission.

To search for products, simply type in your search criteria, and results are returned back to you in the browser.

Google™ screenshots © Google™ Inc. Used with permission.

Matching criteria is returned, including product description, images, pricing, and price comparison options for matching items. You may also use Product Search to generate a shopping list. Click on the "compare prices" button to compare pricing and vendor information for a particular product. Comparison data includes seller ratings, links to the products on their Web sites, and tax and shipping information, as well as pricing. Advanced features, such as "preview this book on Google™ book search," may be available.

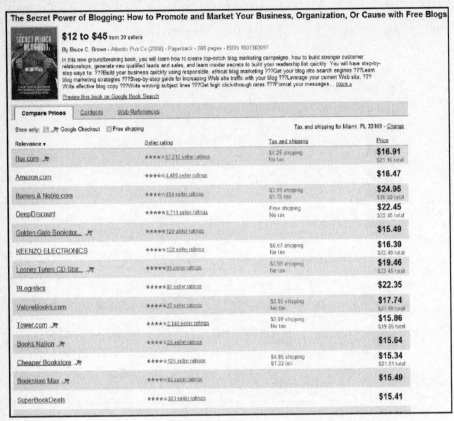

Google™ screenshots © Google™ Inc. Used with permission.

The "contents" link will show you the table of contents for books, and the "Web reference" link will do a search for the product on the Web and pull back exact match criteria, enabling you to do advanced research or reviews of the product. The following screenshot is a sample of Google™ Book Search, which enables you to preview books located in Google™ Product Search.

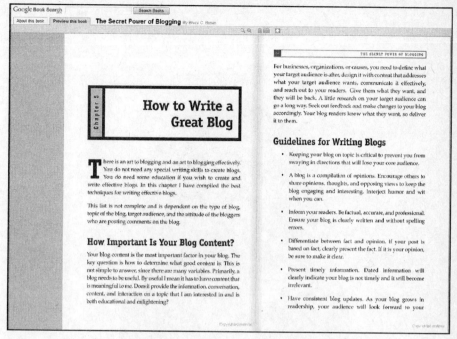

Google™ screenshots © Google™ Inc. Used with permission.

Google™ Product Search is simple to use and highly effective at promoting your products and Web site. Since you are going to do the work to upload your products via the Google™ Base interface, simplify and automate the process with a monthly or fresher data feed to ensure data accuracy is achieved while maintaining an active inventory at all times in Google™ Product Search.

CHAPTER 10

Proven Methods Using Google to Generate Income through Traditional and Affiliate Marketing

This chapter contains information about using Google™ and the Google™ Search Engine to gain media exposure, expand online marketing, and use affiliate marketing, along with other ideas to promote your Web site and products using Google™ to its fullest potential.

Affiliate Marketing & the Google Search Engine

There are two basic types of affiliate marketing. You can be an affiliate of someone else, which means that you sell their products on your Web site and they pay you a commission for each sale. Or, you can offer an affiliate marketing program on your Web site, which allows others to join your network, and in turn, they can sell your products on their Web site, and you pay them a commission fee for each sale. Both are fantastic programs, and when done properly, they can yield substantial results. With the Google™ Search Engine, you can effectively promote your products and Web site as an affiliate of others, selling products on your Web site, or as a company who runs your own affiliate program with others joining your program, selling your products on their site.

Affiliate marketing allows merchants to dramatically increase their marketplace by paying their affiliates to promote their products on a commission formula based on a sale or sales lead. Affiliate marketing is not always about selling products; it can also be used simply for impressions, or "per action." For example, driving traffic from your Web site to the affiliate owner's site may qualify for an affiliate payment. In most cases, affiliate networks are created to sell products and expand the marketplace. In all cases, the concept is to drive traffic back to the merchant Web site. Upon completion of the sale, you are given a commission for the sale. Simply put, if the visitor to your Web site clicks on a link, banner, or product that is an "affiliate" item, and they then go to the merchant Web site and purchase this item, you get paid the referral (or commission). With CPC programs, the affiliates get "credit" based on the number of clicks on ads or banners on their Web sites, while in cost per action (CPA), affiliates only get credit when the site visitor completes a purchase or other transaction on the affiliate merchant's Web site.

Affiliate Marketing Networks

If you are an online retailer, you have two choices with affiliate marketing. You can establish your own affiliate marketing program, or join a well-established, large affiliate network. An affiliate network has enormous reach, and may get you significantly increased market presence over establishing your own affiliate program, but it is not free, and you are restricted to the terms of service of the affiliate network. There are hundreds of affiliate networks — some are good, some are not. Establishing your own affiliate program, or even joining an affiliate program, will require hard work, dedication, patience, and determination, but by using the power of the Google™ Search Engine, you can dramatically increase the visibility and search engine rankings of your affiliate program or affiliate-linked products by optimizing your Web site for maximum organic search engine visibility. Work with the provided Google™ Webmaster guidelines and tools to ensure your Web site is properly indexed and visible within the Google™ database.

Affiliate Marketing Principles

Affiliate marketing has grown in the past decade, and it has exploded in both popularity and profitability. It has expanded into every aspect of the Web and has the potential to be one of the more lucrative ways of generating both sales and revenue. The basic principles of affiliate marketing are sound and have stood the test of time, which are simply. Any commercial link on any Web site is tied to affiliate or pay-per-click marketing in some form or another.

Now that you have a good understanding of what affiliate marketing is, the following is a more detailed overview of the two primary affiliate marketing methods:

- **Joining an Affiliate Program or Network:** This means that you have your own Web site, and you join an affiliate program or network selling other products. Let us say you have a Web site or blog about running. To increase your revenue, you join the affiliate network of a large running shoe merchant. This is free to you, and they provide you with the information to add their products to your Web site. They will provide you with special URLs which will uniquely identify sales that originated from your Web site. You can encourage your site visitors to buy the running shoes by following the image and other information you placed on your Web site, and when they click it, they are taken to the merchant's site, where they can place the order. Once the order is processed and completed, you are notified of the sale and of your commission amount. You will likely have access to an online account to monitor your statistics, revenue, and other vital information. You can change out products as often as you want to keep your Web site interesting. You do not process the sale, handle the merchandise, ship the merchandise, provide customer service, or do anything else. Once the transaction is completed, you have earned your commission. The merchant must do the rest.

- **Create or Manage Your Own In-House Affiliate Program:** This means that you have your own Web site and have products to sell. You want to expand your marketplace beyond your Web site and leverage the power of thousands of other sites to promote and sell your products for you. Those who promote these products for you on their Web sites are your affiliates, and they fall into the category above. They place your products and material on their Web site, and if someone visits their site and clicks on your products, their unique affiliate link takes them to your Web site, where you complete the transaction. You now have the luxury of promoting your products on Web sites all over the world, at no cost to you, reaching millions of people you could not previously reach, and who may not have otherwise known about, you or your products. As each sale is completed, your affiliates earn a commission. At the end of each month, you must pay your affiliates their commission on the sales. Although this means you will earn less profit, since you are paying out 10 percent or more per sale to someone else, you are theoretically selling significantly more products than you could have before, since you now are promoting your products on hundreds or thousands of relevant Web sites. You must maintain your affiliate account status, generate monthly checks, and administer your affiliates (which involves approvals and account maintenance). There is some overhead and work on your part, but this tends to be minimal. As you add new products to your inventory, you add them to your affiliate program, and your affiliates can instantly start promoting them. You process the sale, handle and ship the merchandise, provide customer service, handle the transactions, and do all the rest.

There are several choices in "types" of affiliate marketing software available to you if you wish to build your own affiliate network or install an affiliate program on your Web site. Here are the general options you will have:

- **Affiliate Network:** The software is provided and hosted by the affiliate network provider. You simply join the network and offer your products for sale to other members of the affiliate network. They handle the program administration, reporting, commission payments, and more.

- **Hosted Affiliate Network Software:** The software is not provided to you or installed on your Web server. The software provider hosts it on their servers, and you pay a fee, often monthly, for support and maintenance. All you tend to have on your Web site is a small piece of tracking code; your work is minimal. Since they own and host the software, you instantly benefit from software upgrades, patches, and enhancements, and they are responsible for all the servers, backups, and reliability. Additionally, you get technical support included with the package.

- **Affiliate Network Software (Stand Alone):** You buy the software package outright, and you own the license to use as you see fit. There is a one-time fee, which can be expensive. You install it on your Web server (although often, this is included for free or a small fee), and you integrate it with your shopping cart or inventory management system. This software tends to be quite robust and packed with features, and there are typically no recurring fees unless you want to sign up for upgrades, patches, or other support that is typically limited or not included.

The world of affiliate traffic is full of misconceptions. Following are some facts and realities of affiliate marketing:

- Setting up an effective affiliate traffic program is not necessarily easy, and it will take an investment of time and money, but it can return large dividends.

- Affiliate marketing does not automatically mean a huge increase in Web site traffic. Setting up (or joining) an affiliate program or network alone will not necessarily bring you any noticeable increase in traffic. You will still have to promote your program through other means in order to make it effective.

• You must avoid over-hype and build credibility in your Web site and products.

• Some Web surfers are reluctant to click an affiliate link/ banner. The nice thing is that many affiliate programs have built in methods to help combat this. It all goes back to credibility; if they trust you, this is a non-issue.

• There are no shortcuts. Affiliate traffic is one of the most labor-intensive techniques available, but it is also potentially one of the most effective.

When you approach affiliate marketing, you must ask yourself if you would buy the product you are promoting. This is a key question, because the answer is often "no." Why would you not buy the product? Is it because the product itself is of low quality? Is the language used to promote it too full of hype? Do you have an aversion toward the format in which the offer is available? Would you have a problem buying a product from someone who is a mere middleman and not actually the manufacturer of the product? These are the questions that hold the key to a more effective type of affiliate marketing.

Picking the Right Product

The best affiliate product to sell that you will find is the one that you are familiar with. Anything can be sold if there is a niche to it, and although the niche itself might be small, the competition itself is often even smaller. If you have expertise in a certain field, and you pick a product related to that field, you will have a huge advantage over your competition because you will be able to understand your customers. You will also be able to instantly distinguish a quality product from a low-quality product, and quality counts. As time goes on and you attract more traffic, you build up a portfolio of affiliate products to sell to your existing customers. The idea is to find a customer niche that you understand and know how to cater to, and concentrate on marketing those products through your affiliate program.

Effective Product Web Copy or Sales Material

There are many approaches available to sell products on the Web. Consider why people are browsing the Web. A consistent percentage are indeed out there looking for a solution to a problem, or simply looking for a product to purchase, but most of them are only looking for general information or human interaction. You should cater to those looking for a solution to a problem or a product to purchase. Catering to a small community with a high likelihood of purchase with products you know well is a key to affiliate success. Trying to cater to anyone, without specialization, is typically much less successful. Target your Web copy to your products, and provide detailed information, advantages, reviews, and more to generate interest. Generic banner ads plastered all over your Web site, without else to support them, will not generate conversions. Effective Web copy includes proper keyword density, and Google™-optimized Web pages lead to maximum effectiveness and visibility in the Google™ Search Engine.

Promoting Your Affiliate Program

Starting up a new Web site is like opening a store in the middle of the Sahara Desert. Land is plentiful and cheap, but no one is shopping in the middle of the desert. This is true for any new Web site, not just affiliates. This means that your quest for traffic should never end. You should also employ a diverse array of traffic-gathering techniques.

Affiliate Program Payment Methods

Affiliate programs use different ways to determine the payment method. Each can be successful in its own way, but there are slight differences between each. The three most common methods of payment are as follows.

- **Pay-per-click.** If you enter into this type of method, you will be paying your affiliates a total price that is determined by the number of Web visitors who click on a link on the affiliate Web page to arrive at your business' Web site. These visitors are not required to buy anything; all they have to do is visit your Web site through the affiliate link.

- **Pay-per-lead.** With this type of method, you will be paying your affiliates an amount determined by the number of visitors that leave information at your Web site. All the visitor needs to do is fill out a form on your site, which is then used to further sales and communication with the potential customer. Your goal is to make a sale and make the Web visitor a repeat customer so you can increase your client database and overall sales performance.

- **Pay-per-sale.** If you are using this type of method with your affiliates, you pay a total that is determined by the number of sales you make from the visitors that are sent to your Web site from the affiliate Web site or blog who click on the affiliate links and make a purchase (conversion). The amount you pay is based on either a predetermined amount that is fixed ahead of time for each sale (flat rate) or a percentage of each sale.

The Challenges of Managing Affiliate Marketing

Once you decide to use affiliate marketing, you have choices:

- Develop your own in-house affiliate program

- Use a third-party affiliate platform, such as ClickBank (**www.clickbank.com**) or Commission Junction (**www. cj.com**)

Promoting Your Affiliate Program

No matter what, you must promote your affiliate program, and you can promote it yourself through the Google™ Search Engine. First, you need to get to know your market. Identify where potential affiliates may congregate, whether that be in forums, online groups, or elsewhere. This is critical as you spread the word of your affiliate program. Do not discount the use of blogs, as they are powerful, and because they ping the search engines after each new posting, they are quite search engine friendly. Your affiliate program has to be enticing to a potential affiliate. It needs to be easy to understand, easy to sign up for, and easy to manage. The registration process should be quick, and that the marketing materials at their disposal should be diverse and effective. Use this checklist to make sure you meet the minimum requirements for an effective promotion:

- The affiliate link to join the program should be visible.

- The registration process should be quick and painless, capturing minimum required information (affiliates can add more later) with a solid affiliate agreement and e-mail confirmation.

- The marketing materials you use should be wide-ranging, from banner ads to articles and sales copy. The easier it is on an affiliate to integrate your content into their Web site, the more consistent the click-through rate will be. You will also attract more affiliates, since you will have substantially decreased the workload on them to join and manage the program.

Other promotion ideas to consider include the following:

- Ask your friends and online neighbors to start a topic and "ask" questions in a forum thread that you can interject your affiliate program into. This definitely needs to read as a natural conversation, not a canned sales pitch to promote your affiliate program. Be careful because you are essentially trying to draw in potential affiliates by engaging in a planted online discussion, but others have had success with it.

- Offer promotional incentives to new affiliates, such as "first 50 affiliates receive a 50 percent commission for the first six months."

- Buy endorsements or listings in blogs, forums, and Web sites promoting your affiliate program. You can also list your affiliate program with affiliate directories for free (more on this in later chapters).

The goal with any promotional program is to ensure your affiliate program grows and prospers.

Ideas to Improve Your Site & Affiliate Program

- **Site Design**: Make sure that your Web site is professional and has a great design. You want your Web site to have a clean, tight look so that customers are compelled to return. Professional site design means having a Web site that (1) is easy to navigate, (2) has appropriate logos, (3) has up-to-date information, (4) answers customer questions, and (5) does not look like an amateur site. Use the tools provided in the SEO chapter of this book to ensure your site is indexed with Google™, has Google™ Site Maps, and is optimized for Google™.

- **Honesty**: Do not hide anything from your customers or affiliates. Follow through on what you say you offer with your affiliate program to maintain credibility and trust. You do not want to be identified and exposed as running a fraudulent or dishonest Web site or affiliate program.

- **Testimonials and Product Reviews**: Using customer testimonials and product reviews is a good way to promote the quality and reliability of your products. This is an amazingly effective tactic, which **Amazon.com**™ has perfected with their product reviews. The strongest, most effective referral comes from direct customer testimonials. You can add **Amazon.com**-style product reviews to your Web site by visiting here: **www.review-script.com**. These reviews are also indexed by the Google™ Search Engine, significantly increasing search engine visibility.

- **Tiered Commissions for Top-Performing Affiliates**: If you have highly successful affiliates, you may wish to award them with higher commission rates. Also, you may wish to have other affiliates in special categories with higher commission percentages. Promote the tiered policy through Google™ to entice new affiliates.

- **Promote your URL**: Include your Web site URL on all correspondence, such as e-mail signatures and blog posts — anything that will garner search engine visibility.

Once you have your affiliate program running, you can use Google™ to promote it. This is where the power of the Google™ Search Engine comes in to promote and expand your affiliate program. Of course, using organic SEO (a technique which means that you implement SEO methods to draw natural Web site traffic and rankings) and other methods to maximize the visibility of your Web site and affiliate program in major search engines, including Google™, is critical. You must optimize your site for search engine visibility, and also promote your new affiliate program.

Affiliate Directories

Start plugging your affiliate program into affiliate or associate directories. One of the best is at **http://associateprograms.com**. You can find the submission URL at **www.associateprograms. com/pages/How-to-submit-an-affiliate-program**. Another good one is Affiliate Scout, located at **www.affiliatescout.com/add/**. **Http://affiliateRanker.com**, which is available for submission of your affiliate program at **www.affiliateranker.com/submit.jsp**, is another good one. Search for "affiliate directory" and spend an afternoon submitting your affiliate program to the many directories out there. Some will require you to put a reciprocal link on your Web site to their Web site.

Promoting Your Affiliate Program

In addition to promoting your Web site through organic SEO (essentially, making sure your site is indexed by search engines) and optimizing your site design, there are many more things you can do to promote your affiliate program.

The golden rule before announcing your affiliate program is to ensure you have fully tested it — it is 100 percent functional, easy to find, easy to navigate, and the support mechanisms are in place to support it. A promotional opportunity is a good way to recruit new affiliates. Likewise, they can use this promotional period to promote your affiliate program for you and recruit other affiliates.

You can initiate campaigns within your affiliate program to promote sales volume, total sales amount, or other incentives to inspire affiliates to promote your program and encourage sales. This is a good thing to consider around holiday periods, when shoppers are looking for good bargains.

If you are offering discounts or other promotional materials your affiliates can promote for you, consider also adding them to the many big coupon Web sites, which promote coupons, discounts, and special sales. Try **www.dealnews.com**.

Embrace e-mail marketing as a method to promote your affiliate program. Atlantic Publishing Company produces a monthly "newsletter" that announces new book releases to their customers. Include details about your affiliate program in your e-mail marketing campaigns. In depth information about e-mail marketing is provided in the book, *The Complete Guide to E-mail Marketing: How to Create Successful, Spam-Free Campaigns to Reach Your Target Audience and Increase Sales*. One word of caution, use your trusted e-mail list. Spam does not work, and you will not get quality affiliates by sending out bulk spam e-mails. Keep in contact with your affiliates and customers through regular e-mails that contain useful information, as well as promotional offers.

Consider integrating Google™ AdWords into your overall marketing strategy to promote your affiliate program. Also consider purchasing ad space on Web site or in e-mail marketing campaigns that have content relevant to your products. Although these cost money, they do have a good return on investment and promote your company, products, and affiliate program opportunities.

Establish a blog for your company. Use it to promote communications and viral marketing, and disseminate information through this medium. Blogs are powerful and popular. For more information on blogs, check out the book, *The Secret Power of Blogging: How to Promote and Market Your Business, Organization, or Cause with Free Blogs*. Promote your products and affiliate program through co-workers, friends, other blogs, and other Web sites, and the viral effect (particularly with blogs) will have a measurably positive effect on your overall (and affiliate) sales.

Make your affiliate program, Web site, and blog appealing to visitors and potential customers. It does not matter how cool your Web site or affiliate program is if no one clicks on the links and buys from you. You need to give them a reason to want to join your affiliate program or buy your products. Create this interest, and you will be successful. Do not stuff your Web pages and blog with useless ads and links. Nothing is worse than a page crammed with flashing ads. If you have products to sell, put good descriptions by each one, as in the following example:

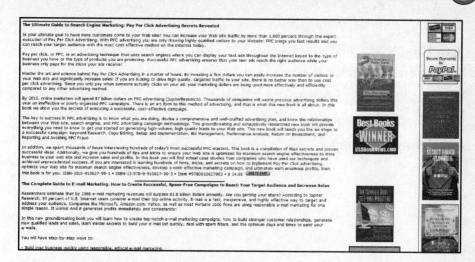

Reprinted with Permission Atlantic Publishing Group, Inc.

Organize your Web site so the navigation is logical and simple so the visitor finds the clearly presented information they would expect to find on the Web page.

Consider writing articles related to your products. You can offer an incentive for signing up with your affiliate program. Offer a free product sample, or something tangible, not another useless download they will toss in the deleted bin.

Subscribe to and participate in online forums and blogs related to your product or marketplace. You can shamelessly plug your products and your affiliate program. Create a link to your Web site and affiliate program in your signature on the forums, and blog and offer advice, or respond to others with information that will peak interest in your company, Web site, products, and blog.

These are just some ideas to get you started. As with any online promotions or long-term plans to promote your Web site, blog or affiliate marketing campaigns take patience and determination, but they can be incredibly successful, and you can easily leverage the power of the Google™ Search Engine to generate Web site traffic and search engine visibility and increase income. For advanced details on Affiliate Marketing, read *The Complete Guide to Affiliate Marketing on the Web: How to Use and Profit from Affiliate Marketing Programs.*

Google Web Services & API's: Harnessing the Power of Google

An API is an application program interface, or a set of routines, protocols, and tools for building software applications. The purpose of an API is that it makes it easier to develop a program by providing you with all the building blocks to "build" the program. Although an API is intended for a developer, Google™ has made APIs available for most of their applications, absolutely free of charge.

A Google™ API will help you because it can automate, streamline and improve the process of updating and exchanging data between your company database and a variety of Google™ applications such as AdWords, Base, Product Search, or Google™ Maps. As this book is not a developer's guide, this is merely an introduction to Google™ APIs, explaining what is available and how they can benefit you. Detailed instruction is available, which you can use in your Web and interface development.

Google Developers Network

Google™ Code is Google™'s Developer Network Web site (**http:// code.Google.com**) for developers interested in Google™-related development. The site contains Open Source code and lists of their service's APIs and current projects. This Web site is packed with API information, source code, blog data, and relevant applications for how Google™ APIs have been implemented by developers.

GoogleAPIs and Tools

There are dozens of APIs and tools available through the Google™ Developer's Network, most of which are listed here:

Android: Android is a software stack for mobile devices including an operating system, middleware, and key applications. It is being developed by the Open Handset Alliance, a group of more than 30 technology and mobile companies. Android was built from the ground up to enable developers to create compelling mobile applications that take full advantage of all a handset has to offer. Developers can create applications for the platform using the Android SDK.

Blogger Data API: The Blogger Data API allows client applications to view and update Blogger content in the form of Google™ Data API feeds. Your client application can use the Data API to reate new blog posts, edit or delete existing posts, and query for posts that match particular criteria.

Chromium: Chromium is the open source browser project behind Google™ Chrome. Built from components that include the Apple WebKit renderer and the new V8 JavaScript™ engine, Chromium provides all the elements of a functional Web browser.

FeedBurner APIs: FeedBurner offers Web services for interacting with their feed management and awareness-generating capabilities.

Gadgets API: Gadgets are simple HTML and JavaScript mini-applications served in iframes that can be embedded in Web pages and other applications. Built-in JavaScript libraries make it easy to create gadgets that include tabs, Flash content, persistent storage, dynamic resizing, and more.

Gears: Gears is an open source browser extension that lets you create Web applications that run offline. It lets you store and serve application resources locally, store data locally in a fully-searchable relational database, and run asynchronous JavaScript™ to improve application responsiveness.

Gmail Atom Feeds: This feed mechanism lets you read your Gmail inbox or labels via any aggregator that supports the Atom XML feed format.

Google Account Authentication: Writing mashups or other applications that exchange data with your user's Google™ services? Use the Authentication service to simplify the process of getting permission from your users.

Google AdSense API: The AdSense API enables you to integrate AdSense sign up, ad unit management, and reporting into your Web or blog hosting platform.

Google AdSense for Audio API: The AdSense for Audio API enables you to integrate AdSense for Audio into a broadcast system, such as a radio automation system. By integrating AdSense for Audio into a broadcast system you give radio stations access to the AdSense for Audio network, which makes their unsold commercial inventory available to thousands of new advertisers through the Google™ Audio Ads program.

Google AdWords API: The AdWords API enables advertisers and third parties alike to integrate directly with the AdWords advertising platform.

Google AJAX APIs: Google™'s AJAX APIs let you implement rich, dynamic Web sites entirely in JavaScript™ and HTML.

Google AJAX Feed API: The AJAX Feed API makes it easy to access and use data feeds in your JavaScript™ applications. You used to need a server to proxy feeds before you could read and manipulate them in mashups; now you can load RSS and Atom feeds from different sources with a few lines of JavaScript code.

Google AJAX Language API: Easily translate and detect multiple languages using JavaScript™.

Google AJAX Search API: The Google™ AJAX Search API lets you use JavaScript™ to embed a simple, dynamic Google™ search box and display search results in your own Web pages, or use search results programmatically in innovative ways.

Google Analytics: Track total page views, unique visitors, and AdWords conversions on your site.

Google App Engine: Run your Web applications on Google™'s infrastructure.

Google Apps APIs: Provides domain administration for Premier and Education Edition customers.

Google Base Data API: With the Google™ Base Data API, you can query Google™ Base data to create applications and mashups, as well as input and manage Google™ Base items programmatically. Your application can upload new data, update or delete existing items, and execute specialized queries to find matches for complex attribute criteria.

Google Book Search APIs: Google™ Book Search is Google™'s effort to make book content more discoverable on the Web. Using our APIs, you too can easily and reliably integrate with this repository from your own Web site or application.

Google Calendar APIs and Tools: The Google™ Calendar Data API and other tools enable you to do many things: create a Web front end for your group's calendar, generate a public calendar based on your organization's event database, create Calendar Gadgets, and much more.

Google Chart API: The Google™ Chart API is a simple tool that lets you create many types of charts.

Google Checkout API: Google™ Checkout provides a streamlined e-commerce checkout process that can be integrated with Google™ AdWords and Analytics to attract more leads and drive better conversion rates. The Checkout API allows you to integrate your site with Google™ Checkout, either by spending 5 minutes and dropping in simple "buy now" buttons, or by stepping through a complete integration of your order management system with.

Google Code Search: Google™ Code Search helps you find function definitions and sample code by giving you one place to search publicly accessible source code hosted on the Internet.

Google Code Search Data API: Enable your apps to view data from Code Search.

Google Contacts Data API: The Google™ Code Search Data API allows client applications to view data from Code Search in the form of Google™ Data API feeds. Your client application can use the Google™ Code Search Data API to query for public source code, function definitions, and sample code.

Google Coupon Feeds: Google™ coupon feeds enable businesses to provide coupon listings that will be included in Google™

search results. Coupon feeds enable merchants to easily distribute coupons for free via the Web. Consumers can also search for, print and redeem coupons for free.

Google Custom Search API: Google™ Custom Search enables you to create a search engine for your Web site, your blog, or a collection of Web sites within minutes. You can harness the power of Google™ to create a search engine tailored to your needs and interests and present the results in your Web site. You can fine-tune the ranking, customize the look and feel of the search results, and invite your friends or trusted users to help you build your custom search engine. You can even make money from your search engine by using your Google™ AdSense account.

Google Data APIs: The Google™ Data APIs provide a simple, standard protocol for reading and writing data on the Web. Google™ Data API is a protocol based on the Atom 1.0 and RSS 2.0 syndication formats, plus the Atom Publishing Protocol.

Google Desktop Gadget API: Desktop gadgets are powerful mini-applications that can live within the Google™ Desktop sidebar, or right on the user's desktop, or even inside iGoogle™ home pages. You create Desktop gadgets using XML and JavaScript™, optionally adding native code for access to Windows® APIs. The Desktop Gadget API enables advanced functionality such as transparency, animation, custom fonts, and personalization.

Google Desktop Search APIs: Use the power of Google™ Desktop in your applications and gadgets, or create indexing plug-ins that let users search any file type — documents, spreadsheets, music files, e-mail, calendar, or your software application's special file type. The Search APIs work with JavaScript™, VBScript, C, C++, C#, and VB.Net code.

Google Documents List Data API: The Google™ Documents List Data API allows client applications to view and search through documents in Google™ Documents using Google™ Data API feeds.

Google Earth API: The Google™ Earth Plug-in and its JavaScript™ API let you embed Google™ Earth, a true 3D digital globe, into your Web pages. Using the API you can draw markers and lines, drape images over the terrain, add 3D models, or load KML files, allowing you to build sophisticated 3D map applications.

Google Finance Data API: The Google™ Finance Portfolio Data API allows client applications to view and update Finance content in the form of Google™ Data API feeds.

Google Friend Connect: Google™ Friend Connect enables Webmasters to quickly and easily enhance their site with community features; what's more, these features leverage visitors' existing social ties.

Google Health API: The Google™ Health Data API allows client applications to view and send Health content in the form of Google™ Data API feeds. Your client application can use the Health Data API to create new medical records, request a list and query for medical records that match particular criteria.

Google Mapplets: Google™ Mapplets are mini-apps that you can embed within the Google™ Maps site. Examples include real estate search, current weather conditions, and distance measurement.

Google Maps API: The Google™ Maps API allows you to create innovative online mapping applications and helps integrate maps and geo-coding into your Web sites. With it, you can easily present your geo-referenced content in any Web browser.

Google Maps API For Flash: The Google™ Maps API for Flash® allows you to add maps to Flash® applications. Based on Action-Script® 3.0, this API enables Flex developers to easily customize maps through a variety of services.

Google Mashup Editor: Google™ Mashup Editor is an AJAX development framework and a set of tools that enable developers to quickly and easily create simple Web applications and mashups with Google™ services like Google™ Maps and Google™ Base.

Google Notebook Data API: The Google™ Notebook Data API allows client applications to view stored data in the form of Google™ Data API feeds. Your client application can request a list of a user's public notebooks, or query the content of a public notebook.

Google Radio Automation API: Google™ Radio Automation is used by radio stations to ingest, manage, and broadcast audio content. Using this API, you can write applications to add func tionality to Google™ Radio Automation or tightly integrate your product with Google™ Radio Automation.

Google Safe Browsing APIs: The Safe Browsing API is an experimental API that allows client applications to check URLs against Google's constantly-updated blacklists of suspected phishing and malware pages.

Google Search Appliance APIs: The Search Protocol is a simple HTTP-based protocol for serving search results. Search administrators have complete control over requesting and presenting search results to end users. The Feeds Protocol enables a customer or a third-party developer to write a custom application to feed a data source into the Google™ Search Appliance for processing, indexing, and serving. The Authorization Protocol enables a customer's Web service to authorize users to access specific documents for searching in real-time, leveraging their existing security and access control environment.

Google Sitemaps: Enables Google™ crawlers to quickly find what pages are present and which have recently changed. You create a file conforming to the site map protocol on your Web server; this file informs and direct Google™ crawlers, improving the time to inclusion in the index.

Google SketchUp Ruby API: Google™ SketchUp Ruby API allows you to manipulate SketchUp models and extend the behavior of Google™ SketchUp.

Google Spreadsheets Data API: The Google™ Spreadsheets Data API allows client applications to view and update Spreadsheets content in the form of Google™ Data API feeds.

Google Static Maps API: The Google™ Static Maps API lets you embed a Google™ Maps image on your Web page without requiring JavaScript™ or any dynamic page loading.

Google Talk for Developers: The Google™ Talk network uses XMPP for its communications protocol, making it easy for client developers to connect and other networks to federate.

Google Themes API: The Google™ Themes API allows you to further personalize the iGoogle™ homepage by specifying your own background images and colors in an XML file.

Google Toolbar API: The Google™ Toolbar API allows you to create custom buttons for the Google™ Toolbar (version 4 and above) using XML.

Google Transit Feed Specification: The Google™ Transit Feed Specification is a common format that transit agencies and other interested parties can use to make public transportation information available through Google™ Transit Trip Planner, Google™ Earth, Google™ Maps, and other tools.

Google Visualization API: The Google™ Visualization API allows you to create visualization and reporting applications over structured data and helps integrate these into your Web sites or Gadgets. With this API, you can easily create visualizations that provide insights from relevant content and embed those in any Web browser.

Google Web Toolkit: The Google™ Web Toolkit (GWT) is an open source Java software development framework that helps you produce user-friendly AJAX applications.

Google Webmaster Tools Data API: Google™ Webmaster Tools Data API allows client applications to view and update site information and site maps in the form of Google™ Webmaster Tools Data API feeds.

iGoogle Developer Home: Gadgets on iGoogle™ now support canvas view and OpenSocial, a common set of APIs, HTML, and JavaScript™ designed to let you easily build social applications.

KML: KML is a file format used to display geographic data in an Earth browser, such as Google™ Earth, Google™ Maps and Google™ Maps for mobile.

OpenSocial: OpenSocial defines a common API for social applications across multiple Web sites. With standard JavaScript™ and HTML, developers can create apps that access a social network's friends and update feeds.

Orkut Developer Home: As a developer, you can create social applications for Orkut users. Orkut supports OpenSocial, a common set of APIs, HTML, and JavaScript™ designed to let developers easily build social applications.

Picasa APIs: The Picasa® APIs enable you to create buttons users can install in the Picasa® client user interface.

Picasa Web Albums Data API: The Picasa® Web Albums Data API allows Web sites and client applications to view and update Picasa® Web Albums content. Using Google™ Data API feeds, you can retrieve and update photo albums, add new comments and photos, and even tag photos automatically. It's the easy way to get photos and albums into your own Web site or application.

Social Graph API: The Social Graph API makes information about the public connections between people on the Web easily available and useful for developers.

Subscribed Links: Google™ Subscribed Links enables you to create custom search results and define search keywords for triggering the results.

V8: Embed V8 in your own C++ application to make your application's objects and methods available to JavaScript™, and to make JavaScript™ objects and functions available to you.

YouTube APIs: YouTube offers open access to key parts of the YouTube video repository and user community, via an open API interface and RSS feeds. Using our APIs, you can easily integrate online videos from YouTube®'s rapidly growing repository of videos into your application.

Google Code University

The Google™ Code University is a Google™ Web site that provides tutorials and sample course content for computer science students and educators to learn about current computing technologies. This site contains tutorials, lecture slides, and problem sets for a variety of topic areas, including AJAX programming, Web security, and more. Google™ Code University is on the Web at **http://code.Google.com/edu**.

Significant information, tutorials, support, and more is available at **http://code.Google.com**.

Google Web Publisher Tools

Google™ provides you with a wealth of Web publishing tools, most of which are covered throughout this book

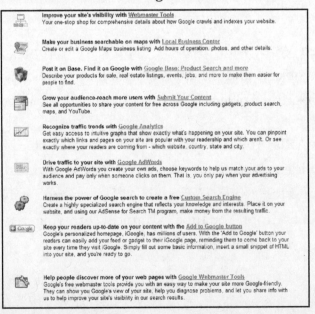

Google™ screenshots © Google™ Inc. Used with permission.

Below are more Web publishing tools provided by Google™:

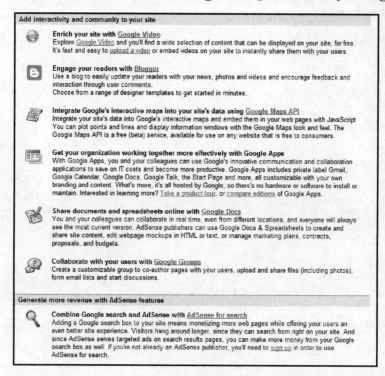

Google™ screenshots © Google™ Inc. Used with permission.

Google and Blogs: A Partnership to Generate Income

A blog is a combination of the words Web + Log. It is a Web site in which short entries or "postings" are made in an abbreviated style format and are displayed in reverse chronological order.

Blogs can be about any subject, and many are about politics, news, world events, public opinion, food, and cooking in addition to personal blogs from celebrities, world leaders, aspiring political candidates, and almost anything else you could possibly think of. Personal blogs are often like online versions of a diary or journal, but they offer interactivity you cannot get with a traditional paper-based diary or journal, or even with a static, HTML-based Web page diary or journal.

A blog uses a combination of text, graphics, images, and hyperlinks to other blogs, Web sites, Web pages, and multimedia content, such as movie or audio clips. One of the features associated with blogging is that blog visitors can leave comments on the blog, thus creating a collaborative dialogue between you and potential customers, donors, or others you may wish to interact with. A blog opens the door to two-way communication between you and millions of people on the Internet.

Blogging is all about linking. As with Web sites, links can help raise blog visibility with search engines. Links to and from blogs to other blogs and Web sites are directly relevant to the popularity and overall visibility and ranking of blogs.

The blogosphere is the compilation of all blogs, including personal, business, political, or otherwise, on all Web sites throughout the Web. The blogosphere is not a physical place or Web site.

The Construction of a Blog

Although this is generalized, and each blog may be slightly different, you can usually expect to find the following:

- **Title**: This provides the blog reader an overall idea of what the blog is about.

- **Date**: The date of the blog's most recent update or post. Blogs are displayed in reverse chronological order, so the most recent post is at the top of the blog.

- **Post Titles**: The title of each blog post.

- **Blog Text**: The actual text each blog post consists of.

- **Blog Post Information**: This is information about the individual or business who wrote the blog. Sometimes this contains contact information as well.

- **Blogger Comments**: This is an area for the readers of a blog to place comments, responses, opinions, or reactions to a blog post. This is not a mandatory field; if your intent is only to "push" information out via your blog, you do not have to accept comments.

- **Previous Blog Posts**: This is the reverse chronological listing of previous blog posts from most recent, to oldest.

- **Archived Posts**: Even the most organized blogs and get unwieldy, it is not uncommon to archive old posts after a preset period of time.

- **Blogroll**: A list of links to other related sites.

- **Advertising**: This is a common sight in the world of blogging. Many ads are prominently featured in free blogging applications. In some cases, you can generate revenue through the use of advertising, but often, these are third-party ads that you allow for use of blogging software.

- **Feeds**: Feeds to push blogs posts automatically to subscribers such as RSS or Atom;

This is where the power of Google™ comes in. **Blogger.com** is a Google™ blog product that lets you create your own blogs for free. Google™ even hosts the blog for you, or you can host it on your server. You can set up a blog in minutes. Blogger is a good choice because it is hosted free on **http://blogspot.com**, and if you want, you can host it on your own Web servers via FTP with the click on a button. There is no software to install on your Web servers.

Who Blogs?

A critical component to the success of any blog is who will participate in the blog. A blog is nothing without participation from subscribers, readers, customers, and potential customers. Millions of people are "bloggers." Bloggers come from every walk of life, including professionals, executives, blue-collar workers, housewives, and techno-geeks. Blogging has exploded in popularity and is now considered to be a communications method of the future. Blogging is much more than simply a "journal," as it was when it was first invented. Blogging is a marketing tool allowing you to communicate and interact directly with your fellow bloggers. The beauty of blogging is its simplicity. Not only is it easy to establish a blog site, it is easy to become an active blogger. You do not need any technical knowledge, special skills, or training to establish a highly effective blog site or become an expert blogger.

Understanding Pings and Trackbacks

Blogging is a way of publishing information to the Web by using "blog" software. You have the ability to publish information quickly, and even to publish new content through e-mail or a cell phone, but the most unique feature of blogging is comments. Comments create the two-way communication between you and your blog readers. Bloggers read your blog and post comments, questions, opinions, and concerns. This dialogue is what makes blogging unique. To take it one step further, your blog readers can also link directly to your blog posts and recommend your blog to others, an act referred to as trackbacks and pingbacks.

Trackbacks are simply a notification method between blogs. They allow a blog reader to send a notice to someone else that the blog might be something they would have an interest in reading.

Pingbacks are a method for Web authors to request notification when somebody links to one of their documents. Typically, Web publishing software will automatically inform the relevant parties on behalf of the user, allowing for the possibility of automatically creating links to referring documents.

Blogger, found at **www.blogger.com**, is entirely free, thanks to Google™. It is a basic, yet effective way to start a blog. Blogger, which was started in 1999, was bought by Google™, so it will continue to be supported and improved upon. Blogger uses standard templates to get you started with an attractive site right away without the need to learn HTML, but also allows you to edit your blog's HTML code whenever you want. You can also use custom colors and fonts to modify the appearance of your blog.

Blogger's simple drag-and-drop system lets you easily decide exactly where your posts, profiles, archives, and other parts of your blog should reside on the page. You can also upload photos and embed them into your blog. Blogger Mobile lets you send photos and text straight to your blog while you are on the go. All you need to do is send a message to go@blogger.com from your phone. You do not even need a Blogger account. The message itself is enough to create a brand new blog and post whatever photo and text you have sent.

Blogging allows you to open two-way communications directly with your customers and attract potential customers to your products or services. The bottom line for blogging is that it increases communications and visibility for your business, organization, or cause. The underlying principles of blogging are a perfect fit into a customer oriented business model, where you want to allow customers, potential customers, readers, site visitors, or fellow bloggers to engage you with two-way communications, which are visible on the Internet to others. You can promote your products, answer questions, engage customers, and give expert advice, tips, and suggestions. A Web site is static in nature, meaning that the content only changes when you change it. By its nature, a blog is ever-morphing as more dialogue is added to it.

Business Blog Communications—How it Works

To understand how a Weblog will impact your business, dramatically improve communications, and increase Web site traffic, you need to understand in detail, exactly how a Weblog works. For explanation purposes, let us just assume that we already have a Weblog for our business, and today, we are going to update it. Here is the process that takes place:

- A resident corporate blogger, or anyone who blogs, writes something and publishes to the blog.

- The blog software updates the blog with an HTML coded blog, and if you are using an RSS feed, the RSS file is also updated.

- Your blog software now "announces" a new update to your blog. This is critical to understand. Blogger actually "pings" the Google™ Search Engine and advises readers that you have fresh content for them to check. The process of notifying search engines of your new content is called "pinging." Essentially, pinging is a program that tells the search engines that your blog has been updated, and notifies them to re-index the content. It is also important to tell blog search engines and news aggregators so that they too can check out all your new content. Telling them you have fresh content is called pinging them.

- After you ping, major search engines such as Google™ (**http://blogsearch.Google.com**), and RSS services will index your blog and retrieve the new content. Another secret to increase search engine visibility is to ping often and use an RSS file to publish Weblog updates, which tends to result in increased search engine rankings.

- Another critical component to Weblogs that makes them distinct from Web sites or bulletin boards is trackbacks. By using trackbacks, also called pingbacks, you can notify other bloggers whenever you cite an article from another site or blog into your own blog. This exponentially increases the communication and visibility of Weblogs. As a blogger reads your blog post, they may write about your post on their blog and enter your trackback link into the trackback section of their blog through their blog software. Once this blog entry is published, the blog is then registered to your trackback blog address. As trackback links increase throughout the blogosphere, your blog post can quickly be referenced by thousands of bloggers on their Weblogs, within a short time period. This feature gives your blog significant promotion through the blogosphere and allows you to know when someone has been writing about your blog post. Whenever you discuss someone's blog or blog post, always include a trackback. On your blog, make sure your trackback address is clearly visible so other bloggers can easily identify it and use it on their blog posts.

Technically, a blog is a Web site. It uses standard HTML formatting and is interpreted by the browser in the same way a regular HTML Web page is. The difference is in the ability to ping and use RSS feeds, along with trackbacks, to automate the process of creating, maintaining, publishing, and communicating with Weblogs.

As blogs become popular, and other blogs post information and trackbacks, the comments grow exponentially, as do the links and page ranks. As you build your blogs, most of this will become clear and you will have a thorough understanding of how blogs are created and how they communicate.

Why You Should Start a Blog

There are several reasons why you should consider blogs, including the following:

- They are free

- They are popular

- They are easy to establish

- They do not require HTML coding skills

- You can open new channels of communication with your customers

- You can promote your business, products, or cause for free

- You can create enormous advertising buzz and promote your Web site across the Internet through trackbacks

- Your blog is posted instantly through pinging, instead of waiting on a search engine to pick up your new Web site content

- You can communicate on a one-to-one basis with customers, collaborators, donators, sponsors, and others

- You can have instant communications channels

- You can schedule blog updates on a specific schedule, such as weekly, monthly, or even daily

- You can use RSS feeds to push your blog updates to subscribers

The goal for any business is to increase profits and sales, grow the customer base, and improve communications. Blogs are the perfect solution to help you achieve all these goals.

Optimizing Your Blog for SEO/Web Site Traffic

An SEO optimized blog, which is updated frequently, tends to get indexed and spidered by the search engines more often than static HTML Web sites do. Since you have the ability to literally create blogs on the fly, without significant time investment or advanced Web design skills, you can quickly and easily promote your Web site. Since you link your blogs back to your Web site (and link often), as your blogs grow in popularity and search engine rankings, so does the resulting traffic to your Web site. Use appropriate keywords in blog posts and in your blog headlines. Your blog posts need to be relevant, on-topic, keyword-rich, and contain useful information. Content should be original and clearly organized. As your blogs grow in popularity, your search engine rankings and Web site traffic will increase.

Effective use of trackbacks in your blog posts will dramatically increase visibility and traffic for your blog. Trackbacks are more than just placing a URL link in your blog to another Web site or blog.

Already pinged:

- http://ggwdblog.blogspot.com/2007/06/get-publishing-in-my-book-blogger.html#comment-8415195899569979412

Google™ screenshots © Google™ Inc. Used with permission.

Those are some basics for when you visit a blog. By implementing these practices, you will grow traffic to your blog and Web site. The No. 1 rule is that if you find a site or blog you like, bookmark it, and visit often. Comment on the blog posts when they are of interest or you have an opinion to share. Subscribe to the blog RSS/Atom feeds. Share articles among blogs, and use trackbacks to other articles of relevance. Spread the word about a good blog or Web site through your blog, Web site, or e-mail.

For both your blog and your Web site, keywords and key phrases are critical for increasing search engine visibility and generating Web site (and blog) traffic. Search engines use keywords, Web site content, and meta tags to rate your Web site. Think of what the content of your Web site or blog is and how you would search for it. Those keywords or phrases should be on your home page or blog so they are indexed by the search engines as keywords relevant to your Web site or blog.

Links are critical for search engine rankings of your Web site and your blog. Frequently changing content helps with search engine rankings, which is why blogs do so well in search engines. Change your Web site content frequently, and keep publishing blog posts on a regular basis. Review both your blog posts and your Web site content for keyword-rich phrases. Replace any extraneous material that adds little or no value with phrases loaded with keywords. Write quality, relevant articles and publish them at other article Web sites with a link back to your site and blog.

Your titles need to tell readers what a post is about, and to ensure search engines pick up on your keywords and key phrases. Your blog needs to be of value to the reader, not just another marketing tool for you to sell stuff. Think of a Web site as the sale vehicle for the Web and blogs as the "resource staff" where information is posted, questions are answered, and background information is provided to help inform a potential customer about your business, organization, products, or services. When you hook them for the sale, they can always go to your Web site for the "sales pitch" and to place an order.

Do a quick search on "blog directories," and you will find dozens of directories you can submit your blog URL to. Although it will take some time, you will see results. Two such directories can be found at **www.icerocket.com** and **www.bloggernity.com**. Also, you can search blogs by using Google™ Blog Search, at **http:// blogsearch.Google.com**.

Use your Blog Roll, which is simply a collection of blogs that you visit often, or feel are useful, and you choose to list them on your

Web site homepage or blog. This is a good way to build relationships between yourself and other bloggers. Keep your Blog Roll a living list by adding to it often, as appropriate.

Blogger

Blogger started out as a small, independent company in the late 1990s. In 2002, **www.blogger.com** was bought out by Google™. So, although you go to **www.blogger.com** to create your blog, you will be using your Google™ account login information to access your blog.

To get started, navigate in your browser to **www.blogger.com**:

Google™ screenshots © Google™ Inc. Used with permission.

Click on the "Create your Blog now" arrow to continue. If you already have a blog with blogger.com, you simply log in to access your account.

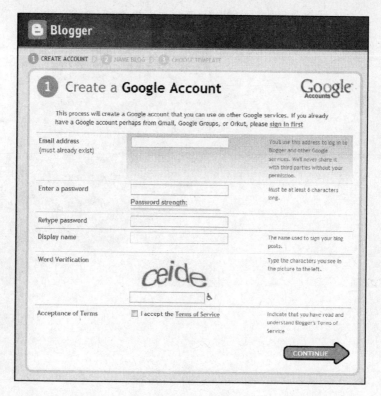

Google™ screenshots © Google™ Inc. Used with permission.

You must have a Google™ Account to access your Blogger blog or create a new blog. Follow the instructions to create a blog.

More Tools to Harness the Power of Google

As you know by now, Google™ is much more than the world's most powerful search engine, and by employing the tools and applications offered by Google™, you can generate increased income levels. There are a variety of other tools Google™ offers, most at no cost to you, to enhance your Web site, communicate better, improve customer sales, and expand your sales base. You may have heard of many of them and already use them on a daily basis, but there are others you may not know about that may be of tremendous value to you.

While many of these tools are not directly related to marketing or advertising, you may find that this culmination of Google™'s products and services offers significant value.

Google Checkout

Located at **http://checkout.Google.com**, Google™ Checkout is a fast, convenient checkout process. Customers who use Checkout can buy from you quickly and securely, using a single username and password, and you can use Checkout to process their orders and charge their credit or debit cards.

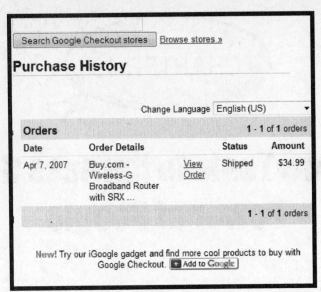

Google™ screenshots © Google™ Inc. Used with permission.

You can use Google™ Checkout with your Google™ Base data feeds. Instructions for how to do this are available at **http://base. Google.com/support/bin/answer.py?hl=en&answer=25396**. Google™ Checkout has specific policy and restrictions which are outlined in the Google™ Checkout Content Policy: **http://checkout.Google.com/support/sell/bin/answer. py?answer=75724&hl=en**.

If you wish to use Google™ Checkout on your Web site as your primary or alternative payment method, it may increase your sales volume because Google™ is recognized and trusted; Google™ Checkout has grown in popularity, similar to the way PayPalSM has exploded in use. Google™ Checkout is fast and convenient, and under certain conditions, you can process customers' orders and charge their credit or debit cards for free. Since Google™ checkout can be integrated with Google™ Base, Google™ Product Search, and Google™ AdWords, the Google™ Search Engine will drive customers to your Web site, and offering Google™

Checkout gives your customers the confidence they need to buy online. With Google™ Checkout, you can even automatically add the Google™ Checkout logo directly to your AdWords ads and Product Search listings.

Google™ screenshots © Google™ Inc. Used with permission.

Google™ Checkout will cost you 2 percent + $0.20 per transaction. With Google™ Checkout, there are no monthly, set-up, or gateway service fees. Google™ Checkout tends to be much less costly than traditional merchant accounts. If you advertise with Google™ AdWords, you will also be eligible for free transaction processing for some or all of your Google™ Checkout sales each month. Currently, for each $1 you spend on AdWords each month, you can process $10 in sales the following month for free through Google™ Checkout. You should review the latest fee schedules, available at **http://checkout.Google.com/support/sell/bin/topic.py?topic=12153**.

Because Google™ Checkout uses a single sign-on, it simplifies the checkout process from your Web site and lets frequent shoppers pull their critical shipping and billing data automatically. A Google™ Checkout Merchant's Forum is available and contains a wealth of relevant information, advice, and support: **www. Google.com/support/forum/p/checkout-merchants?hl=en.**

Gmail

Located at **www.Google.com/accounts**, Gmail℠ is a new kind of Web mail, built on the idea that e-mail can be more intuitive, efficient, and useful. Here is a summary of Google™'s Top Reasons to use Gmail℠:

1. Built in anti-spam filters

2. Built in search capability to eliminate searching and sorting e-mails

3. Capability to organize replies into conversations — your messages are grouped with the responses they receive, even as new replies arrive

4. Google™ Chat is built into Gmail℠ — you can even archive and search them

5. Built in labels and filters to organize your e-mails

6. Accessible anywhere on the Web and via your mobile device

7. Virtually unlimited storage space.

8. No pop-up or banners ads; instead, you get text ads with relevant content links

9. Keyboard shortcuts and built-in contacts

10. Free

11. For organizations, use Gmail℠ for your enterprise-wide business, along with Calendar, Chat, Google™ Collaboration, and more, for a minimal fee

Other features include quick PDF preview, built-in text capability from Gmail℠, Gmail℠ themes, voice and video chat, emoticons, and much more. Google™ Gmail℠ also protects personal e-mail accounts if you choose to use Gmail℠ as a primary business account, and keep a personal e-mail account private. Plus, it is accessible anywhere in the world. The automated grouping of messages and all the replies in conversations is an incredibly powerful feature. Instead of tracking dozens of e-mails on a particular topic, and hoping you do not forget to save any or file them in the proper place, Gmail℠ does the work for you. It always associates all the e-mails together, so you never lose any piece of an e-mail exchange with friends, clients, and customers.

Google™ screenshots © Google™ Inc. Used with permission.

Google Talk

Located at **www.Google.com/talk**, Google™ Talk allows you to Instant Message and call your friends through your computer. You can also host video chat within Gmail℠.

YouTube

Located at **www.youtube.com**, YouTube® allows you to watch, upload, and share videos. If you have not visited YouTube, you are missing out on some good Web content. YouTube, which was founded in 2005, was bought by Google™ in 2006, and was one of the most publicized acquisitions in Google™ history. Your videos can be distributed on YouTube for free, and you can embed them into your Web site, blog, RSS feeds, social networking site, and mobile device through YouTube with links to you Web site, generating site traffic. Adding YouTube to your Web site keeps your site fresh and keeps your site visitors interested and entertained. With YouTube, you can join the Web's largest collection of online videos.

Google Custom Search Engine

Located at **www.Google.com/coop/cse**, the Google™ Custom Search Engine allows you to harness the power of Google™ search to create a free custom search engine that reflects your knowledge and interests. Specify the Web sites that you want searched, and integrate the search box and results into your own Web site.

Orkut

Located at **www.orkut.com**, Orkut is an online social networking community. With Orkut, you can maintain existing relationships with pictures and messages, and establish new ones by reaching out to people you have never met. Do not underestimate the power of social networking and its potential impact on Web site traffic, Internet marketing opportunities, quality inbound links, search engine visibility, and more. Orkut is not yet at the same level or familiarity as MySpace® or Facebook®, but it is growing in popularity and is entirely free.

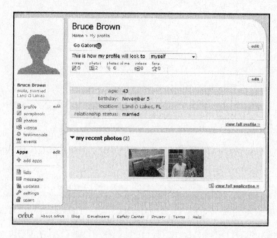

Google™ screenshots © Google™ Inc. Used with permission.

iGoogle

Located at **www.Google.com/ig**, iGoogle™ provides you with the ability to customize content and personalize your home page and Web browser. This customization lets you select what information you want to see and gives you instant access to the data you want at a glance. You may select and organize information and content such as Gmail, News and other headlines, weather, stock quotes, movie show times, Google™ Maps, calendars, and more. You need a Google™ account, and then you simply select your options and default data, such as zip code, in the setting console:

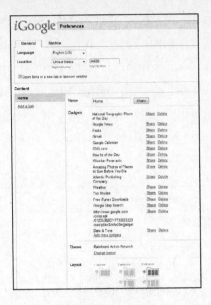

Google™ screenshots © Google™ Inc. Used with permission.

Your Web page is then displayed based on your customized content. While iGoogle™ is not likely to make you money, it will make you more efficient and deliver the data you need to you, instead of making you look for it elsewhere. Google™ AdWords ads will appear in iGoogle™:

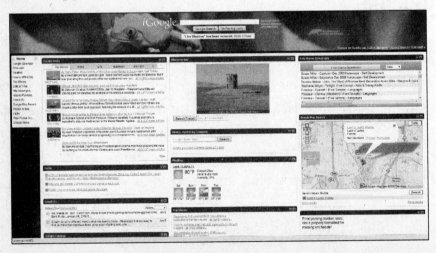

Google™ screenshots © Google™ Inc. Used with permission.

Google Local Business Center

Located at **www.Google.com/local/add/splashPage?hl=en-US&gl=US**, Google™ Business Center lets you harness the power of the Google™ Maps to make your business visible to others searching with Google™ Maps, at **http://maps.Google.com**.

Google™ screenshots © Google™ Inc. Used with permission.

Millions of people search Google™ Maps every day, and a free listing on Google™ Maps makes it easy for them to find you. Simply click on the "add new business" or "add data feed," and follow the simplified instructions to create and list your business for free.

A sample Google™ Map is pictured on the following page.

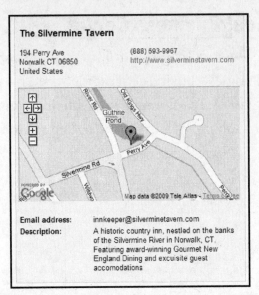

Google™ screenshots © Google™ Inc. Used with permission.

More Helpful Google Applications

Google Finance (http://finance.Google.com/finance) – Interactive business news, charts, business Information, and market news

Google Product Search (www.Google.com/products) – Find and compare products from online stores

Google Images (http://images.Google.com) – The most comprehensive image search on the Web

Google Local (http://maps.Google.com/maps) – Local maps, business locations, and directions

Google Maps (http://maps.Google.com/maps) – Detailed maps, directions, and points of interest

Google News (http://news.Google.com) – Search news articles and headlines

Google Patents (www.Google.com/patents) – Full text search of U.S. Patents

Google Scholar (http://scholar.Google.com) – Search scholarly papers

Google Specialized Searches (www.Google.com/options/specialsearches.html) – Perform highly specialized searches (i.e. government, universities, etc.)

Google Toolbar (www.Google.com/tools) – Adds a powerful search bar to your Web browser

Google Video (http://video.Google.com) – Search videos on Google™ Video and YouTube

Google Web Search (www.Google.com/webhp) – Search millions of Web pages

Google Web Search Features (www.Google.com/help/features. html) – Allows you to search by key topic

Google Code – (http://code.Google.com/) Google™ API's and Source Code

Google CO-OP – (www.Google.com/coop/) Google™ Co-op is a platform that enables you to customize the Web search experience for users of both Google™ and your own Web site

Google Labs (http://labs.Google.com/) – A look at the ideas from Google™ Laboratories which are not quite ready for prime time release

Google Blogs (www.blogger.com/start) – All inclusive blog tools and Web site

Google Calendar (www.Google.com/accounts/) – Full featured online calendar, event planner, & scheduler

Google Docs & Spreadsheet (www.Google.com/accounts/) – Free Web-based word processing and spreadsheet program that keeps documents current and lets the people you choose update files from their own computers

Google Groups (http://groups.Google.com/) – Create mailing lists and discussion groups

Picasa (http://picasa.Google.com/) – Find, edit, and share your photos

Google SketchUp (http://sketchup.Google.com/) – Developed for the conceptual stages of design, as a powerful, easy-to-learn 3D software tool

Google Talk (www.Google.com/talk/) – Instant Message and call your friends through your computer

Google Translate (www.Google.com/language_tools) – View Web pages in other languages

GoogleMobileMaps(www.Google.com/gmm/index.html?utm_ source=us-et-more&utm_medium=et&utm_campaign=gmm) –

The power of Google™ Maps on your mobile phone

Google Mobile (www.Google.com/mobile/) – The power of Google™ on your mobile phone

Google SMS (www.Google.com/intl/en_us/mobile/sms/) – Google™ Text Messenger service

Google Pack (http://pack.Google.com) – A free collection of essential software

Google Webmaster Central (www.Google.com/ webmasters/#utm_medium=et&utm_source=bizsols&utm_ campaign=sitemaps) – Essential tools for Webmasters

Google Analytics (www.Google.com/analytics/) – Google™ Analytics tells you everything you want to know about how your visitors found you and how they interact with your site;

Google Personalization – (www.Google.com/) Launch your Google™ Browser then click the "personalize this page" link in the top right hand corner to customize your browser

Interviews with Google Experts

I interviewed numerous individuals who achieved success with Google™ by using applications such as Google™ AdWords, Google™ AdSense, Google™™ Product Search, and Google™ Base, as well as individuals who achieved remarkable success though SEO and the Google™ Search Engine.

Interview with Dr. Robert C. Worstell

"How can I get to the top of Google™'s Search Engine Rankings?" What practical and realistic advice can you give someone who is starting out with a new Web site or online business to achieve optimal success?

As odd as it sounds, your first action is not to try for top rankings. Sure, the majority of online businesses get the majority of their traffic from Google™ — at least to start with. But your first actions are building the backend, which will handle that traffic when it comes. That means handling pages of content which are linked to each other, plus a working e-commerce engine of some sort — even if you are only promoting as an affiliate sales point.

You have to run your business for the long-term. Nothing in this universe is "get rich quick," and most of your "competition" is from people who have this mind set — but the ones who get and keep their rankings are those who build their sites carefully and continually. So get your business in order, and slate your time so that you'll be able to dedicate a certain amount of time to making your business succeed.

To get rankings, you have to know what Google™ and other search engines are looking for. Search engines are trying to duplicate how people look for and use Information. Google™™ has done this best so far, and thus has become the industry leader. People use certain short combinations of words to find things. These are called "keyword phrases." Some are used and searched for more than others. Some of these keyword phrases are used on more Web sites and pages than others.

When you look at search pages in Google™, it will tell you how many pages exist with that combination of words on them. That number is the apparent competition for that keyword phrase. You need to establish what keyword phrase you actually want to rank for.

The simple steps are:

a. Establish what people are looking for. Find the keyword phrases that suggest your product and ensure your product is something people need or want. You want keyword phrases that have around 100 hits per week, but less than 2 million in competing sites, as a rule of thumb. While Google™'s KeywordExternalTool can help you estimate demand, Wordtracker and Competition

Research provide online tools to give you some more accurate free estimates on hits.

b. Check those keywords in "quotes" to find out how many sites are looking for that particular phrase. Many sites will match a three or four-word phrase, but fewer will have that exact phrase on their site. Also, you want to check for those sites that have that phrase in their title and in their incoming links. Use this query: inanchor:"(keywordphrase)" AND intitle:"(keywordphrase)" in Google™ to see what your real competition is. There are several free sources found under the term "competition estimator" that will allow you to do this for free online.

c. You want to build your site, which can be just a few pages, with the keyword chosen based on your research:

1. In the title

2. In your page description

3. In headings (h1 and h2)

4. In links between the pages of your own site

5. And in every graphic on that page

6. As well, your content has to be about that keyword phrase — not something else. Don't just repeat your keyword over and over on a page, but if you're offering Bengal Tigers, don't write about Tiger Woods.

d. Try to only work with one main keyword phrase per set of pages. Lots of keywords is a spammers trick and will get you penalized. Related keywords are fine, but you can only get so many keywords in the above. Concentrate on a single one, or a couple. Later, you can build more pages that concentrate on other related keyword phrases you want to rank for.

e. Now, start blogging and getting social media out there. Blogs and social media are looked for by Google™™ because they are new, fresh content — and because social media is voted on and peer-reviewed. However, the top spots in Google™ are very competitive. One or two posts on a subject won't stick around. If they point to your Web site, and use the same keywords in their links to that site, your Web site will show up in the top few and stay there. The subject of social media is a wide and evolving one, but if you blog and comment on others' blogs using your keywords and linking to your site, that will be a good start. And, if properly done, you can see results in minutes — literally. But the trick is to blog and add content regularly and consistently.

What do you think are the benefits (or drawbacks) from using Google™ AdWords? Is Google™ AdWords a recommended investment, and can it truly generate Web traffic and revenue for an online business?

PPC can be done. Unfortunately, the bigger corporations have started getting wise to this, so overall, the ad word rates have increased tremendously. This means that for a small business starting out, it's another uphill climb. To use PPC, you need to concentrate on narrow niches and be very left-brained about it — constantly analyze your ads, phrasings, and where you are placing your ads, as well how much to pay for second or third compared to first place. Big Box stores will concentrate their ad dollars on the most popular items. Oddly, this is also where the profit margins are the least. Set up your product line on handling a niche that has decent traffic looking for it (and little competition, as above) and then start testing ads. There are many, many good books (as well as many flaky ones) that define how to use PPC and AdWords for a business. These above are the broad strokes.

Once you have your keywords based on demand and competition, then check out what the PPC is going for. If people are buying PPC, demand for competing products is confirmed. But just because PPC rates are low doesn't mean there isn't demand, it just means advertisers don't have something to sell in that niche.

What do you think are the benefits (or drawbacks) from using Google™ AdSense? Is Google™ AdSense a viable source of income?

Most people don't make a lot of money from AdSense. However, if you have a high traffic site, this is sensible. Write-ups on making the most money from AdSense indicate that it is a good idea to run the biggest ad blocks you can and put them in the most visible areas of your site — top, left-center.

Unfortunately, only search engines really appreciate all the content on your page when visitors have to look at ads first. Search engines also ignore ads and serve up the content further down the page that's relevant. Most Internet users train themselves to ignore ads — and a huge block of ads on your site might get you more bounces. Personally, I go elsewhere when I see pages with ads like this because that author is selling ad space, not working to provide useful content.

So, AdSense is mostly used as supplementary income. A handful of people are using it to make a decent living from, but they concentrate on having great content and attracting tons of traffic, because it is still a numbers game — only a small percentage of any site's traffic actually clicks on ads unless that site is actually designed to get people to click through. But their business, in that case, is selling ad space, which is a minority of businesses out there.

If your business is making, selling, and delivering widgets, then concentrate on those widgets.

Have you ever used Google™ Product Search or Google™ Base? What practical advice can you give someone who is considering using these two Google™ applications?

The short advice is to have your backend ready first. There are certain e-commerce applications that will upload your products to Google™ Base with little work, and others with which you have to do several steps to do so. You want to be able to upload from an Excel sheet or something similar, so that you aren't having to put up products one at a time. Your time is very valuable. And as you expand to hundreds of products, you either have to take the time or hire someone to do it for you.

Selecting an e-commerce engine that does this right off the bat is sensible. This goes back to the point of running your business as a business, including picking tools that work from the get-go.

Is implementing a blog, such as Google™'s Blogger, recommended? Will having a blog increase traffic for an online business?

A blog will definitely increase Web site traffic. Google™ is watching blogs for fresh content and gives them priority in rankings. And you can have as many free Blogger blogs as you want, covering different subject areas.

Successful blogs serve these functions:

1) Information

2) Speed

If you look up the most popular blogs, you'll find they are minimal and short posts. People can find and read what they are looking for quickly. Further, those blogs with the largest followings are really always linking to other places for top information about a product, and that is what keeps people coming back. They've become a trusted authority for their particular niche-subject area.

I'd suggest you have one Blogger blog (unless you are really informed in several different subjects and can write in volumes) and another blog section on your own site. The Blogger blog is for the short, utility-type posts — and you tweak the template so that links to your own site (using those keywords above) are prominent. Always link to your own site in the title. Activate the "show link" field so that you can always point your title as a link to your own site, or any page in your site. This is a great way to build your own incoming links.

Having a second blog on your own site is for the longer posts, your product reviews, and guides. The shorter, pithy Blogger posts will point to these longer reviews (make sure you link to the permalink of that post, not the site itself). You'll spend time crafting your reviews and product descriptions. Then you find different relevant actions occurring in the popular press and on the Internet that relate to that product. Link the two together via your Blogger blog. This strategy has you constantly promoting your business products or services indirectly — which works better than conventional marketing.

Google™ seems to create new applications and tools on a consistent basis, such as Google™ Product Search, Google™'s APIs, Google™ Maps, Chrome, and more. Are there any specific Google™ applications an online business should use to increase traffic and/or Web site visibility?

There are many great tools a small business could use to promote itself and its products or services. Here are a few key ones:

- Use Google™ Alerts to find data about your keywords and products, as well as your industry and who is talking about you and your company.

Setting these up is quite simple, just go to **www.Google.com/ alerts** and create the search you are looking for. Once there, you have the option of having it sent to you as an e-mail or subscribing to it as an RSS feed (see Google™ Reader below). Google™ Alerts will automatically search the Web, blogs, and news for items related to your keywords and deliver them to you. You can also set up a search to tell you who has commented about your blog, product, or company — or you. By using alerts, you can find out what conversations are ongoing about anything and then blog about it yourself, or simply go to that site to comment, leaving an in-bound link to your site.

- Use Google™ Reader to accumulate data for you, and present it in a format you can digest readily.

Having a news reader simply saves you time. And Google™ Reader is constantly being improved. You no longer have to spend time going out to sites to find out what people are saying about your keyword niche, but can simply see their actual article without all the ads and other distractions — or the wait for their site to load. As mentioned, you can also get your Google™ Alerts showing up in your Google™ Reader, so you can keep on top of all the latest data in a single window. Once you know what the conversation is out there, you can either blog about it or visit the site to comment there. And, sharing items in Google™ Reader is a great way to facilitate your subscribers to keep on top of what you think is important about your niche.

- Use Google™ Analytics to track exactly what your traffic consists of and what you can improve on your site.

This is a simple script you install in your template, or on every page of your site. It will tell you what your traffic is, what pages they went to, what's most popular, what keywords are being used, and so on. The great part is that if you have multiple blogs and sites, you can track them all from one location. You can also set up campaigns so you can see how it is performing. This is another vital tool to tell you what you are doing that is successful, and how to improve what you are doing. The most vital point of promotion is in the metrics.

- YouTube and Google™ Video — vital promotion.

Video has seemingly taken over the Web — like YouTube. Videos can give people a visual and auditory sampling of your product. Popular how-to videos show exactly how to use your product, or how to install it. And, when you put your own link in the description, it will bring traffic directly to your site. The trick is also to upload your video to several remote servers and then embed that video on your site — this saves you bandwidth and provides a service to your viewers. And don't forget that when you have your video up and going, you can now use the original files to create a video CD or DVD, which can be sold or used as promotion by itself. Another tip — you can set up your videos to show up on your Blogger blog in the sidebar.

- Google™ Sets can tell you what Google™ thinks are related words to your keyword searches.

When you use this tool, you'll see what Google™ thinks should be in your description of that subject on your site. You'll get an inkling of how Google™'s algorithms will process your keywords this way. It can also tell you what related keywords you can use — or what related products you should be offering your customers, as well.

I also use several tools for the business itself, not just for promotion.

- Use Gmail for all business and personal e-mail.

This is because it has better filters and search capacity than other e-mail systems. You can access it from any Internet-connected computer (or device), so you are able to stay in touch with all your associates with little effort. Their spam filters are probably the best available. The practical tip here is to use another "throw-away" address for all sign-ups that require an e-mail address, then, only give out your Gmail address to those you trust. You can access Gmail via Google™ Reader, and also Google™ Toolbar. Another feature is Google™ Chat, which is plugged into the side of Gmail — but can be popped out into its own window, meaning you can coordinate with your associates without having to call — and share links and documents near instantly.

- Use Google™ Docs for all business documents.

This is a dead simple way to keep all your files and make them available to everyone in your business. It also makes sure that you can all have the latest version of a file. Google™ Docs imports and exports into every major format. If you receive a Word Doc, you can export it as a PDF, for instance. This file was edited in Google™ Docs and output to Word. I saved the original file to Google™ Docs, which opened another window so I could start editing it right away, instead of downloading it to my computer and then waiting for another application to start up. Because somewhere small business start-ups don't even have their employees working under the same roof, this is a quick way to keep up and coordinated, as you can share and e-mail files quickly — even write Web pages, all online.

- Get the Google™ Toolbar to speed your own Web searches and prevent most distracting pop-ups. Also, this can track your searches and will provide additional related terms and approximate counts of pages. In that way, you can look for keywords by competition. The toolbar is very customizable, so you can add more searches to it. All of this makes your time more efficient.

What are the most common mistakes made by businesses that are trying to harness the power of the Google™ Search Engine and achieve top search engine rankings?

a. The biggest mistake is to try to use conventional marketing gimmicks instead of learning about how the Internet actually works. The Internet is a huge collection of social communities. Consider how you search and what you look for, as well as what you throw away as useless or ignore. Spammers are trying to use conventional marketing gimmicks to get your money, and are despised because they are out of touch with people who would actually want their product.

If you don't personally like the way something looks, or how it comes across, chances are, your potential clients or customers won't either. Google™ started off correctly in delivering what people want and gaining their trust in the process. Trust is the first thing you have to establish when you go online with your products. It doesn't mean writing better sales pages. It means providing actual substance people can use regularly. Valuable content will get you repeat traffic to your site and eventually give leads.

The bottom line is to get people subscribing to your site. Meaning they follow what you say and constantly return for more information. As you have links to your products, they will eventually click on these links and a certain percentage will buy your stuff. This business model is quite different for people creating an online business than a traditional brick-and-mortar business. Some actually succeed because they actually give away incredibly valuable information in bulk — and then simply ask for donations to their charity. Others start by giving away a really good e-book (which equates to a loss-leader, conventionally) and so gets potential buyers interested in services and products which they must purchase/invest in.

Build trust, get subscribers first — concentrate on servicing them with what they want, and then your sales will follow. But that's all promotion, isn't it?

b. To keep on top in the search engines, you have to narrow your focus — very narrow. Find exactly what niche you need to start in and really concentrate on that one single area. Tune all your pages to that specific set of products which service that niche. Don't try for hundreds of products and to become the big-box store all at once.

Stay focused and build out from a base of steady, new, useful content about your particular niche. People will come to you to buy your product when you have proved over a longer period of time that you know what you are talking about and have helped them with their particular problem. That is what defines a niche: a specific solution for a specific problem. Most small businesses start out by scratching their own itch, and then offering that solution to the broader public who also has that same itch.

One criteria for your niche is that you can create lots of content about it on a routine basis — and can do so easily. With a blog, it doesn't matter if you just have a short paragraph — go ahead and put it out there. Just make sure it links back to your site with a relevant keyword. Now, do this every day, or several times per day — always on the same subject — and shortly, you'll have several posts about that subject, which all point back to your site. A year would give you several hundred posts if you keep at it. (Practically, you could blog at a set time each day, talking about another facet of your product or its service. This would develop a habit of constantly commenting and promoting.)

c. Search engines are actually only the start. As you build a following of subscribers, you will start getting more traffic from other sources and your search engine traffic will become a smaller percentage. This doesn't mean you change things drastically when you find that happening. You keep doing what really created that traffic, which was routinely providing valuable, informative content to people who are interested, and then serving them better than anyone else.

The basics of business are routine, no matter where you are on this planet or whether you are online or offline. Provide a valuable product, let people know it exists, make it easy to acquire and use, and make sure they are satisfied with their service or product. Then they will become evangelists for your product and recommend you to their friends. These steps are the heart of business and commerce. They haven't changed since time began. So keep these in mind as you work to get search engine rankings as a small part of your actual business cycle.

It seems that quality inbound links have a significant effect on Google™ Search Engine Rankings?

Actually, this may have the biggest effect on rankings, if you take everything into account. PageRank™ (Google™'s original algorithmic estimation of a page and a site's value) has been devalued and continues to be.

Partially, this is due to the rise of social media — where people are exchanging data more rapidly than ever before while voting and ranking the value of this data between themselves. Google™ and other search engines are playing catch-up because most popular social networking and bookmarking sites have their own search function now. Plus, people are able to follow their own group of influences and are less dependent on search engines to find the content they are looking for. It's like word of mouth on steroids. In order to stay relevant, search engines have to constantly find and provide data from all these many social sites — each of which serve an increasing number of social niches.

The inbound links to your site come from the people who are using your keywords to tell other people about your site. While you can do futile (and time-consuming) work to exchange links, mostly, these backfire. This happens if your inbound links come from an unrelated site, it looks like a spammy effort to raise the value of your site. Some people have found themselves dropping in PageRank™ simply because someone with a lot of unrelated outbound links has linked to them — so they got penalized as well.

Your best way to get a lot of inbound links is to provide great content, which people link to. However, in order to let people know that your content exists, there are a couple of perfectly valid strategies to get your links out there:

a. Find other sites that are talking about your keyword subject and leave comments along with your Web site link. Of course, you use Google™ to search for them, particularly Blog search, as I outline above. Make sure your comments are not promo, but actually contribute to the conversation ongoing.

b. Forums (search for "[keyword phrase] forum") are also great places to contribute your expertise through comments.

c. Through your Google™ Alerts (see above), you can blog about other people's sites if they don't have comments open — many sites look for incoming links and check out why they are being linked to. Blog platforms like WordPress auto-notify their authors when someone links to their blog.

d. And you can backtrack people who link to you and return the favor or leave a comment on their blog or article in order to get links.

The trick in all of this is to let Google™ do your heavy lifting in terms of finding places that can give you incoming links. The underlying principle is not to try to generate a lot of incoming links personally, but rather to create great and valuable content that people want to tell other people about.

If you were to give three pieces of advice to someone who wants to achieve success and high rankings using the Google™ Search Engine, and other applications & tools provided by Google™ for their business, what would they be?

a. Realize that Google™ deals in information. It might be the 900-pound Gorilla in the room, but it is still only one tool to use. It's not the end-all, just a way to get there. Google™ depends on its popularity — which is serving up information people want as fast as possible. If you use Google™ as a Swiss Army Knife, then you'll see how to make your business profitable and successful very quickly. But the people who just try to "game" Google™ wind up blocked and basically have to start over. Coordination and Cooperation are the key points to keep in mind in any online business venture.

b. Subscribe to the various blogs Google™ keeps itself. If you follow Matt Cutts, for instance, you'll be constantly informed about the changes Google™ is making to eliminate spammers and make the viewing experience better. Google™ is evolving along with the Internet. By keeping track of what Google™ itself is saying, you can adapt more quickly and stay on top of your game, which keeps you successful and expanding. Blogger has a blog about itself, for instance. So does Gmail and Google™ Maps. Of course, there's the official Google™ Blog. Google™ has a loyal community of users. By telling people what they are up to, they empower that community and foster that loyalty. When you know what they are up to, you can see quickly whether the changes they are making will be of immediate benefit to your company. Google™'s Webmaster Blog (**http://Googlewebmastercentral.blogspot.com**) is a key one for keeping up with all things Google™.

c. Keep it real. Google™ ranks by real use. In fact, they hire people just to check out and personally vote on the usefulness of sites. Your Web pages reflect your own approach to your business and how you relate to your customers. Google™ is going to give the highest rankings to the most useful and relevant sites. If you set your site up to begin with so that people can find useful content that will actually improve their lives, then you'll be way ahead of the get-rich-quick crowd, who have shallow attention spans and quickly leave the scene. The best strategy is always to work for the long-term and keep building more and more great content into your site every week. The more valuable content you have, the higher you'll stay on the rankings and will tend to defeat any other competition for your chosen keywords. If you keep every page optimized so that Google™ and other search engines can quickly find what they are looking for, you'll stay way ahead of 90 percent of the other sites out there.

Dr. Robert C. Worstell, M.msc, Ph.D., has been designing Web sites since 1997, before Google™ became mainstream. He has written, edited, and published over four dozen books, mostly in the lines of self improvement. The "Go Thunk Yourself" book series was written by Dr. Worstell as the result of research into the single underlying success model all best-seller self -mprovement books and their writers used. He also lives on and operates a working farm in rural Missouri.

Interview with Will Critchlow

"How can I get to the top of Google™'s Search Engine Rankings?" What practical and realistic advice can you give someone who is starting out with a new Web site or online business to achieve optimal success?

First, I would tell them not to focus on rankings, and certainly not to focus on rankings alone. It is far more important to think about how you are going to build a business online — Google™ search traffic should be just one channel. There are a load of technical things we will come onto in terms of details of getting traffic from search rankings, but if you only remember one thing, I would suggest that it is "think about how you can make your Web site the kind of place people want to find when searching for the appropriate key phrases." From there on, it's technical stuff and a load of effort and networking.

What do you think are the benefits (or drawbacks) from using Google™ AdWords? Is Google™ AdWords a recommended investment, and can it truly generate Web traffic and revenue for an online business?

AdWords is one of the most targeted forms of advertising ever invented and has fantastic return on investment for many businesses. There are two critical things to remember — first, that if you do it wrong, it can cost a lot of money, so never stop learning and testing. Second, it is not really an investment unless you capture lifetime value from the visitors. If you are always dependent on AdWords for new visitors and customers, then it is always going to be an expense. Neither of these are uniformly bad things — the first means you can compete against much larger players, and the second just means that you have to factor that it in as cost of sales.

What do you think are the benefits (or drawbacks) from using Google™ AdSense? Is Google™ AdSense a viable source of income?

The main benefit of AdSense is the ease with which you can get it set up. My experience has always been that as soon as the revenue from AdSense is significant, there are better ways of monetizing most sites.

Have you ever used Google™ Product Search or Google™ Base? What practical advice can you give someone who is considering using these two Google™ applications?

We have clients who do. There is little downside to them, beyond the effort needed, and it can be one more sales channel.

Is implementing a blog, such as Google™'s Blogger, recommended? Will having a blog increase Web site traffic for an online business?

Having a blog does not magically create visitors or business. It is a big commitment to keep a blog going, and there is little worse than a blog that is not maintained. Having said that, done properly, it can be one of the most effective online marketing tools. We would recommend integrating it into the main site (**www. example.com/blog**) rather than using example.blogspot.com. If you can't do that, at the very least use a sub-domain (**http://blog. example.com**), which can be set up in very low-cost ways — using **www.wordpress.com**, for example.

Google™ seems to create new applications and tools on a consistent basis, such as Google™ Product Search, Google™'s APIs, Google™ Maps, Chrome, and more. Are there any specific Google™ applications an online business should use to increase traffic and/or Web site visibility?

I have heard a lot of good things about widgets (e.g., for iGoogle™) but have not experimented myself. If you are selling a product online, AdWords is the only absolute "must try."

What are the most common mistakes made by businesses that are trying to harness the power of the Google™ Search Engine and achieve top search engine rankings?

Thinking that if they can find the magic bullet, hire the right consultant, or pay for the right tool it will magically take care of itself. If it sounds too good to be true, it probably is. Building a business online is hard, just like building a business offline, and while consultants and experts can definitely help, you are unlikely to find someone who can just "sort it" for you. Building a business online needs your blood, sweat, and tears.

It seems that quality inbound links have a significant effect on Google™ Search Engine Rankings?

Yes — quality inbound links are probably the biggest single factor taken into account by Google™'s algorithm. Every business that wants to succeed online needs a strategy and a plan for getting people to link to them. You could write a whole book on the subject, but the simplest piece of advice I can give echoes what I said previously: "Think about why people would want to link to your site and build your business from the beginning so that they would want to."

If you were to give three pieces of advice to someone who wants to achieve success and high rankings using the Google™ Search Engine, and other applications & tools provided by Google™ for their business, what would they be?

Build search engine success into the Web site plan from the beginning — build the business so the Web site is the right answer for the search queries you want to rank for and build something that people will want to link to

Ensure that all Web site development you do is search engine friendly. Too often, we see basics overlooked that put hurdles in the way and mean it is doomed to failure from the start. If you build a search friendly site, then you can do an awful lot of things yourself to build the kind of success you need to be able to afford expensive consultants to help you take it to the next level.

Monitor what people are saying about your business as you market it. Engage with them — network and build contacts to help promote your stuff — and give yourself a chance to respond if there is anything negative breaking. We use our tool at **http:// reputation.distilled.co.uk** for this.

Will Critchlow is a director of Distilled — a fast-growing company in the field of search engine marketing and online reputation issues. He has a background in math and statistics which he studied at the University of Cambridge. His opinions are regularly sought by national press in the UK on subjects from future developments in search to online reputation monitoring and management. He has worked with many of the largest Internet companies in the world and on online reputation issues with clients including international corporations, high-profile individuals, celebrities and politicians.

Contact: will@distilled.co.uk
   www.distilled.co.uk
   +44 (0)20 7183 0767
   10 Maltings Place
   169 Tower Bridge Road London SW16 6JD

Interview with Jason Green

"**How can I get to the top of Google™'s Search Engine Rankings?**" What practical and realistic advice can you give someone who is starting out with a new Web site or online business to achieve optimal success?

Here are three steps that can help when building a Web site:

1. Content: You will probably need a lot. Provide the most informative content on whatever topical area they are looking to have strong results in the Google™ search engines for. Make sure your content is informative, authoritative, and well written (no typos, misspellings, or grammatical errors).

2. Distinguish yourself: Provide tools, functionality, and resources that are unique within your area of focus. Look at what your top competitors are doing and do it better, faster, and more thoroughly.

3. Code: Well-written code is important. Use the WC3 HTML validation tool to ensure that your markup adheres to established standards.

What do you think are the benefits (or drawbacks) from using Google™ AdWords? Is Google™ AdWords a recommended investment, and can it truly generate Web traffic and revenue for an online business?

AdWords can be an extremely beneficial tool for Web sites to promote qualified traffic increases. It will begin having an effect almost immediately and provides excellent tracking to help fine tune the marketing campaigns. A word of caution: you can very quickly move through your allotted budget without seeing a significant impact to your bottom line. Some keyword areas will produce a very high volume of traffic without resulting conversions on your page. Without proper research for the right keywords and a constant eye on traffic statistics, AdWords campaigns may have you spending far more money than you are earning.

What do you think are the benefits (or drawbacks) from using Google™ AdSense? Is Google™ AdSense a viable source of income?

AdSense can be a great additional revenue stream for a Web site. If your site is well trafficked you can profit nicely from visitors clicking on Google™ provided ads from your Web pages. There are some possible drawbacks to AdSense. The most frequent are impaired usability and diminished attractiveness of the page. This is usually only a problem if the ad placements are excessive or interrupt the visitors experience on the Web page. Ad positioning and style should clearly distinguish them from your content.

Have you ever used Google™ Product Search or Google™ Base? What practical advice can you give someone who is considering using these two Google™ applications?

I have worked with Product Search and Google™ Base, both lending themselves as valuable tools for various SEO campaigns.

The benefit of these services really took off when Google™ began including product search results into relevant Web search results. My advice for anyone using Google™ Base would be to keep your product feeds consistent and regularly check your Google™ Base account for feed errors. If you are using an XML feed, create a template that you can use to update your feed.

Is implementing a blog, such as Google™'s Blogger, recommended? Will having a blog increase Web site traffic for an online business?

Blogs can be a great way to increase the value of your Web site to visitors. This is especially so if your blog features real discussions and dialogue by the experts in your organization. By increasing your value as a resource for your relevant topics, you should increase your Web traffic through the search engines. You should also increase the amount of time a visitor is spending on your page, thus increasing exposure to your brand and likely improving conversions as well. The real value of the blogging platform is that it allows for the frequent inclusion of timely information and encourages visitor participation. The only way a blog can hurt your Web site is if the posts are of poor quality, infrequent, or allow for unmoderated comments that will quickly be exploited by spammers.

Google™ seems to create new applications and tools on a consistent basis, such as Google™ Product Search, Google™'s APIs, Google™ Maps, Chrome, and more. Are there any specific Google™ applications an online business should use to increase traffic and/or Web site visibility?

Google™ provides a wealth of tools and resources for online businesses. The key to successfully using these tools is to know which ones are relevant to your specific organization. Businesses should make use of as many tools as they can, as long as they are obviously relevant to the business. For example, an online music store with downloadable files probably has little use for Google™ Maps. An informative Web site about medical insurance probably has little use for Google™ product search. One Google™ offering that I use quite often is Google™ Gadgets. Google™ gadgets are little programs that can be used either on a Web site or in the Google™ Desktop Sidebar. Creating gadgets is quite simple and is a great way to promote your business, as Google™ will host your gadget in their gadget directory. If you create something clever and original, it will get used by Web site owners and Google™ desktop users. Just make sure that your gadget is appropriately branded and contains a link to your Web site.

What are the most common mistakes made by businesses that are trying to harness the power of the Google™ Search Engine and achieve top search engine rankings?

There are so many mistakes that businesses make in an attempt to achieve top rankings in the Google™ search results; I would have a hard time listing them all. Here are two common mistakes we often see when approached by a client looking for professional help with their search engine optimization:

1. Poor link-building efforts: Often, a Web site owner will have heard that links are good for promoting high ranking search results. So they go about putting up links on every page they can find that will let them. This is not a good idea. Your page will become associated with pages having nothing to do with your area of business, and your site's credibility as an authority will be degraded. As far as links are concerned, the notion of the more the merrier only applies when the links are from relevant Web sites.

2. Black Hat SEO: Many new Web sites often first look for help with budgets and time-frames being their first priority instead of long-term success and credibility. They make a poor decision of hiring an SEO to implement a so-called "Black Hat" SEO campaign for their Web site. "Black Hat" refers to very aggressive SEO tactics that attempt to game Google™ and/or other search engines into furnishing a Web site at the top of their results. Though they are poten-

tially less expensive, and they can possibly achieve faster results, Black Hat techniques are a violation of Google™ rules. When Google™ finds out that Black Hat techniques are being used to promote your site, and they will find out sooner or later, your site will likely be banned from being served in the search results, possibly forever. Businesses should look to work with SEO firms that offer a clear, long-term strategy for success, and abide by Google™'s rules.

It seems that quality inbound links have a significant effect on Google™ Search Engine Rankings?

This is absolutely correct, but SEOs have become so hyper-focused on the whole business of inbound links that it has taken away from what I feel is the larger part of the equation: what you do with your own Web pages. Securing high quality inbound links to a Web site is definitely an important part of any comprehensive SEO campaign (just how important is determined by the competitive landscape within a given area of focus). I think that a good guiding approach to link building is to keep in mind that the best links are those that are given naturally by people who like what you have to offer. This is accomplished by having an awesome Web site.

If you were to give three pieces of advice to someone who wants to achieve success and high rankings using the Google™ Search Engine, and other applications & tools provided by Google™ for their business, what would they be?

1. Educate yourself with tools such as this book to have a better understanding of how the various tools available from Google™ can be utilized for your Web site. Google™ offers great tutorials on how to use its various products.

2. Master Google™ Analytics. Check out Google™'s Conversion University for assistance.

3. Intelligent Keyword Research: Google™ AdWords has a free keyword research tool to identify the best search phrases. This process is greatly improved by collaboration: get everyone involved. General keywords drive more traffic but have lower rates of conversion. Specific keywords often have great conversions with much lower traffic. Understand your goals and find the balance.

Jason Green is a professional SEO consultant based in Reno Nevada. Jason is credited with a variety of technical accomplishments, including the development of AXP technology, the S.I.R.E. Project, and Second Generation SEO (SEO2g). Jason is cofounder of Frequency Marketing, where he works to keep his clients on top of the search engine results.

Contact Information:

Jason J. Green e-mail: Jason@findthefrequency.com

Frequency Marketing

3105 Susileen Drive Reno, NV 89509

Interview with Dan Soha

"How can I get to the top of Google™'s Search Engine Rankings?" What practical and realistic advice can you give someone who is starting out with a new Web site or online business to achieve optimal success?

I receive this question often. If this is a question of the paid search results, which it often is, the answer is to use search engine marketing tricks and techniques in conjunction with increasing CPC bids. I recognize that it is a simple question, but more often than not, people have no understanding of what is going on in the search engine results and rankings.

On the other hand, this question holds some true merit when asking how one gets in the top of the "natural search" results:

a. The words I repeat over and over are: "think colloquially." When you are building a Web site in an effort to appear on the search engine results, you need to target your customers as they view you. In other words, you need to speak in the language that your customers are using because those are the words that they are going to be searching. The Web site must always be built with the users' search queries in mind.

b. It sounds like an obvious answer, but it is one that is commonly overlooked: the Web site needs to have words. It's commonly overlooked because you can make some really attractive Web sites by designing text with images. Images of text are not good enough, the content must be written in actual text. A quick way to see what the search engines see is to view the source code of your Web site.

c. Avoid SEO tricks. My rule here is that if you are doing something that you feel is fooling the search engines into ranking your Web site highly, and you are able to explain the process in words, then you are wasting your time and risk potentially banning your Web site from search results. A basic rule of Computer Science and Programming is that if you can explain it in words, then a good programmer should be able to portray it in code. In other words, Google™ will inevitably unravel the trick, search Web sites for this trick, and will either make the effect of the trick null or penalize the Web site by as grave as a banning — something that can be almost impossible to turn around.

What do you think are the benefits (or drawbacks) from using Google™ AdWords? Is Google™ AdWords a recommended investment, and can it truly generate Web traffic and revenue for an online business?

The major benefit of AdWords is that it is easy to track its performance in real time. Unlike almost all other sources of advertising, where advertisers and marketers have to estimate the success (or failure) of a given advertising campaign, with AdWords, you can use tracking tools like Google™ Conversion Tracking to determine whether each individual click has led to a customer or lead. There are no drawbacks in my eyes. As long as your business has a metric of success, which nearly all businesses do, you can track the success of your AdWords campaigns accordingly. Search engine marketing will work for almost all businesses, it's really just a matter of determining at what cost-per-click and how granular it makes sense to do so.

What do you think are the benefits (or drawbacks) from using Google™ AdSense? Is Google™ AdSense a viable source of income?

The benefit of AdSense is that it ads a source of income to Web sites that weren't previously generating income. The major drawback here is that you are creating a middleman in the income-generating process. Google™, with AdSense, is generating revenue off your Web site, and the user advertising is generating revenue as well. Often, you can generate more revenue by connecting yourself closer to the advertiser's business model. If you can advertise directly for that advertiser, or sell related products online yourself, then you could potentially generate more revenue by doing so. On the other hand, these statements make the assumption that the placement of the advertiser's ad, via AdSense, on your Web site is justifiable, which it often is not. Advertisers often use content match (the advertising side of AdSense) improperly and, in doing so, Web sites are getting paid more than they should. As a Web site owner, you need to test all advertising opportunities and see which combination is the best for you.

Is implementing a blog, such as Google™'s Blogger, recommended? Will having a blog increase Web site traffic for an online business?

Absolutely. Blogs are fantastic for creating traffic. Google™ gives more value to Web sites that are being constantly updated and blogs are a great way to do so. Furthermore, users will comment to your blog and, in doing so, they too are creating content for your site. When it comes to content, more is better, because more is more. Another benefit of blogs are that they force Web site owners to speak colloquially. It's amazing that when people build Web sites, they have their Collegiate-level English hats on, but when it comes to blogs, they tend to speak just as their customers speak.

On the same token, potential customers speak in the same language that other potential customers speak, and the Web site will benefit accordingly when people respond to your blog.

It seems that quality inbound links have a significant effect on Google™ Search Engine Rankings?

Correct. I feel that the best strategy in getting quality inbound links is by creating the content that will lead to this exposure and interest. Avoid paying for links, as doing so is not a good long-term strategy. On a related note, avoid linking out to Web sites, as that will decrease the value of your own Web site.

Dan Soha has years of experience as a Search Engine Marketer, both creating advertising campaigns and overseeing the SEM strategy for companies ranging in budget from five figures to seven figures monthly. He has developed innovative techniques that draw not only on his skills in marketing and advertising, but also on his academic background in the field of Algorithm Theory, having graduated from UC Berkeley with a degree in Computer Science. This experience and knowledge has allowed him to unravel search-engine-bidding algorithms and to create bidding and management strategies that are both unconventional and highly effective. As the Principal and SEM Specialist of Five Mill Marketing, he provides his expertise along with custom-tailored SEM strategies to clients in such varied fields as lead aggregation, retail, broker, and brand advertisement. He lives in San Francisco.

Contact Information:
  Dan Soha
  Principal, Founder, and Search Engine Marketing Specialist
  dan@fivemill.com

Interview with Joy Brazelle

"How can I get to the top of Google™'s Search Engine Rankings?" What practical and realistic advice can you give someone who is starting out with a new Web site or online business to achieve optimal success?

When you launch a new Web site or online business, unless you've been doing a lot of prep work, it is unlikely that your site is going to show up in the first few pages of the search engines results as a natural result.

The good thing is that there is another option. You can pay your way into the results. The first three results at the top of the page and the ten results on the right side of the page are paid ads — Google™ AdWords.

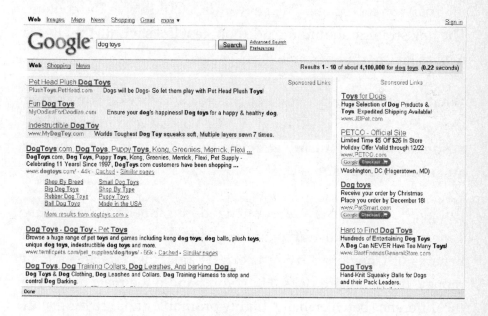

Google™ screenshots © Google™ Inc. Used with permission.

Anyone can open a Google™ AdWords account and write the ads that appear in these spots. It just takes $5 and a few minutes to get started. Within minutes, you can see your ad appear among the paid results.

Unlike the paid results, showing up in the natural results can take weeks, months, or may never happen. There are lots of factors that go into optimizing a site to show up in the natural results (such as content, navigation, site structure, and links). One key, piece of advice is that if the Web site is optimized for good human experience, it is likely that it will also be optimized for a good search engine experience.

So when creating a new Web site, do your homework. Plan for each page; create an optimization plan that includes the keywords to optimize for and the link strategy (both external and internal) for each page. The keywords should drive the content. The link strategy should include both text links within the site, as well as link partners from external sites.

What do you think are the benefits (or drawbacks) from using Google™ AdWords? Is Google™ AdWords a recommended investment, and can it truly generate Web traffic and revenue for an online business?

Google™ AdWords is a recommended investment that can truly generate substantial traffic and revenue, if done correctly. The benefits of Google™ AdWords can be amazing; lots and lots of money. But there are risks. How you handle the risks can make the difference between being highly profitable and throwing your money away.

Risk 1: Bad Ads. Just because anyone can create an AdWords account and write ads does not mean that everyone does this well. Research the competition and write better, more interesting, more relevant ads that really give the searcher a reason to click. This may not be difficult but does take time.

Risk 2: "Set it and forget it." This is the mistake most unsuccessful advertisers make. Google™ AdWords is an art (writing good ads) and a science. Google™ gives you the tools to monitor the success (or lack of success) of your ads. Measure, rework, improve. This is the key to profitability.

Risk 3: Your competitors. Because what you pay is based on several factors (your history [click-thru rate], relevance, quality score plus what your competitor is willing to pay), your competitors can outfox you two different ways: they can decide to outbid you regardless of the price, or they can consistently improve their ads, which will also drive up the price you will have to pay.

Risk 4: Click Fraud. Click fraud is a reality of pay-per-click. Click fraud can take several different forms:

- Competitors clicking your ads and spending your budget

- Web site owners displaying AdSense on their sites can click the ads so they make money

- Web site owners displaying AdSense on their sites can create complicated programs that automatically click their ads and grow their bank accounts

- Spam or arbitrage sites that "pump in" paid content and trick less savvy Internet users into clicking an ad when they think it is real content

Monitoring your AdWords traffic using Web analytics can help you detect fraud. With the proper proof, you can work with the search engines to get credit for the fraudulent clicks.

One key thing to remember is that it takes more than just driving lots of traffic to your site to be successful. The traffic needs to be qualified, converting traffic in order for you to achieve the biggest benefit, positive return on your investment.

What do you think are the benefits (or drawbacks) from using Google™ AdSense? Is Google™ AdSense a viable source of income?

The obvious benefit of displaying Google™ AdSense ads on your Web site is the money. With very little work, your Web site can become a cash cow.

The drawback to displaying the ads on your Web site is that it is frustrating to some more Internet-savvy visitors. The ads can detract from the credibility of your site. People are sick of seeing ads when they are looking for actual content.

Also, there are many businesses built around tricking less savvy visitors into clicking ads while looking for actual content.

The bottom line is that as long as the ads complement the content of your site and don't detract from the user experience, Google™ AdSense can be a nice additional revenue stream.

Have you ever used Google™ Product Search or Google™ Base? What practical advice can you give someone who is considering using these two Google™ applications?

Google™ Product Search is not as popular as some other shopping sites. It is free and not too technically difficult, so it is definitely worth listing your products on Google™ Product Search. I would warn that because of the potentially low traffic volume, you should not expect that Google™ Product Search will generate a huge revenue stream. It will give searchers one more opportunity to find your product.

Google™ Base does not even compete with Craigslist℠. That said, there may be an opportunity to add listing your products in

Google™ Base while there is not much competition. Initial traffic may be low, but if Google™ does start promoting Google™ Base with more effort and money, traffic volumes could increase.

Is implementing a blog, such as Google™'s Blogger, recommended? Will having a blog increase Web site traffic for an online business?

Having a blog is a great compliment to a Web site. Not only does it help with SEO by linking, but it also creates the opportunity to have a greater presence on the SERP (Search Engine Results Pages). Blogging is a responsibility. You must follow some basic rules to have a successful blog.

- Limit personal posts. Many people are turned off by too much information. Your blog should represent your personality, yet still be professional.

- Blog often. People will not return to your blog if your content is stale. Set a schedule for blogging and stick to it.

- Be interesting. Be aware that there are thousands of other blogs out there competing for your readers' time and attention. Write useful, interesting posts. Don't just add to the unwanted noise that is out there.

Google™ seems to create new applications and tools on a consistent basis, such as Google™ Product Search, Google™'s APIs, Google™ Maps, Chrome, and more. Are there any specific Google™ applications an online business should use to increase traffic and/or Web site visibility?

If you have a Web site, and are concerned with increasing traffic and sales (or other conversion events), the most important product that Google™ has launched is Google™ Analytics. The only way to consistently improve your Web site is to understand what visitors are doing (or aren't doing) when they get to your Web site. Driving traffic to your site is meaningless unless the visitors are doing what you want them to do on your site (buying things, signing up for newsletters — whatever your business model is).

What are the most common mistakes made by businesses that are trying to harness the power of the Google™ Search Engine and achieve top search engine rankings?

The most common mistake that I've heard people complain about is hiring a firm that makes unrealistic claims or guarantees rankings. So many companies have fallen victim to fraudulent claims. If a company seems to be promoting something that sounds too good to be true, it most likely is. So don't be disappointed. There are no guarantees with search engine optimization.

Another common mistake is assuming your traditional ad agency or the firm that is running your pay-per-click campaign can also optimize your site for natural rankings. Search engine optimization is a specialty. It is worth it to either seek out a professional or take the time yourself to understand the search engines algorithms and other factors that are key to success in natural rankings. Don't let another company learn SEO on your dime.

A common misconception is that rankings can happen overnight. Appearing top in the natural rankings can take weeks, months, or possibly not happen at all. Search engine optimization takes time and discipline.

Often, companies think it is okay to fool the search engines or employ Black Hat tactics. This may be a win in the short term.

But the search engines always wind up on top. It is not worth the temporary good rankings to risk being banned by the search engines when they find that you are using Black Hat tactics.

The most dangerous mistake with search engine optimization is becoming complacent with your good rankings. You never know what your competition is doing. So while you may enjoy ranking No. 1 for key terms today, you may wind up dropping to the bottom of the page, or worse virtually, disappearing from the rankings at all. Search engine optimization is a discipline that must not be ignored or taken for granted.

It seems that quality inbound links have a significant effect on Google™ Search Engine Rankings?

Having quality inbound links is so important to rankings. Because it takes a lot of time and effort people either try to find an easier way (buying links) or ignore linking altogether. The best approach to linking to find relevant, complementary sites, contact the site owner, and ask for a reciprocal link.

Internal text links are also important, as they help the search engine spiders navigate deeper throughout your site.

If you were to give advice to someone who wants to achieve success and high rankings using the Google™ Search Engine, and other applications and tools provided by Google™ for their business, what would they be?

1. Be smart. You can make a lot of money with Google™, but you must have the proper expectations. When launching a new site, do your homework and prepare your site to rank well naturally. But don't be surprised if you do not

show up in the rankings immediately after your launch. Be prepared to pay for clicks (AdWords). The key to making money with paid clicks is to know how much you can pay for a click, profitably, and set your limits accordingly. An online merchant sold a product that retailed for $150. Knowing his profit margin and costs, he was perfectly happy paying $75 for enough clicks to generate a sale. Then he got smart. He figured out what his conversion rate was. He figured out which type of clicks generated sales (from search engines not from the content network). He then used his analytics to see exactly which key terms and phrases were generating sales. He stopped paying for the keywords that weren't converting. He monitored the copy of the ads that were resulting in sales and reworked the ones that weren't working. Within four weeks he went from paying $75 for a sale to paying around $20.

2. Be prepared. Successful search engine optimization takes time and planning. Before you launch your site, do the research. Know what terms you plan on optimizing for and create content based on those key terms. Make your site easy for humans to navigate and the benefit will be that the search engines will find your site "user friendly" to.

3. When paying for clicks, take the time to create relevant, well-structured campaigns and ad groups. The more targeted the ads are to the keywords you purchase and the content of your site or landing pages, the more successful your ads will be. Be prepared to monitor your campaign using both the reporting that Google™ provides in your AdWords account and other analytics (Google™ Analytics or another product that allows you to segment out the paid-clicks to analyze that traffic separately).

4. Don't be evil. If you want to earn money using AdSense, don't create a spammy site with nothing but ads. Create interesting content and supplement the pages with ads along the right side or towards the bottom of the page.

Also, if you are using AdSense, don't commit click fraud. You may be tempted to click, because each time an ad is clicked on your site, you make money. But remember that someone has to pay for the clicks. And you wouldn't want someone to fraudulently click on your ad.

AdWords Blog Posts by Serengeti Communications:

http://endlessplain.com/2008/03/18/anAtomy-of-a-successful-ad-group/

http://endlessplain.com/2008/03/25/keyword-research-a-really-good-place-to-start/

http://endlessplain.com/2008/04/01/making-sense-of-the-numbers/

http://endlessplain.com/2008/05/06/avoid-the-single-theme-use-analytics-to-find-long-tail-keywords/

http://endlessplain.com/2008/08/05/three-ways-to-track-revenue-a-comprehensive-guide/

http://endlessplain.com/2008/09/30/the-10-most-common-ways-to-waste-a-lot-of-money-on-ppc/

http://endlessplain.com/2008/08/26/5-bad-ppc-symptoms-that-usually-are-not-click-fraud/

Joy Brazelle is vice president of Serengeti Communications. Brazelle has more than ten years experience in Internet Consulting, with a strong focus on analytics. Knowing that you cannot improve what you do not measure, she has made analytics a priority during her years helping clients build and grow their online presence.

Prior to joining Serengeti, Brazelle was the Director of Professional Services at ClickTracks, a Web Analytics software company. As Director of Professional Services for ClickTracks, Brazelle worked with hundreds of customers helping educate them on how to understand their analytics and use the information to improve their online marketing.

Brazelle has been a member of the Web Analytics Association since its launch in May 2006. When she's not working, Brazelle can be found playing with her two dogs or hanging out with her husband on the beach, unsuccessfully learning to surf.

Contact Information:
Joy Brazelle
jbrazelle@sereneticom.com
843-283-9355

Interview with Kent Lewis

"How can I get to the top of Google™'s Search Engine Rankings?" What practical and realistic advice can you give someone who is starting out with a new Web site or online business to achieve optimal success?

Having been in the world of search engine marketing (SEM) since 1996, I've had a unique opportunity to experience the evolution of the industry. That said, the fundamentals have changed little over the years: relevant content, clean code, and link credibility. I've written an article outlining the "3Cs of SEO" (available below). Beyond gaining visibility in organic search results, it's important to also understand the fundamentals of pay-per-click (PPC), and more recently, social media, both of which are integrated into search results.

www.anvilmediainc.com/seo-building-blocks.htm

www.anvilmediainc.com/social-media-marketing-optimization-article.html

What do you think are the benefits (or drawbacks) from using Google™ AdWords? Is Google™ AdWords a recommended investment, and can it truly generate Web traffic and revenue for an online business?

The benefits of PPC (or specifically Google™ AdWords) include instant visibility in search results for target phrases, measurability, and a pay-for-performance model that essentially provides a degree of free branding on an impression basis. While PPC doesn't automatically generate a positive return on investment (ROI) for every company, it does perform well for most businesses that manage it effectively. I've written an article on implementing a PPC campaign (below), which includes testing the following elements: account structure, keyword selection, ad copy, and landing page elements. The downside to AdWords is that it doesn't generate long-term equity in search results: you only show up when your ads perform well and you have money to spend. My recommendation is to focus on mastering the fundamentals of SEO and use PPC to augment visibility in key search results. Ad-

Words is also an excellent tool for evaluating keywords for SEO, as well as marketing messaging and positioning.

www.anvilmediainc.com/pay-per-click-advertising-article.htm

What do you think are the benefits (or drawbacks) from using Google™ AdSense? Is Google™ AdSense a viable source of income?

Google™ AdSense can generate incremental income for companies with significant traffic and valuable content. If your site doesn't have unique and relevant content to an audience, it's unlikely to attract enough visitors to generate meaningful revenue. As an advertiser, Google™'s content network can be a viable extension of AdWords, creating new opportunities for awareness and visitors to your site at a more affordable rate than AdWords.

Have you ever used Google™ Product Search or Google™ Base? What practical advice can you give someone who is considering using these two Google™ applications?

To ensure our clients maximize visibility in Google™, we typically recommend, if not implement and manage, Google™ Product Search and Google™ Base accounts for clients. While not optimal for every company, GPS and Google™ Base offer manufacturers and retailers of commodity products a powerful way to connect to customers deep into the purchase cycle. Both platforms are very cost-effective, and if properly optimized, can generate meaningful revenue.

Is implementing a blog, such as Google™'s Blogger, recommended? Will having a blog increase Web site traffic for an online business?

We are big fans of blogs as a marketing tool for ourselves and our clients. While Blogger is an affordable and reasonably robust platform, we typically recommend WordPress, as it's inherently search-friendly and easy to use. I believe blogs are generally best-served through leadership and expert resource platforms (i.e., our Reputation Watch blog). Blogs can also be a powerful tool for reputation management and influencing search results (i.e., my Lockergnome blog). We've all but abandoned our Blogger site, which I believe is a general industry trend, as the platform doesn't seem to be as relevant or powerful as other platforms, like WordPress and Typepad. I've included an article outlining fundamental business strategies for blogging below.

www.anvilmediainc.com/corporate-blogging-tips-article.htm

www.lockergnome.com/kentlewis

www.reputation-watch.com

Google™ seems to create new applications and tools on a consistent basis, such as Google™ Product Search, Google™'s APIs, Google™ Maps, Chrome, and more. Are there any specific Google™ applications an online business should use to increase traffic and/or Web site visibility?

Google™'s most powerful tools for maximizing visibility in search results include AdWords, Analytics, and Webmaster Tools. We encourage our clients to utilize Google™ Analytics to better understand marketing efforts and user behavior. Webmaster Tools also offers unique measurement and reporting options. Google™ Apps may not aid in generating site traffic, but could be invaluable for small business and startups looking for a cost-effective alternative to Microsoft® Office. Larger or more technically-savvy companies may create powerful hooks into Google™ with the API, but that's not as common.

What are the most common mistakes made by businesses that are trying to harness the power of the Google™ Search Engine and achieve top search engine rankings?

The most common mistakes made by businesses looking for a big win with Google™ include: using Grey or Black Hat tactics to increase organic visibility, implementing a half-baked AdWords campaign and not properly leveraging social media to "own" Google™'s OneBox (aka Universal Search). Companies that resort to Black Hat (rule breaking) SEO tactics, like keyword-stuffing and IP spoofing may generate short-term visibility, but run the risk of getting black-listed by Google™. I've seen this happen to clients in the past, where they lose up to 80 percent of their Google™ traffic, and we then have to dig them out and get them back into good graces. A poorly implemented or managed AdWords campaign can quickly sink a company, due to poor performance (getting suspended due to low Quality Score), over-spending media budgets, or generating too few conversions and thus no ROI. With Google™'s OneBox, businesses must claim their listing in the Local Business Center in order to appear in the Google™ Ten Pack (the Google™ Map with ten businesses listed by location).

www.anvilmediainc.com/search-engine-marketing-philosophy.htm

www.anvilmediainc.com/black-hat-seo-article.htm

It seems that quality inbound links have a significant effect on Google™ Search Engine Rankings?

Indeed, quality inbound links are a key component of achieving visibility in organic search results. In fact, link strategies tie into roughly 70 percent of the most critical factors in achieving top rankings on Google™ (according to an SEOmoz study - below). You may recall that the third "C" in my 3Cs article is credibility, with a primary focus on inbound links. If you understand where the founders of Google™ came from (Stanford), it helps to understand why they chose PageRank™ (aka Google™ Juice or BackRub) as key criteria in their algorithm. John Battelle's book, *The Search*, does a great job of explaining the mindset behind PageRank™.

www.seomoz.org/article/search-ranking-factors

http://battellemedia.com

If you were to give three pieces of advice to someone who wants to achieve success and high rankings using the Google™ Search Engine, and other applications & tools provided by Google™ for their business, what would they be?

In order to achieve high rankings in Google™ (and other search engines) I recommend the following:

1. Create and optimize relevant, valuable content on a Web site built on W3C-compliant code and generate quality inbound links, including social media profiles.

2. Leverage free Google™ tools like Analytics, Local Business Center and Webmaster Tools to test, tune and measure your Web presence.

3. Consider more advanced strategies and tactics, like online reputation management (ORM) and search engine marketing public relations (SEM PR) to further maximize awareness, credibility, traffic, and sales.

www.anvilmediainc.com/online-reputation-management-article.htm

www.anvilmediainc.com/sem-pr-article-part1.htm

www.anvilmediainc.com/search-social-media-marketing-integration-article.htm

As President of Anvil Media, Inc., Kent Lewis is responsible for managing operations, marketing and business development to achieve the search engine marketing agency's mission: to build Anvil into the one of the most respected search engine marketing agencies in the world. Current Anvil clients include Extensis, gDiapers, Nautilus, Lucy Activewear, Oregon State University, PC World, Planar, Point6, Tea Collection and Yesmail. He is also founder and acting President of Formic Media, a search engine marketing (SEM) agency focusing on the small business market. Lewis is also cofounder and former President of SEMpdx, a trade organization for SEM professionals based in Portland, Oregon. With a background in integrated marketing, Lewis left a public relations agency in 1996 to start his Internet marketing career at a Web development firm, where he also created a free monthly life style e-zine. Shortly thereafter, he built and managed his first search engine marketing team at local full-service marketing agency before cofounding

Wave Rock Communications, and later, eROI. Lewis was also Director of Marketing and Business Development at http://good-guys.com, an online electronics retailer. In 2001, Lewis created pdxMindShare, an online career community and Portland-area networking event. He is also an adjunct professor at Portland State University, where he teaches eMarketing and SEM workshops. In 2003, he founded a charity fundraiser event, Anvil's Annual Get SMART Gala, to raise awareness for SMART (Start Making a Reader Today), for which he also sits on the board. Lewis is a member of EO, a global organization for entrepreneurs, and is a recipient of Portland Business Journal's Top 40 Under 40 Award. When he's not working or hanging out with his family, he likes to write about his travels and life experiences on his blog, The Kent Lewis Experience.

Contact Information:

> *Kent Lewis | President | Anvil Media, Inc.*
> *2189 NW Wilson St. | Portland, OR 97210*
> *503.595.6050 x223 v | 503.260.6700 c | 503.223.1008 f*
> *www.anvilmediainc.com | Twitter/Skype profiles: kentjlewis*
> *www.reputation-watch.com | The reputation resource blog*
> *www.pdxmindshare.com | Portland's career community*

Interview with Matt Malden

"How can I get to the top of Google™'s Search Engine Rankings?" What practical and realistic advice can you give someone who is starting out with a new Web site or online business to achieve optimal success?

The goal of the search engines is to help users find the best Web sites and Web pages that match their needs. By building a reputation as a source for quickly finding the most relevant Web sites, search engines grow their user base, search volume, and advertising revenues.

The advertising arena is undergoing a tremendous paradigm shift. The Internet is supplanting traditional mediums of the past, including television, radio, and print, because of its ability to more precisely target prospects, to enable more cost-effective advertising, and to quantifiability measure return on investment (ROI). If a new Web site or business is not embracing search engine marketing as a core part of its go-to market strategy, it's highly likely the company won't survive its infancy.

The first thing I would tell clients trying to get to the top of Google™'s search engine rankings is to understand what goes into achieving top rankings. First, it's impossible for anyone to guarantee the top ranking. There are way too many variables that contribute to rankings, including the fact that additional competitors appear and vanish, as well as each search engine has a different ranking algorithm, which changes over time. However, if a client takes the time to understand how rankings are determined, they can take steps to increase the likelihood of their Web pages being displayed higher on the search engine results pages. As an example, Web pages can't be all things to all people. So, they should consider what queries (i.e., keywords) they would like their page to achieve high rankings for. Then, focus the content, headlines, meta tags, URL, and more based on those target keywords. At the same time, it is critical that one appreciates that search engines and their algorithms are evolving in their level of sophistication. The search engine algorithms evaluate criteria which indicate whether your page is valuable to searchers. So, while tuning your pages for search engine ranking, make sure to use any advice as merely a guideline within the constraints of creating a great Web site and great Web pages, otherwise it's unlikely that anything you do will rank high in the search engines.

What do you think are the benefits (or drawbacks) from using Google™ AdWords? Is Google™ AdWords a recommended investment, and can it truly generate Web traffic and revenue for an online business?

As I mentioned above, using Google™ as an advertising medium is growing increasingly critical to a business' success as it provides cost-effective targeted marketing. While not as cost effective as natural search (free), paid search is experiencing dramatic growth because of its effectiveness. Because of the pay-per-click (PPC) advertising model, now advertisers must pay only when people are actually interested in their products or services. The challenge of using paid search advertising is that search engines are designed with complex features to address the complex needs of expert search engine marketers. As a result, there is a steep learning curve for novice marketers. Second, in order to determine whether your keywords and bidding strategy are effective, it is critical to drive early results. These early results are most easily achieved by overbidding initially and then refining bids over time. Thus, the initial launch of search engine marketing campaigns can be significantly more expensive than the steady state. The good news is that Google™, the other search engines and third-parties are developing products, tools and other techniques to reduce the learning curve and up-front investment.

What do you think are the benefits (or drawbacks) from using Google™ AdSense? Is Google™ AdSense a viable source of income?

Google™ AdSense can sometimes be an effective advertising medium. While less effective than AdWords, AdSense ads are displayed on content sites where the interest level in finding new sites is not as strong. However, due to the pay-per-click, pay-per-action, and other monetization models, the expense can be less costly managed based on the value of those placements.

Is implementing a blog, such as Google™'s Blogger, recommended? Will having a blog increase Web site traffic for an online business?

To acquire customers, Web sites need to acquire traffic. Many entrepreneurial people have figured out creative ways to do this. For instance, on the Web site "Where the Hell is Matt?" (**www.wherethehellismatt.com**), an entrepreneur has made videos of himself dancing in various geographies all over the world. As a result, his site receives an enormous amount of traffic by developing a cult-like following — enough traffic that he's even managed to secure his own sponsor. Similarly, blogging is another mechanism to drive traffic. If you put up valuable content, people will come to your site to read your content and other users will link to your content. Both will drive traffic, plus, the latter will help increase your rankings on the search engine results page.

Google™ seems to create new applications and tools on a consistent basis, such as Google™ Product Search, Google™'s APIs, Google™ Maps, Chrome, and more. Are there any specific Google™ applications an online business should use to increase traffic and/or Web site visibility?

Google™ has done a world-class job of leveraging their success in Internet advertising and anticipating the evolving needs of both businesses and consumers.

Google™ Analytics allows Web site owners to understand and profile the traffic to their Web site by a variety of different dimensions — such as geography, date, time of day, or content.

Google™ Maps allows your visitors to understand geographic data in a graphical format-whether you use this for helping people find your physical location or visualize more operational data.

Google™ Docs has a great capability to easily create online customer surveys and quickly aggregate the results.

What are the most common mistakes made by businesses that are trying to harness the power of the Google™ Search Engine and achieve top search engine rankings?

One of the most common mistakes for businesses trying to harness the power of Google™ is a lack of preparation. In order to win in any game, it's important to understand the rules and the competitors. Google™ is no different. Understanding how it works, and how your competitors are using it to their advantage is paramount. Another common mistake is to focus on "optimizing for free." Search engines are more cost effective than any other medium in history, but unless you spend time and money tuning your pages, perfecting your content, building links and purchasing paid search advertisements, you won't succeed. The key is to test different techniques and then double-down on those techniques that deliver results.

It seems that quality inbound links have a significant effect on Google™ Search Engine Rankings?

Quality inbound links have a significant effect on Google™ Search Engine Rankings. While many believe that Google™ Page Rank is no longer the best indicator of inbound link popularity, everyone agrees that achieving quality inbound links is enormously important. Google™ has evolved their algorithm and due to the creation of link farms, reciprocal links and other non-organic link building techniques, they have placed an emphasis on quality inbound links (those inbound links that come from quality sources unlikely to be affected by nefarious SEO manipulators). These quality sites typically include highly reputable Web pages, educational Web sites (.edu), and government Web sites (.gov).

If you were to give three pieces of advice to someone who wants to achieve success and high rankings using the Google™ Search Engine, and other applications & tools provided by Google™ for their business, what would they be?

Due to the explosive growth of the Internet advertising space, there is a whole industry designed to complement and augment the technology provided by the search engines. In the early stages of this market, the offerings primarily consist of consultants as well as tools designed for early adopters. As the market continues to mature, be on the lookout for packaged applications that automate and optimize the process of search engine marketing.

1. Start early. All the best advice and techniques described in this book take time to execute. It takes time to get links from other Web sites, it takes time to drive traffic from paid search and it takes time to tune your messaging and content.

2. Get help. In the early days, anyone could be effective in search engine marketing. The only difference was whether you were going to be moderately successful or wildly successful. Now, the competitive landscape has significantly changed. Investigate the various products and services that can help you cost-effectively drive results.

3. Make sure that whatever product or service you select is reputable and has references and demonstrable results. If someone offers to help you drive traffic to your Web site, and their Web site looks like they are a used car salesman, chances are, they are a used car salesman who is just trying to branch out into search engine marketing.

Matt Malden is the CEO and Founder of Yield Software, a leading provider of search engine marketing software. Yield Software enables companies to increase revenue by automating, simplifying and optimizing the process of marketing on the Internet.

Prior to Yield Software, Malden spent nine years as an executive at Siebel Systems. As Vice President and General Manager, he grew the call center product division from inception to over $500 million in annual revenue. Next, he designed, launched and managed a joint development effort with Microsoft and IBM in building a next-generation, service-oriented software architecture. In addition, he led Siebel's division focused on products for the public sector.

Malden also held positions in software development at Oracle Corporation and in financial and strategic planning at Pacific Telesis Group.

He holds numerous patents in the areas of user interface design, computer telephony integration, call scripting, and advanced queuing and routing algorithms.

Malden earned his MBA from The Wharton School at the University of Pennsylvania where he was recognized as a Palmer Scholar (top 5 percent of graduating class). He received his bachelor's degree in Computer Science and Economics from The University of Michigan.

Contact Information:

Matt Malden

CEO, Yield Software

1700 S. Amphlett Blvd., Suite 202

San Mateo, CA 94402

www.yieldsoftware.com

650-357-7100

matt.malden@yieldsoftware.com

Interview with Teri Ross

"How can I get to the top of Google™'s Search Engine Rankings?" What practical and realistic advice can you give someone who is starting out with a new Web site or online business to achieve optimal success?

It is important to understand that Google™ became successful as a result of their ability to deliver superior relevant search results, which is a manifestation of their proprietary algorithms. Not only are those algorithms a closely-held secret, but they are constantly evolving. As a result, getting to the top of the search engines, and staying there, is an ever-evolving craft that requires a combination of art and science. My advice to clients is that they budget three to five times the cost of building the site for marketing strategies such as search engine optimization, inbound link development, paid advertising, and social media marketing, all of which are important to search engine rankings.

What do you think are the benefits (or drawbacks) from using Google™ AdWords? Is Google™ AdWords a recommended investment, and can it truly generate Web traffic and revenue for an online business?

The advantages to Google™ AdWords are that it has the ability to instantly drive targeted traffic to a Web site and that it requires no long-term contract. The disadvantages are many, including constantly rising costs, a lower trust level on the part of the consumer (compared to organic listings), limited messaging capabilities due to character limits, and click fraud. We tend to see higher bounce rates from AdWords traffic than from organic traffic.

Having taken over hundreds of AdWords accounts from companies who had been managing their campaigns in-house, it is apparent that Google™ has made it appear as if managing AdWords campaigns is much easier than it actually is. While setting up the account is fairly straightforward, there are literally hundreds of tiny details that can make a difference in not only the effectiveness of the campaigns, but the cost. Many AdWords customers are not as well educated on the nuances as they should be, and as a result we see many campaigns where as much as 75 percent of the ad spend is being wasted.

We advise clients to start out using AdWords as a strategy for identifying the keywords that are driving traffic and conversions, and use that information to optimize the site for organic listings. The objective is to cut back on the AdWords spend and get traffic from the organic search results.

What do you think are the benefits (or drawbacks) from using Google™ AdSense? Is Google™ AdSense a viable source of income?

If a Web site needs to rely on Google™ AdSense as a source of income, then they need to rethink their online marketing business and strategy. Not only do AdSense ads detract from the objectives of a Web site, but by their very nature, they are designed to drive traffic away from a site — the very traffic Web site owners work so hard to get. The only Web sites who make an appreciable amount of money with AdSense are the arbitrage sites that buy a domain name and then fill the site with related AdSense Ads.

The only place where AdSense is of value is in the free social media sites, such as LinkedIn™ — which allows the site owner to offer the service for free in exchange for the AdSense ad revenue. Whether the ad revenue actually covers operating costs or generates a profit is something only these site owners can identify.

Have you ever used Google™ Product Search or Google™ Base? What practical advice can you give someone who is considering using these two Google™ applications?

I have used them — with limited results. I think Google™ was late to the game on these products. eBay® and Amazon.com® have really captured this market.

Is implementing a blog, such as Google™'s Blogger, recommended? Will having a blog increase Web site traffic for an online business?

The answer to this is unique to each Web site, and contingent on the target audience, products or services being sold, the messages to be delivered through the blog, and available resources. Blogging is a real time commitment. Questions that need to be asked include the following:

- What is the objective?

- Who will be the voice of the blog?

- How often should you post?

- Should you allow comments?

- How to handle negative comments?

- How much blogging competition is in the specific market?

The bottom line is blogging is one of many marketing strategies that can be considered for a Web site, but it needs to be considered in the context of all of the other marketing objectives and available resources.

Google™ seems to create new applications and tools on a consistent basis, such as Google™ Product Search, Google™'s APIs, Google™ Maps, Chrome, and more. Are there any specific Google™ applications which an online business should use to increase traffic and/or Web site visibility?

The tools at the top of my list include

- Webmaster Tools: Tools to ensure your site is easily crawled and indexed by Google™.

- Local Business Center: A tool that allows a business to be identified on Google™ Maps for local searches.

- Custom Search: A tool for on-site search. Not only does this enhance the site visitor's experience, but knowing the search terms visitors are using on a Web site is very valuable marketing intelligence for any company.

- Analytics: What gets measured gets managed. By using the business intelligence from Google™ Analytics, Web site owners can continue to improve their results.

- Web site Optimizer: Test and optimize site content and design in order to increase revenue and ROI.

What are the most common mistakes made by businesses that are trying to harness the power of the Google™ Search Engine and achieve top search engine rankings?

- Not thinking about search engine optimization until after the site has been built, or after they have spent significant dollars on Google™ AdWords.

- Not taking advantage of the Google™ tools

- Focusing on search engine optimization in the coding of the site and ignoring the requisite inbound links, which is at least 1/3 of a site's SEO "score."

- Not taking advantage of social media sites for the development of inbound links.

- Forgetting to distribute press releases, articles, and videos to other sites where they can become inbound links

If you were to give three pieces of advice to someone who wants to achieve success and high rankings using the Google™ Search Engine, and other applications & tools provided by Google™ for their business, what would they be?

1. Start on keyword research, with the objective of not only identifying optimal phrases to target, but also learning about the competitors in your market.

2. Make search engine optimization a fore thought, not an afterthought. Numerous studies have identified SEO as the most cost effective online marketing strategy (after e-mail marketing). It is much more cost effective to optimize a site from the ground up, as opposed to retrofitting it.

3. Be sure to use all of the free tools Google™ makes available.

Teri Ross has been providing strategic direction to Web site development and online marketing projects since 1995. She built the first and only online trade publication dedicated to technology in the apparel industry, http://techexchange.com, which she sold in 2002. She has defined, crafted, and implemented online marketing strategies and campaigns for both B2B and B2C. She specializes in online marketing strategy development, search engine optimization, paid advertising ad management, and Web site analytics. She enjoys leveraging her left and right brain skills into facilitating the cooperation of marketing and IT departments. She is a Google™ AdWords Advertising Professional, an Open Directory editor, a member of the Search Engine Marketing Professional Organization (SEMPO), a member of the Minnesota Interactive Marketing Association (MIMA), and an eBay® Trading Assistant.

Contact Information:

Teri A. Ross

President, Imagine That Consulting Group, Inc.

2229 Sherwood Court

Minnetonka, MN 55305

Office 952.593.0776

Cell 612.384.7206

teriross@imaginethatinc.us

Interview with Heather Lutze

"How can I get to the top of Google™'s Search Engine Rankings?" What practical and realistic advice can you give someone who is starting out with a new Web site or online business to achieve optimal success?

Make sure you are connecting with searches when they are ready to buy. So often we jump to our ego keywords we would love to see our Web site listed under in Google™. We need to connect with our searching customer and give them a great user experience with exactly what they request when they are ready to buy.

What do you think are the benefits (or drawbacks) from using Google™ AdWords? Is Google™ AdWords a recommended investment, and can it truly generate Web traffic and revenue for an online business?

Google™ AdWords is a great way to get visible and findable very fast for a fixed amount of money per click. However, I often see business owners make tragic mistakes because they dump a bunch of high-level, non-targeted keywords, set U.S. or International Delivery and are very upset with the results. AdWords is a bit too easy for most businesses. They do not put in the time and thought process to see how and when they want customers to see them in their decision making process. Google™ is a worthwhile investment as long as the homework has been done to build a very targeted keyword list that gives searchers a great user experience from keyword, to ad text, to final landing page on their site. This is the only way any business can truly get the ROI on an AdWords account and receive quality score with each click.

What do you think are the benefits (or drawbacks) from using Google™ AdSense? Is Google™ AdSense a viable source of income?

AdSense is a great model if you have the core Web sites with significant traffic to garner the clicks needed to make money with AdSense. Advertisers are getting savvier with the content network and they are turning off this function. Advertisers also understand the impulsive nature of a content click verses a sponsored results click. What are they willing to pay for to get a visitor to their site? If a content click is less valuable and less qualified then a keyword driven sponsored results click, the choice is simple. Make sure you have a great infrastructure for your current sites with good traffic to ensure AdSense success.

Is implementing a blog, such as Google™'s Blogger, recommended? Will having a blog increase Web site traffic for an online business?

Blogging comes back to the keyword selection again. If you know your core keyword is "Internet Marketing Denver," and you name your blog "blog.InternetMarketingDenver.com," then you are setting a precedence that you deserve and belong to be indexed under that term. Then as you post on an ongoing basis, you keep filtering this keyword in your titles and body copy of your blogs. This keyword usage has to be with the user experience in mind. Don't make the content too repetitious or unreadable in your efforts to insert keywords. Have a keyword plan that has your most converting terms that you are focusing on for SEO. Then blogging and other Web initiatives take their cue from this plan. We are no longer picking keywords out of thin air; we know which phrases get us business from our site.

Google™ seems to create new applications and tools on a consistent basis, such as Google™ Product Search, Google™'s API's, Google™ Maps, Chrome and more. Are there any specific Google™ applications which an online business should use to increase traffic and/or Web site visibility?

1) Google™ Optimizer: **www.Google.com/websiteoptimizer**

This is an amazing free tool that lets you test landing page elements in a multi-variant manner. These tools used to cost many thousands of dollars to run and execute. This can exponentially help increase your conversion rates on your landing pages you are using for PPC. If you can come up with the high converting recipe for your pages, then you are truly connected with what visitors expect want from a paid search campaign. You will also realize a happier visitor and a higher conversion rate as well.

2) Google™ Local Business Center: **www.Google.com/accounts/**

We start a Google™ Local business account for every client who has any ability to sell or market their services on a local level.

Then we connect this in with their local ads in Google™ AdWords. This increases the visibility for their listings in Google™ Maps and in the localized searches displayed with a map in the search results.

What are the most common mistakes made by businesses that are trying to harness the power of the Google™ Search Engine and achieve top search engine rankings?

The most common mistake is using AdWords campaigns that lacks negative keywords. You must tell Google™ who you are not. If you sell high-quality leather purses for Coach, then you don't want to be displayed under knockoff, counterfeit, or fake when they type in "Coach Leather Purse." This is essential to run a profitable and targeted AdWords campaign. Another major mistake is that people do not understand their campaign settings and do not turn off content delivery. They also keep to geo-targeting set to International when they only sell in the US. This will cost your account because you are paying for clicks that you cannot deliver your product to and you have frustrated the visitor who wanted your product or service outside the U.S.

It seems that quality inbound links have a significant effect on Google™ Search Engine Rankings?

We advise all clients to go after link bait links first. Write a diagram on your Web site for users to download. If this is a valuable and informative giveaway, then you will get people linking to your site just to have access to that resource. Then we recommend that you go after the obvious linking opportunities like vendors, clients, and partnerships. See if they are willing to endorse your site if you give them a testimonial for their site and link it back to your site. This creates goodwill between clients and vendors and you get a great link back. The key with linking is that you consider the quality of the site you want a link from, then you ask for an anchor text link with your core keyword that is hyperlinked back to your site. Finally, are you willing to give them a reciprocal link back on your site? We consider links in three levels:

- Gold: High Page Rank link, content related, anchor texted, and non-reciprocated

- Silver: High Page Rank link, content related, anchor texted, and reciprocated on your site

- Bronze: A link on a page with lots and lots of links that are grouped by category but still content related and anchor-text linked

If you were to give three pieces of advice to someone who wants to achieve success and high rankings using the Google™ Search Engine, and other applications & tools provided by Google™ for their business, what would they be?

1. Start with pay-per-click. Test keywords, ad text, and landing pages for the best possible conversion event. Once you have at least a 90-to-120-day testing time, then choose your top converting keywords with for your SEO campaigns.

2. Make sure you take the time to build your Web site with PPC converting terms in mind. Craft your Web site in clear and hierarchical page themes that tell a search engine who you are by keyword on each page. Pick one or two related

keywords per page and optimize that page for those only. You win the SEO game by not generalizing to everyone, but niche your business to a select few who will buy.

3. Only endeavor to start social media after steps one and two are done. You have no business driving traffic to a site that is poorly conceived and constructed. Also be committed to blogging once a week, at minimum. If you can meet this standard, then you can start Twitter™, Facebook®, and MySpace® work. You have to be active participants in this arena or it will be a real waste of time.

A nationally recognized speaker, trainer, and consultant in search engine placement, cost-per-click models, natural search, and ad campaign tracking, Heather Lutze's speaking engagements are conducted in the same irreverent style of her book, "The Findability Formula" — delivering equal parts information and entertainment. Lutze taught Yahoo! Advertiser Workshops for two years across the US from 2006 to 2007.

Lutze is a member of the National Speaker's Association, the Colorado chapter of the NSA, and the Meeting Industry Council (MIC). She is a Certified Google™ AdWords Professional (one of only three in the country), has her Yahoo! Search Marketing Ambassador Certification, and is a Lead Trainer for the prestigious PPC Summit. She is also a senior editor for the Search Engine Marketing Journal (SEMJ).

Lutze began her Internet career as a Web designer and then became a paid search manager at a large dot com in Denver.

In July of 2000, Lutze founded Lutze Consulting in response to Web site owners who had paid for Web sites that weren't performing. Indeed, it was her clients' frustration with getting traffic to their sites that was her inspiration for mastering the art of search engine visibility.

Contact Information:

> *Heather Lutze*
>
> *Director of Strategy and Owner of Lutze Consulting*
>
> *Speaker and Consultant*
>
> *Lutze Consulting*
>
> *14 Inverness Drive East, A212*
>
> *Englewood CO 80112*
>
> *303-841-3111*
>
> *hlutze@lutzeconsulting.com*

Interview with Ken Vitto

"How can I get to the top of Google™'s Search Engine Rankings?" What practical and realistic advice can you give someone who is starting out with a new Web site or online business to achieve optimal success?

Showing up in the Top 10 results on Google™ for a competitive search term requires many actions, not just a one or two. Ultimately, it comes down to good, focused content and many well-respected links to that content.

When looking for information, most people would want to find good content about the subject in question. Because Google™ wants to present the best choices to the searchers, Google™ must judge the value of the content on each page. Having details and keeping it focused will give a page a better chance of showing up than a page that does not have details and is not focused.

Even with great content, a Web site would be a waste of time and money without a way for Google™ to find this good content.

The Internet is just a bunch of links presented in a fancy format. The more links that go to the same Web page, the more likely Google™ will believe that content is important.

Content and links to the content is what the Internet is all about. Getting top Google™ search result rankings is also about content and links to the content; it is mastering the finer details that make the difference. It is not easy; if it was, then everyone would have top Google™ search result rankings.

What do you think are the benefits (or drawbacks) from using Google™ AdWords? Is Google™ AdWords a recommended investment, and can it truly generate Web traffic and revenue for an online business?

A Google™ AdWords campaign is great to use when targeting a key phrase for the first time or for a new Web page. Since it takes a minimum of a few months to start showing up naturally in a Google™ search, using AdWords can get you immediate placement in the sponsored links section and you will show up in a better position with the more you pay.

For Web sites that make money through affiliate programs and AdSense, using Google™ AdWords to generate traffic can be very profitable. link arbitrage, making more on affiliate or AdSense links leaving the site than the amount you paid for incoming AdWords traffic, is possible and can be lucrative. The key to making money with this technique is to do a lot of research, have good instincts, and get lucky sometimes.

What do you think are the benefits (or drawbacks) from using Google™ AdSense? Is Google™ AdSense a viable source of income?

One drawback to using AdSense would be the appearance it gives. Having AdSense ads could give the appearance that the Web site is designed just for ads, which could make people have less trust in the content.

Have you ever used Google™ Product Search or Google™ Base? What practical can you give someone who is considering using these two Google™ applications?

Google™ Base can generate a fair amount of traffic to a site. I use a combination of articles and product listings to create additional traffic to my sites.

Is implementing a blog, such as Google™'s Blogger, recommended? Will having a blog increase Web site traffic for an online business?

Google™ favors blogs by spidering them more often for fresh content. Blogs are a great way to generate traffic as well as provide links to other Web sites. Creating unique, quality content is the key, just like with any Web site.

Google™ seems to create new applications and tools on a consistent basis, such as Google™ Product Search, Google™'s APIs, Google™ Maps, Chrome, and more. Are there any specific Google™ applications which an online business should use to increase traffic and/or Web site visibility?

Google™ Analytics is one of the most valuable tools. Analytics provides the information needed to tell if your techniques are effective. This allows you to see what works and what might need to be changed. You can also derive information to improve Web site features like navigation, shopping carts, and more.

What are the most common mistakes made by businesses who are trying to harness the power of the Google™ Search Engine and achieve top search engine rankings?

People duplicate the same content in too many places and create links with duplicate information. Do not use automated processes to spread content and links across the Internet, this will create duplicate content which may have a negative effect. Having the same exact content spread across the Internet wastes resources. Imagine a massive library with the same book in several different places at the same time; it takes extra effort to keep track of copies are not needed.

It seems that quality inbound links have a significant effect on Google™ Search Engine Rankings?

You will likely place a high value on an opinion from a trusted friend, like Google™ does when a trusted Web site provides a link to another site. A link is like a suggesting a good place to find valuable information. Without this value system, only the number of links would be the judge

If you were to give three pieces of advice to someone who wants to achieve success and high rankings using the Google™ Search Engine, and other applications & tools provided by Google™ for their business, what would they be?

1. Create new, single topic pages with great content often.

2. Build links to your pages from external pages with similar, great content.

3. Drive traffic not only to your site, but to the external pages that link to your site.

Ken Vitto, the director of marketing at GizMac Accessories LLC., has been with the company more than three years. During his years at Giz-Mac, Vitto established two e-commerce sites and generated dozens of Top 10 Google™ result rankings for very competitive search terms. With the significant increase in visitors to their Web sites, GizMac was able to substantially reduce poor performing advertising while increasing sales further.

Currently, GizMac uses little to no advertising and relies primarily on Internet exposure for sales. Vitto has refined his skills of search engine optimization through staying current on the latest trends, and the Giz-Mac Web sites have benefitted.

Contact Information:
Ken Vitto
ken@xrackpro.com
GizMac Accessories LLC.
2295B Jefferson Street
Torrance, CA 90501
(310) 320-5563

Interview with Dave Collins

"How can I get to the top of Google™'s Search Engine Rankings?" What practical and realistic advice can you give someone who is starting out with a new Web site or online business to achieve optimal success?

Getting to the top is easy, which is why so many SEO companies offer Top 5 Ranking guarantees. Getting to the top for the right keywords, however, is a different story altogether.

First of all, subscribe to a keyword database like WordTracker, and spend some time on keyword research. You have to know what people are looking for; your guesses won't even be close.

Create good, solid, and targeted content. Fill your Web site with well-written, informative and original content that will be of interest to your site visitors.

Next, make sure that the pages are correctly setup for the engines — for example, using keywords in the page titles, description meta tag and the body. But it's important not to be tempted into shortcuts — avoid trying to trick the search engines at all costs. Such tricks don't work and might you get in trouble.

Finally, be patient. Spread the word of your Web site, and try to get as many legitimate incoming links as possible. Search engine success can't be sped up, so accept that it will take time.

What do you think are the benefits (or drawbacks) from using Google™ AdWords? Is Google™ AdWords a recommended investment, and can it truly generate Web traffic and revenue for an online business?

Google™ AdWords gives you instant reach to the whole world. Unlike regular SEO, you can start putting your ads in front of the right people immediately, and track the results.

AdWords is a recommended investment, but be careful. Losing money on Google™ AdWords is incredibly easy, and the system is in many ways set up to make sure that happens. Take time to really learn how the system works, or get a professional to do the job for you.

AdWords can certainly create targeted traffic at a very reasonable cost, but not unless you know what you're doing.

What do you think are the benefits (or drawbacks) from using Google™ AdSense? Is Google™ AdSense a viable source of income?

My advice is simple: don't do it.

It cheapens your Web site. If I'm interested in buying whatever you sell, I might question why you're prepared to risk losing me for the sake of an ad that may earn a few cents. If you're really that desperate for money, do I really want to buy your product?

Also, you might well be advertising your competition on your own page. I'm sure they would be delighted to take away one of your potential customers at the cost of only a few cents, but why would you let them?

If you're lucky, your competition may start running AdSense ads on their Web sites. If so, make sure that your ad appears there. This is the best use of AdSense for your business.

Have you ever used Google™ Product Search or Google™ Base? What practical can you give someone who is considering using these two Google™ applications?

I've worked with both. My experience suggests that your time might be better spent on other Google™ channels — Google™ AdWords and SEO.

Is implementing a blog, such as Google™'s Blogger recommended? Will having a blog increase Web site traffic for an online business?

A blog can be beneficial, but there are conditions. You need to be able to write well. You need to have targeted content that will be of interest to people who may buy your goods. You need the time to write regularly; once a month isn't going to produce results. You need traffic to your Web site. Spending an hour a day when three people a week read your comments is pointless.

Google™ seems to create new applications and tools on a consistent basis, such as Google™ Product Search, Google™'s APIs, Google™ Maps, Chrome, and more. Are there any specific Google™ applications an online business should use to increase traffic and/or Web site visibility?

It really depends on what you're selling, but irrespective of what that may be, and what markets you operate in, you really can't go wrong with SEO and Google™ AdWords. My advice would be to dip your toes in cautiously when exploring. If you find it pays off, then devote the necessary time and resources as required. But bear in mind that many of these possibilities are effectively in beta anyway, so invest your time cautiously.

What are the most common mistakes made by businesses that are trying to harness the power of the Google™ Search Engine and achieve top search engine rankings?

Trying to cheat the system. If I had a dollar for every Web site I've seen with text that doesn't read well, as it's been "over-optimized" for Google™ at the expense of the visitor, I would have retired years ago.

There's always someone, somewhere who believes he has the secret to ranking highly on Google™; he's wrong. Believing their methods and theories is like paying for a get-rich-quick book.

Aside from those lucky enough to inherit or win fortunes, everyone else has to work hard and develop their skills to make money. The same rule applies to search engine success.

If you were to give three pieces of advice to someone who wants to achieve success and high rankings using the Google™ Search Engine, and other applications & tools provided by Google™ for their business, what would they be?

1. Build content. The more targeted content you can put on your Web site, the better. Articles, resources, downloads, samples, white papers, ideas, newsletters, and blogs.

2. Make sure that there are targeted incoming links. Use press releases extensively, find bloggers to link to you, add your site

to targeted Web sites and directories, and do everything you can to get as many legitimate incoming links as possible.

3. Avoid tricks. Don't pay for links, don't use hidden text, and avoid cunning tricks. Don't even consider link farms, and don't even think about anything that goes beyond common sense. Most tricks will be ineffective. A few can get you in serious trouble.

Dave is the founder and CEO of SharewarePromotions, and has been working within the online software industry since 1997. Collins likes to think of himself as the pretty face of the organization, but in reality oversees the Google™ AdWords and marketing work for all of clients. Other areas of expertise include server log analysis and procrastination.

Contact Information:
dave@sharewarepromotions.com
www.SharewarePromotions.com

Interview with Dale Lenz

"How can I get to the top of Google™'s Search Engine Rankings?" What practical and realistic advice can you give someone who is starting out with a new Web site or online business to achieve optimal success?

My number one tip is to have good content. If you are publishing something that people want and need, it will work toward the top in time.

What do you think are the benefits (or drawbacks) from using Google™ AdWords? Is Google™ AdWords a recommended investment, and can it truly generate Web traffic and revenue for an online business?

AdWords will indeed generate traffic, but you have to make sure that you are getting the desired results from the traffic. You have to know what you want the traffic to do (buy something, subscribe to a newsletter, or visit your site again). It is important to use Google™ Analytics along with AdWords.

What do you think are the benefits (or drawbacks) from using Google™ AdSense? Is Google™ AdSense a viable source of income?

AdSense can turn off some users. Most people are used to seeing AdSense on sites, but that still doesn't mean they like it. Determining if you want to use AdSense all goes back to the purpose of your site and what your overall monetization plan is.

Have you ever used Google™ Product Search or Google™ Base? What practical advice can you give someone who is considering using these two Google™ applications?

I have looked at Google™ Product Search and found that **www.amazon.com** is a much better source for product information.

Is implementing a blog, such as Google™'s Blogger, recommended? Will having a blog increase Web site traffic for an online business?

A blog is a great way to work content and keywords into your site. **www.RouteBlast.com** is a very simple, fast, and easy-to-use online mapping and routing site. If you want to find the distance between multiple cities, there is no faster site. A challenge when creating RouteBlast was the fact that the interface is so simple, there is not a lot of wording on the site. Google™ has a hard time finding sites like this, so a blog can help by getting related content on the same domain.

Google™ seems to create new applications and tools on a consistent basis, such as Google™ Product Search, Google™'s APIs, Google™ Maps, Chrome, and more. Are there any specific Google™ applications which an online business should use to increase traffic and/or Web site visibility?

Google™ creates so many great tools it is hard to keep track of them all. Wikipedia seems to have a good list of all the Google™ tools. I use Google™ Docs for 90 percent of the things I had done with Microsoft products. Google™ Analytics is pretty much standard on any Web site, and the Google™ Maps API was used to build **www.RouteBlast.com**.

What are the most common mistakes made by businesses that are trying to harness the power of the Google™ Search Engine and achieve top search engine rankings?

I have heard of companies trying to find tricks to get a top search engine rank. Google™ is pretty secretive on how they rank their search results. It all goes back to the fact that nothing is better than hard work; get good content and have other sites link to it.

If you were to give three pieces of advice to someone who wants to achieve success and high rankings using the Google™ Search Engine, and other applications & tools provided by Google™ for their business, what would they be?

1. Have good content

2. Network with other similar sites and share links that will be appreciated by your users

3. Read blogs published by folks at Google™; they sometimes provide information about changes or upcoming features

Dale Lenz is a proud father and husband who has worked more than ten years in the transportation and logistics industry. Lenz is cofounder of Two Lane Tech, a commercial software development company. He has a passion for entrepreneurship and believes in several principals for business success: focus on the customer, give employees the tools and training they need to do the job, and have written goals, policies, and procedures.

Contact Information:

Dale Lenz

Cofounder

Two Lane Tech, Inc.

PO Box 672

Ames, IA 50010

515-598-2232

dale@twolanetech.com

www.twolanetech.com

www.RouteBlast.Com

Interview with Jason Shindler

"How can I get to the top of Google™'s Search Engine Rankings?" What practical and realistic advice can you give someone who is starting out with a new Web site or online business to achieve optimal success?

To get listed at the top of Google™'s Search Engine Rankings, you simply need to convince Google™ that you are the correct answer for a specific question. It sounds simple, but in fact, this is an almost impossible task.

Unfortunately, Google™'s formula for determining which sites are the correct answer is a secret, and it is always changing. We don't know exactly what they use, and they are always improving the algorithms involved. We're not completely in the dark, though. We have some ideas of what criteria they use.

The criteria of the Google™ algorithms are as follows:

- The content of your site: All search engines scour the text of your site to see what it is about. Remember to think like a customer — if you think you are a piping engineer, but everyone knows you as a plumber, you should make sure that your site says "plumber" and not "piping engineer."

- Links back to your site: Think of the Web as a popularity contest. If 30 people say your site is great, and only 10 say your competitor is great, search engines may rank your site higher. Get sites that are relevant to your business to place a link to your site on theirs. You can often entice them to do this by placing their link on your site.

- Alt tags: These are words that you write that describe pictures on your site. Google™ can't usually read a picture, even if there are words in it. By using this special tag, you can tell Google™ (and visually impaired users) what is inside a picture.

- Meta tags: These are words that you write that describe what your site is about.

By considering all of these things, you'll get your site listed higher in search engines like Google™.

What do you think are the benefits (or drawbacks) from using Google™ AdWords? Is Google™ AdWords a recommended investment, and can it truly generate Web traffic and revenue for an online business?

I highly recommend Google™ AdWords. Here's why.

There are two ways to get listed in Search engines — by getting listed in the organic search results and by paying for an advertisement like Google™ AdWords. Organic search results are hard to control. Even if you are hiring someone, it may work and it may not work.

With AdWords, at least you know that when you spend money with Google™, you are getting something out of it. For example, as a plumber, if someone searches for "plumbing emergency" and they are located in your geographic area, that is a good lead

That said, you still need to monitor an AdWords account to make sure that you are advertising under the right keywords and your ad is appropriately written.

What do you think are the benefits (or drawbacks) from using Google™ AdSense? Is Google™ AdSense a viable source of income?

Google™ AdSense is an easy way to make a few dollars off of a site that generates some traffic. In comparison to selling the ad space yourself, or other methods, it is relatively less lucrative. I recommend AdSense to people who want to test out the waters of advertising without having to do a lot of work. If your priority is to make a lot of money, consider selling the ad space yourself.

Have you ever used Google™ Product Search or Google™ Base? What practical advice can you give someone who is considering using these two Google™ applications?

Google™ Product Search is a great tool to use if your Web site sells non-unique products. It allows retailers to publish a list of products that are for sale to Google™. For example, if you sell "widgets," you might tell Google™ what types of widgets you sell and how much they cost. A person searching for widgets using Google™'s search engine might see that your company sells what they are looking for and purchase them from you.

In my experience, this works well with vendors with competitive prices on products that other vendors sell as well. It does not work well for products that are one of a kind, or for vendors where service is more important than price.

Is implementing a blog, such as Google™'s Blogger, recommended? Will having a blog increase Web site traffic for an online business?

Google™'s Blogger service is one of many services available to help people post blogs. If you are going to start a blog, you should answer yes to these three important questions:

1. Do you plan to post a new article each month? If the answer is no, then do not start a blog. A blog that is not updated looks worse than not having one.

2. If you allow comments, do you have a plan for monitoring them for inappropriate content? Having a comment that is inappropriate can be a much bigger negative than not having a blog at all.

3. Do you plan to post the blog to your own site? Posting the site to your own domain will help generate good content that a search engine could use to index your site. Leaving it on **www.blogspot.com** will help, but not as much as putting it on your own site.

In general, having a blog can help generate more content for a search engine to index, and thus increase traffic.

Google™ seems to create new applications and tools on a consistent basis, such as Google™ Product Search, Google™'s APIs, Google™ Maps, Chrome, and more. Are there any specific Google™ applications an online business should use to increase traffic and/or Web site visibility?

Anytime Google™ or anyone else comes out with a new product, you need to take some time to read between the buzzwords and hype, and objectively answer the following question: "How does this tool help me accomplish my business goals?" If you can't answer the question, or if the answer is "not sure," it is better to stick with strategies that consistently work to provide a good product or service at a good price at the right time.

What are the most common mistakes made by businesses who are trying to harness the power of the Google™ Search Engine and achieve top search engine rankings?

The biggest mistake people make is thinking that if I do "x," it will drive my rankings much higher and I will make millions of dollars. Having that type of attitude makes you a victim for scams. Having good content on your site that describes what you do is much more important than any tricks you might read about.

Jason Shindler is the owner of Curvine Web Solutions. He has 9 years of experience developing Web applications and Web sites for businesses. During his career, he has worked in many settings — including universities, municipalities and large private businesses. He is proficient in many different Web application platforms, including Microsoft®'s ASP and ASP.NET platforms, PHP, Java™, and Perl.

Before starting Curvine Web Solutions in 2005, Shindler was the CIO of a Web development firm in Florida. As a co-owner and CIO of Silver-scape Technologies (later renamed 352 Media Group), Shindler managed the company's programming staff and technical operations. Shindler also worked as a Web application developer for the University of

Florida and the City of Gainesville, Florida.

Shindler is a graduate of the University of Florida. He holds a B.S. in Telecommunications in 2001, with an outside concentration in Computer Science.

Contact Information:

Jason Shindler

CEO, Curvine Web Solutions

phone: 425-818-9096

jason@curvine.com

www.curvine.com

Interview with Joe Niewierski

"How can I get to the top of Google™'s Search Engine Rankings?" What practical and realistic advice can you give someone who is starting out with a new Web site or online business to achieve optimal success?

Be patient. Google™ looks at how long a site has been up and how often it is updated, among a lot of other factors. Too often someone will say "I'm going to set up the perfect page and get a high ranking on Google™." Then, when it doesn't happen right away they abandon the page and move on. That dooms the page to never being ranked high, no matter how well it was set up originally. It's better to keep tweaking the same page, making it better and better, all the while keeping in mind that it's often a slow process of moving up.

What do you think are the benefits (or drawbacks) from using Google™ AdWords? Is Google™ AdWords a recommended investment, and can it truly generate Web traffic and revenue for an online business?

We use AdWords and make millions of dollars in profit off of it every year. But you have to do it right. Like any medium, the initial testing phase it may cost you money. However, if you implement the tracking techniques you will identify where to trim the fat and where there is more to gain.

If you have a large enough budget, you should look into hiring a company to handle your AdWords for you. They usually work for a percentage of your ad spend and are often trained by Google™ themselves, so they know tricks you would never have considered.

What do you think are the benefits (or drawbacks) from using Google™ AdSense? Is Google™ AdSense a viable source of income?

AdSense is a great tool if you have an information based site. They basically supply you with ads so that you don't have to have your own advertising sales department. If you sell products on your site, you can still use AdSense as an extra source of income, however there is more work to do to make sure that competitors' ads are not running on the site next to your products.

Is implementing a blog, such as Google™'s Blogger recommended? Will having a blog increase Web site traffic for an online business?

Definitely. But do your blog correctly. Most blogs online are simply someone grabbing content from other sites and posting one thing every day. In order to get the most pick up from search engines, and to keep the readers coming back, you need to have interesting content updated on a regular basis. Daily is best, but weekly will suffice if it is all you can handle. If you're only going to update your blog monthly forget the blog format. A month is too long for people to remember to come back. You should turn it into a newsletter, and make people subscribe if you are doing it monthly. That way they need not remember.

Google™ seems to create new applications and tools on a consistent basis, such as Google™ Product Search, Google™'s API's, Google™ Maps, Chrome and more. Are there any specific Google™ applications which an online business should use to increase traffic and/or Web site visibility?

There is not a single business in the world that needs to be using everything that Google™ offers. But Google™ does offer something for every business. Publishers should definitely be on Book Search. Programmers and developers should pay close attention to Google™ Code. It takes some creativity on your part to determine what aspects of the vast Google™ empire can help your business, so go to **www.Google.com/intl/en/options/** and check it all out. You're sure to find something that you should utilize.

What are the most common mistakes made by businesses who are trying to harness the power of the Google™ Search Engine and achieve top search engine rankings?

Don't try to trick or cheat the system. Google™ is either way ahead of you or fast on your heels at making their system disregard what you have concocted. Years ago, you could get great placement by putting thousands of keywords in white on white at the very bottom of your page. Google™ is much more sophisticated and a stunt like that gets you kicked to the back of the line. Build solid, keyword rich pages with text that makes sense to real people. Read up on the tactics recommended by the top experts.

It seems that quality inbound links have a significant effect on Google™ Search Engine Rankings?

Yes. Links from quality sites only, though. Don't set up link communities or spend tons of time trading links with sites that don't have much to do with what you do. If you sell telescopes, a link to your site from **www.nasa.gov** will be of much greater value than a link from less reputable site.

If you were to give three pieces of advice to someone who wants to achieve success and high rankings using the Google™ Search Engine, and other applications & tools provided by Google™ for their business, what would they be?

1. Test. Don't assume something will work and put a huge budget behind it. Make it prove itself making dollars from nickels before you let it make millions from thousands.

2. Track. You'll never know if your tests work if you don't accurately and continuously track every aspect. If you don't plan on tracking fully, steer clear altogether.

3. Be Brave. Once you find something that works on a small scale, put more force behind it. It can be nerve racking but it is the only way to get the benefits out of all of your hard work.

Joe Niewierski, the vice president of marketing & promotion at PostcardMania, became a published writer after graduating with a B.A. in Advertising from the University of South Florida. Before his 6 year tenure at PostcardMania, Niewierski worked as a graphic designer for two national advertising agencies, Bernard Hodes Group and Chenoweth & Faulkner, branding campaigns for several of their corporate clients. In 2001, upon discovering his exceptional talent, PostcardMania CEO Joy Gendusa hired Joe to head up her marketing division. In 2005, PostcardMania was hailed as the nation's fastest-growing direct mail postcard marketing firm by Inc. Magazine. PostcardMania is a full service postcard direct mail marketing company which includes graphic design, printing, highly-targeted mailing list acquisition, and mailing services with free marketing advice, printing 4 million and mailing 2 million postcards representing 35,000-plus customers in over 350 industries each week.

Contact Information:

Joe Niewierski

VP Marketing, PostcardMania

404 S. MLK Jr. Ave.

Clearwater, FL 33756

Phone: (727) 441-4704

Fax: (727) 442-5130

joe@postcardmania.com

You can also contact:

Ferris Stith

Director of Public Relations, PostcardMania

404 S. MLK Jr. Ave.

Clearwater, FL 33756

Phone: (727) 441-4704 ext. 342

Fax: (727) 442-5130

ferris@postcardmania.com

CHAPTER 15

Google Case Studies

This chapter highlights success stories and real-life examples of how others achieved enormous success with the Google Search Engine, Google AdWords, Google AdSense or other Google related applications and Search Engine Optimization for the Google Search Engine.

CASE STUDY: IMPORTANCE OF USING ANALYTICS TO IMPROVE RETURN ON INVESTMENT

Submitted by Joy Brazelle

The site www.UsedGolfBallDeals.com is an e-commerce site whose owner understood the power of online marketing. E-mail campaigns had always generated sales. He knew the potential of pay-per-click was huge. The problem was that there was no time to learn how to run Google AdWords campaigns. So he decided to outsource.

Things seemed to be okay. He found an agency, explained his goals and let the agency set up and run the campaigns. That is when the problems started. The site, www.**UsedGolfBallDeals.com,** is a business that is run by the numbers. Money is spent to make money. Between the agency fees and the cost of the clicks, Google AdWords was not a money maker.

This news was shocking as most every other business owner that talked about Google AdWords described it as a super money maker. The owner decided that it was worth the time to learn how to make money with Google AdWords.

He took a slightly different approach, though. Instead of finding a book or an online course to learn AdWords, he decided to first select a Web analytics solution to track the campaign. He wanted to ensure that there was no guess-work with the campaigns; that every decision was based on facts and numbers.

To accomplish this, some prep work was involved:

- Modifying the shopping cart to make sure the dollar value of each sale was captured in the analytics

- Doing keyword research to see which (organic) keywords had historically resulted in sales

- Creating targeted campaigns and ad groups based on specific products

- Writing interesting ads with offers and calls to actions

- Ensuring that every add had a unique destination URL (and the destination was the product page, not the home page)

The campaigns were launched, set to run for a limited amount of time and then the analysis began.

With all of the prep work done it was easy to see at a glance which ads were performing and which were losing money.

The ads that were not working were rewritten. The modified ads ran for a finite amount of time. If they did not start generating a positive ROI, money was shifted away from those ads to the positively performing ads.

Soon www.UsedGolfBallDeals.com was enjoying the payoff. Google AdWords had become a super-money maker.

CASE STUDY: CLICK FRAUD - WHAT IT ISN'T, WHAT IT IS, AND WHAT TO DO ABOUT IT

Submitted by Joy Brazelle

Click fraud is something every advertiser should be aware of. Click fraud means different things to different people.

Click fraud began years ago when advertisers realized they could use up their competitors' budgets simply by clicking on their ads. As soon as Google realized this problem, they took steps to fix the problem. They couldn't prevent a competitor from clicking on an ad, but they could ensure that the advertiser wouldn't have to pay for this competitor's fraudulent click.

Over the years, as Google AdSense has become more and more popular, click fraud has become more sophisticated. Because Web site owners make money when the Google ads they have on their site are clicked, there is financial incentive for them to click the ads. Click fraud has evolved from Web site owners and their friends clicking on ads on their site to the creation of robust programs, automated 'bots' that systematically click these links.

Google has dedicated many resources to stay on top of the click fraud problem to make sure that advertisers don't have to pay for unwanted, invalid clicks. But it seems as soon as Google figures out how to combat one type of click fraud, the hackers get more sophisticated.

For that reason it is important to monitor to make sure that your campaigns don't fall victim to click fraud. The first step in monitoring is to understand what click fraud is and what click fraud isn't.

What it isn't: It is easy to blame poorly performing ads on click fraud. But that is not the case. Most ads that don't do well are not the fault of click fraud. There are many causes for ads that just don't work (low click-thru rate, negative ROI).

The most common causes of ads with a low click-thru rate or negative ROI are not click fraud.

The ads - poorly written ads that are boring with no offer nor call to action. Many advertisers treat writing their ads as a chore. It is obvious when that is the case.

The landing page - when pay-per-click is treated like a chore, many corners are cut and short cuts are taken. Often rather than thinking through which pages are the most appropriate or create custom landing pages, all ads go straight to the home page.

The campaigns and ad groups are too broad. Yet another risk when treating pay-per-click as a chore makes it is easy to create one or just a few campaigns and ad groups that include lots of unrelated keywords. It is definitely worth taking the time to create many targeted campaigns each containing ad groups with keywords that are very relevant to each other.

A little time and effort can fix these non-performing ads.

What it is: But click fraud does exist. You just need to know what to look for to detect it.

The first step is to realize that if you are doing pay-per-click correctly the campaigns will behave fairly predictably. So the biggest red flag is when a campaign veers from the norm. If a campaign gets a spike in traffic (unless there is some seasonality or other logical reason) or drop in ROI, there is a concern and you should look deeper. Here are a few things to look for:

Campaign traffic that shows a high bounce rate with a high average time on site should be a red flag. If a high percentage of your campaign traffic (e.g. 75-80 percent) leave you site almost immediately, it is not logical that the average time on your site would be high unless the visitors who were interested in the site stayed on your site for a really, really long time. This would indicate, then, that the campaign was actually good and effective, however there is something going on that is causing the high percentage of short visits (bounce). That something could be click fraud.

No page views - Any human traffic should account for at least one page view.

No keywords - If you have opted out of the Content Network option for this campaign, all of your campaign traffic should be coming to your site from search results pages, so you would logically expect to be able to see which keywords were driving traffic for each ad.

No referrer - Since you are paying for traffic to your site from another site, there logically should not be any traffic from the campaign with no referrer.

Strange geographical traffic - One red flag that is an increase in traffic from countries, states or regions where you know that you are not running campaigns. If you see a large percentage of campaign traffic from countries, states, or regions where you know that you are not running your campaign, then it is almost always worth contacting Google to pursue a credit.

What to do about it: The best approach to take when you feel you've found campaigns that are a victim of click fraud is to be calm and professional. Do not be aggressive or unprofessional. If you have a Google account manager, contact him or her. Explain that you've found some questionable traffic and ask if they can escalate. Know that the departments that are involved in finding and fighting click fraud at Google are always incredibly busy. If you have the proof (your Web server logs files, analytics reports, etc.), you may just be able to work with your account manager to negotiate a credit for a portion of the clicks in question.

CASE STUDY: WORKING WITH GOOGLE TO GET A CREDIT

Submitted by Joy Brazelle

A manufacturer of enriched infant food had been running a campaign for about 8 months. Each month the campaigns maintained a decent click-thru rate and an impressive conversion rate of about 5 percent. During the 9th month they noticed something alarming — the conversion rate dipped below 1percent. There had been no major changes to the campaign or the Web site, no existing competition had introduced specials, and there was no new competition. The advertiser began an investigation.

In reviewing their log files they found they were receiving campaign traffic from many sites despite the fact they never participated in the Content Network.

They approached their Google account rep. The account rep escalated the issue to the click quality team. Within a few weeks the account rep offered the advertiser a credit for the invalid clicks.

CASE STUDY: WRITING GOOGLE ADWORDS

Submitted by Joy Brazelle

Stephanie was a single, stay-at-home mom looking for a way to make extra money. Before starting a family, Stephanie had enjoyed a career as a copywriter. One day in talking with a friend who worked at an ad agency, she learned about pay-per-click and Google AdWords. Her friend showed her the ads on Google's search results page. What immediately struck Stephanie were the ads. She asked her friend to show her more. The more ads she saw, the more she saw the pattern of boring, non-compelling ads.

She saw her opportunity. Stephanie knew from her days of copywriting that there was an art to writing a compelling classified ad. From what she had seen with her friend, many of the Google ads seemed to be simply thrown together with little or no thought.

But she was intimidated by what she thought was the technical nature of Google AdWords. Stephanie was torn because she was convinced that she could write better ads than what she was seeing. But she was non-technical, not Internet savvy, and didn't know where or how to get started.

Her friend showed Stephanie a Google AdWords account and the structure of the campaigns. Stephanie felt that with a little practice, she definitely could become comfortable going online and creating ads. In learning about the click-thru rate, Stephanie was confident that she could write an ad that was better than the other ads on the page and therefore more likely to get clicked.

Armed with confidence and the technical knowledge she needed Stephanie was excited, but stuck. She was unsure how she could make money. She couldn't position herself as an expert because she was a novice who was just certain that she could write a better ad. How was she going to find clients?

She called her friend again and explained her dilemma. Her friend introduced her to Trada, an online marketplace where advertisers open up their pay-per-click ad budgets to optimizers who select the most effective keywords, ads and click bid prices. The best keywords and ads (ads that get the clicks below the advertiser's bid price) make money. The best optimizers make a lot of money.

Here's how: Advertisers put their PPC campaigns onto Trada's marketplace with a fixed bid price. Individuals (known as optimizers) who have experience in PPC or expertise in a particular subject matter work on the campaigns by selecting the most effective keywords, ads and click prices. Optimizers profit when their keyword is searched and their ad is clicked in the Sponsored Links section of Google. Optimizers earn the difference between the advertiser's bid price (60 cents, for example) and the click price on Google (say, 40 cents). In this scenario, the advertiser would pay 60 cents for the click, Google would charge 40 for the click and the optimizer makes the difference - 20 cents.

This strategy is known as keyword arbitrage. Optimizers make a small profit on each click, but when taken over dozens of campaigns and thousands of keywords, they can earn several thousand dollars each month).

This was perfect for Stephanie. She signed up as an optimizer. She picked out a few advertisers who she was familiar with and immediately began creating keywords and writing ads. Her ads got clicks and she started making money.

Falling back on her copywriting experience, she refined the way she wrote ads. Rather than just thinking about an ad as a three line, character constricted format, she wrote long, descriptive ads. She then reworked and reworked them until they met the character limit. She took a similar strategy with keyword generation by tightly coupling her keywords with her ad content.

The time she spent writing thoughtful, interesting, compelling ads paid off. Stephanie is extremely happy making a lot of money doing what she really enjoys.

Joy Brazelle is Vice President of Serengeti Communications. Brazelle has more than ten years experience in Internet Consulting with a strong focus on analytics. Knowing that you cannot improve what you do not measure, she has made analytics a priority during her years helping clients build and grow their online presence.

Prior to joining Serengeti, Brazelle was the Director of Professional Services at ClickTracks, a Web Analytics software company. As Director of Professional Services for ClickTracks, Brazelle worked with hundreds of customers helping educate them on how to understand their analytics and use the information to improve their online marketing.

Brazelle has been a member of the Web Analytics Association since its launch in May 2006. She stays plugged into the current world of analytics by participating in Facebook groups from 'Web Analytics World' to 'ClickTracks Addicts.' When not working she can be found playing with her two dogs or hanging out with her husband on the beach, unsuccessfully trying to learn to surf.

Contact Information:
Joy Brazelle
jbrazelle@sereneticom.com
843-283-9355

CASE STUDY: USING GOOGLE MAPS API FOR ONLINE MAPPING MASH-UP WEB SITE

Submitted by Dale Lenz

The Google Maps API lets you embed Google Maps in your own web pages. There are lots of Web sites using Google Maps for all kinds of applications. The API allows developers to use the Google Maps & data, and make some great sites. Web sites using the Google Maps API take many forms ranging from serious to silly. The Google Maps API is a free service, available for any Web site that is free to consumers.

We wanted to create a Web site that people could use to find distance calculations. The site **www.RouteBlast.com** was designed to allow users to get mileage calculations fast & easy. I like to travel, and sometimes like to take a weekend drive. Often times I know I want to drive about 200 miles and would really like to visit a short list of cities. My old method involved pulling out my truckers atlas, putting a pin on my origin location and then I would tie a string to the pin to make a circular covering the area I could travel to within 200 miles. I would then scan the map and see which of the selected cities were within range. As much fun as that sounds, I often ended up sticking myself with the pin or breaking the string. Using **www.RouteBlast.com** I can now enter my origin location along with my list of multiple destinations and get immediate results as to how far each city is from the origin.

Site visitors use **www.RouteBlast.com** for all kinds of reasons, but pretty much I get the same message from all of them... "I can't believe how fast it is." The site is so fast, because of a couple things.

1 - A great developer, who knows his way around Google Maps API & is one of the best in the business.

2 - Google, powers the whole thing, requests are sent to Google server and results are returned with amazing speed.

Unlike many of the Google tools, the Google Maps API does take some technical skills. There are software companies that will do custom Google Maps projects for clients, and you can feel free to contact me with ideas or questions about their individual Google Maps project.

The site also uses Google Analytics to track user traffic. Currently, we do not have advertising on the Web site, but may use Google Ad Manager & Google AdSense to monetize the project.

Dale Lenz is a proud father and husband who has worked over ten years in the transportation and logistics industry. Lenz is cofounder of Two Lane Tech, a commercial software development company. Dale has a passion for entrepreneurship and believes in several principals for business success which transcend industry: focus on the customer, give employees the tools and training they need to do the job, and have written goals, policies, & procedures.

Dale Lenz
Cofounder
Two Lane Tech, Inc.
PO Box 672
Ames, IA 50010
Phone: 515-598-2232

e-mail: dale@twolanetech.com
www.twolanetech.com
www.RouteBlast.Com

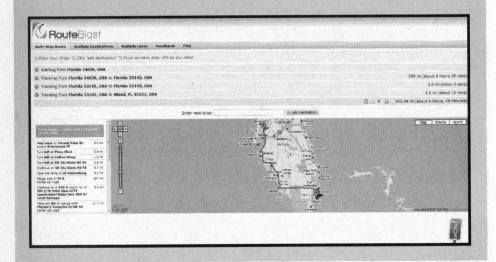

CASE STUDY: LICE ICE - NATURAL HEAD LICE TREATMENT <WWW.LICEICE.COM>

Submitted by Teri Ross

The customer came to us with a B2C Web site needing search engine optimization. In order to identify what we needed to optimize, we first installed Google Analytics, where we learned that more than 75 percent of the traffic was to an image of head lice that was found in Google Images. The graphic was on a landing page by itself with no Web site or product identification, which made the traffic to the site of no value. We began a Web site redesign by researching keywords and competition in the Google AdWords Keyword Tool and Google Search, and then tested the phrases in Google AdWords. After identifying the optimal phrases to use, we restructured the site and wrote new search engine optimized copy.

While the original site had versions in English and Spanish, which made site updates rather cumbersome, this time we used the free Google Translate tool, which will translate any Web page into the language the visitor chooses from the pull-down menu on each page.

After the new site was launched, we used the Google Webmaster Tool to delete all of the old pages from the Google database. With the use of Google Analytics we identified a 242 percent increase in organic search engine traffic for targeted phrases within 4 weeks of launch, an 87.49 percent increase in pages per visit, a 135 percent increase in average time on site, and an 86.42 percent reduction in the bounce rate (visitors exiting from the page they landed on). Online sales have remained constant, while retail store sales have picked up significantly (prospects need this head lice treatment immediately). The head lice images still drive a lot of traffic from Google Images, but now the images are surrounded by related information and product links, which allows the traffic to drive sales, both online and offline.

We monitor the company's online reputation and press coverage with the use of Google Alerts. We are in the process of creating videos that will be hosted on YouTube, which is owned by Google.

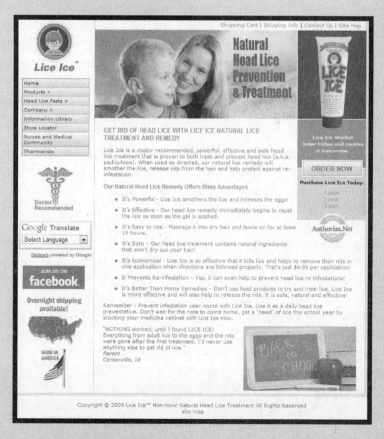

CASE STUDY: BENCHMARK IMAGING & DISPLAY <WWW.BENCHMARKIMAGING.COM>

Submitted by Teri Ross

This large format printing company creates trade show displays and exhibits, signs and banners and portable displays. They came to use seeking an increase in traffic through search engine optimization, an increase in Web site conversions, as well as an improvement in their Google AdWords campaigns. In reviewing their product offerings and the site structure of their five year old site, it was determined that we would build a completely new site.

After reviewing their Google Analytics, we identified that they hadn't been configured properly to track the online conversions, which we remedied. It should be noted that while installing Google Analytics is relatively simple and straightforward, the software needs to be programmed to support the unique key performance indicators and calls to action of the Web site being analyzed. In addition, there are a growing number of third-party plug-ins that will enhance the business intelligence in Google Analytics. Professional assistance is recommended.

We then reorganized their Google AdWords campaigns by adding phrases to test, and fine tuning the ad groups so as to better identify the optimal keyword phrases and messaging to target for our search engine optimization efforts on the new site.

With the benefit of the knowledge obtained from both Google Analytics and Google AdWords, as well as a competitive analysis completed using Google Search, a new site was created. We added Google Custom Search on the site, which would not only help visitors on the site find the information they were looking for, but helped the site owner to see what visitors were looking to find. This is valuable business intelligence for future product and Web site development.

After the new site was launched, we used the Google Webmaster Tool to identify and remove the URLs from the Google database that were no longer valid. Google Analytics identified a 380 percent increase in organic search engine traffic within 3 weeks. It should be noted that this result is highly unusual, as organic traffic generally takes months to demonstrate results. We attribute these better than average results to both the effectiveness of the search engine optimization, as well as the number of inbound links to the Web site, which is an important component to SEO.

CASE STUDY: RALPH ROSENBERG COURT REPORTERS, INC. <WWW.HAWAIICOURTREPORTERS.COM>

Submitted by Teri Ross

This company is the largest court reporting firm in Hawaii. They came to us looking for more traffic to their Web site. Due to the nature of their business and target audience, we needed to drive traffic for both local and national searches. Our strategy was to search engine optimize the Web site for local searches, and to use regional specific keywords in nationally targeted Google AdWords campaigns. We used Google Analytics, Google AdWords, the Google keyword tool and the Google Webmaster tool in the design, development, management and marketing of the new site we created. We also used the Google Local Business Center to get each of their locations in the Hawaiian Islands listed with Google Maps for the benefit of local search results.

We monitor the company's online reputation and press coverage with the use of Google Alerts.

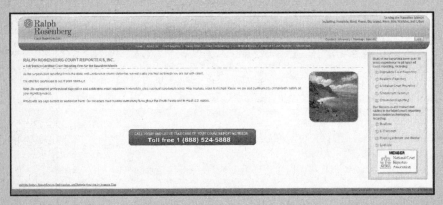

CASE STUDY: BUSINESSCARD2
<WWW.BUSINESSCARD2.COM>

Submitted by Teri Ross

This is a social marketing site that helps business professionals to be found by new prospects as well as to manage their online reputation. As a result, search engine visibility is important to the site's marketing efforts. We used the Google Keyword Tool for our keyword, competitive and trend analysis as the foundation of our search engine optimization efforts. Google Analytics and the Google Webmaster Tool play an important part in identifying opportunities for ongoing improvement. We monitor the company's online reputation and press coverage with the use of Google Alerts.

Teri Ross has been providing strategic direction to Web site development and online marketing projects since 1995. She built the first and only online trade publication dedicated to technology in the apparel industry, www.techexchange. com, which she sold in 2002. She has defined, crafted, and implemented online marketing strategies and campaigns for both B2B and B2C. She specializes in online marketing strategy development, search engine optimization, paid advertising ad management and Web site analytics. She enjoys leveraging her left and right brain skills into facilitating the cooperation of marketing and IT departments. She is a Google AdWords Advertising Professional, an Open Directory editor, a member of the Minnesota Interactive Marketing Association (MIMA), an eBay® Trading Assistant, and a certified ski instructor.

CASE STUDY: HEADZUP ENTERTAINMENT <WWW.HEADZUP.TV/WUHZUP/INDEX.PHP>

Submitted by John Shay

Headzup Entertainment, based in Seattle, Washington, publishes the world's first daily political cartoon for cell phones and the Internet. The company's Headzup cartoon is specifically designed to be downloaded to cell phones where the tiny video clips can be played and then shared freely with others as picture messages. This mobile content distribution model is referred to as "catch and release comedy." Fans who "catch" a Headzup on their cell phone typically personalize the clip by adding their own text message before "releasing" the clip back into the wild. Once on a cell phone, Headzup clips have been known to traverse the globe within minutes; passing from cell phone to cell phone. Due to the viral nature of the content, the distribution pattern within the global cellular networks can become geometric whenever users forward a Headzup clip to multiple cell phones.

The core business challenge Headzup faces is the same faced by every other new media content producer — catalyzing and expanding a loyal fan base while simultaneously developing scalable lines of revenue capable of driving the business forward. Google AdSense has played a critical role in helping Headzup meet this challenge.

It may surprise readers to learn that having extensive experience in cellular networks and new media did little to prepare Headzup to tackle those core business challenges. This was due primarily to the fact that cellular networks operate under a subscription based business model rather than an audience driven business.

That is to say, content sold to a mobile user and billed to a cellular network account has little to do with the popularity of the content and more to do with availability and discovery. Unlike the Internet where users can freely browse a wide selection of content; access to content on cellular network portals is tightly controlled by network operators. As a result, the ease with which content can be found and purchased on a mobile portal is dictated not by audience appeal but by contractual placement. With limited selection, the content that sells best on network operator controlled portals is usually the content users discover first.

To better understand how this works it may be helpful to imagine the Internet as a collection of countless vendors competing head-to-head selling similar goods and services to an endless stream of browsing consumers. In this framework, the consumption of new media content is driven nearly entirely by popularity and rapid discovery. A company offering popular content that is easy to find and purchase will always be more successful than a company offering anything less.

Cellular network operated portals turn this model upside down by offering a limited selection of content in a highly controlled environment. Compared to the highly competitive Internet model described above, cellular network portals operate much like quickie-marts attached to 24-hour gas stations. Instead of offering a wide selection of low-cost goods these captured-audience outlets intentionally limit you're choices to the high margin late-night food groups of sugar, nicotine, alcohol, and fat.

For most early-stage mobile content providers, such as Headzup, the cellular portal business model is a dead end. The premium pricing and limited shelf space represent a double barrier of entry that very few companies, much less startups, are able to overcome.

Rather than expend considerable resources working to land a coveted spot on cellular network portals, many mobile content startups focus their efforts on building an Internet audience. Furthermore, with the surge in popularity of Internet ready mobile phones, such as the Apple® iPhone®, mobile content providers are now positioning themselves to tap a burgeoning mobile Internet audience. As mobile consumers navigate their way past the constrained network operator portals to the content rich Internet, mobile content providers are beginning to take advantage of AdSense supported services.

In addition to the traditional Web site content related ads that made AdSense the leader in contextual advertising, Headzup is now actively exploiting these additional AdSense services:

AdSense For Domains - A service introduced in the fall of 2008, AdSense for domains enables partners to monetize their portfolios of undeveloped domains. For example, Headzup has owned the domain **www.bloggger.com** (note the triple-g spelling) for years with thoughts of developing it into a 3G mobile blog property. Rather than having that domain sit idle, Google's AdSense for domains allows the domain to generate modest revenue by displaying Google contextual advertisements.

AdSense For Search - Allows Web site owners to offer custom Google searches tied to Google's contextual advertising engine. Web site owners earn revenue from advertisements relevant to the custom searches.

AdSense For Feeds - Places contextual ads in RSS feeds managed by Google. Introduced in the fall of 2008, this service turns any podcast or vodcast feed into a revenue source.

AdSense For Mobile Content - Similar to traditional AdSense block ads for Web sites, AdSense for mobile content enables ad placements on portals designed specifically for cell phones and other mobile devices. As the number of Internet ready mobile devices increases, Headzup anticipates this service to become its fastest growing line of revenue.

AdSense For Content Host - Also introduced in the fall of 2008, this AdSense service enables the monetization of YouTube hosted video content embedded on third-party Web sites such as The Huffington Post, Democratic Underground, and Air America Radio. For Headzup, this service revitalized third-party collaboration efforts. Although collaboration was already strategically important, this service added a revenue incentive to work already underway.

When combined with the cost savings and audience reach associated with YouTube hosted content, integrating these Google AdSense services into their business model has provided Headzup with a robust mobile content business model that is independent of the cellular network operators.

John Shay was director of International Business Development for Hutchison Whampoa Americas Limited. While at Hutchison he was tasked with evaluating and securing best-of-breed technology, applications, games, and content in support of Hutchison Whampoa 3G cellular network launches worldwide. Shay also served as Director of Business Development for Hutchison's streaming media subsidiary, Vidiator Technology, where he spearheaded Vidiator's successful acquisition of Eyematic, a 3D avatar animation and video motion capture company.

Prior to joining Hutchison-Whampoa, Shay was director of IPv6 Business Development at Zama Networks. As a next generation Internet startup, Zama was building the first native IPv6 (Internet Protocol version 6) network bridge between the US and Asia.

Prior to Zama, Shay was with RealNetworks where he was recruited as the original product manager for the RealAudio server product line. Shay was instrumental in establishing RealAudio as a ubiquitous streaming media solution by gaining broad firewall industry support for Real's streaming media protocol, RTSP.

Shay later served as International Business Development Manager. In this role he spearheaded the introduction of RealNetworks technology to telecommunication and broadcast companies throughout the world, including ABC News, BT, DT, FT, BBC News Online, ITN, Korea Telecom, SK Telecom, KBS, Hong Kong Telecom, RTHK, China Central Television, Chungwha Telecom, NTT, TBS, Telstra, Australian Broadcasting Corp., SingTel, Embratel, Globo Television, Telmex, Televisa, and Cable & Wireless. He is also credited with conceiving and executive producing the landmark Princess Diana and Hong Kong Handover Cybercasts.

Shay also produced multi-player interactive games at Sierra On-Line for AT&T's ImagiNation Network. He has worked in the software industry since 1989, having started as a UNIX and VMS software engineer developing geophysical software for Sierra Geophysics, Halliburton, and Western Atlas. Mr. Shay holds advanced degrees in chemistry and geophysics.

john@headzup.tv, **www.headzup.tv**.

Summary

Google is much more than a power search engine, and it is much more than the most popular search engine on the Web. Google™ is a critical tool in your arsenal to build your business, grow income, increase Web site traffic, and achieve unparalleled levels of financial success. The goal of this book was to provide you with practical advice, knowledge, and understanding of the tools and applications of Google™, and how you can harness them to achieve financial success and increased income. If you design your Web site with sound SEO fundamentals, in conjunction with Google™ Webmaster Tools and other Google™ applications, you will have taken significant strides toward online success. The efforts you achieve will not only yield results on the Google™ Search Engine, but from all major search engines. Pay-per-click marketing, AdSense, AdWords, Blogs, Google™ Base, Google™ Product Search, Gmail, Google™ Checkout, You Tube, and others will empower your Web site to achieve success over your competitors. Learn from the wisdom, advice, mistakes, and practical experience of the experts interviewed as you apply the principles laid out in this book.

Ten Reasons to Follow the Guidelines in this Book:

1. Google™ is the No. 1 search engine in the world. You can significantly increase your search engine visibility and rankings in the Google™ Search Engine, yielding increased Web site traffic and increased revenue.

2. You can reach millions of potential customers every day through Google™ AdWords.

3. You can generate residual revenues by simply adding Google™ AdSense ads onto your Web site or blog.

4. You can harness the power of blogs by creating your own free blog in minutes.

5. Blog posts on Blogger ping the Google™ Search Engine instantly; your blog and Web site will be indexed, often by the most powerful, popular search engine on the Web.

6. You can implement all the techniques in this book yourself. You do not need a Web development, technology, or consulting staff.

7. Google™ offers a wide variety of applications, Web services and APIs, such as Google™ Maps, Google™ Earth, Google™ Base, and Google™ Product Search — all of which are free and can be incorporated into your Web site design.

8. You do not need to be a Web design master to get top rankings in Google™ and other search engines, and you do not have to pay anyone to do it.

9. Google™ is constantly adding more tools and applications. You can constantly improve and enhance your Web site and blog, and reach an even wider customer base.

10. You can generate increased income for your business.

Nothing is more gratifying than achieving success based on your own efforts. This book is designed to arm you with the skills, tools, and knowledge to succeed with Google™. The rest is up to you. I am 100 percent confident that investing your time and energy into using the tools and application of Google™ will pay you back with significant financial dividends many times over. I wish you success with your online business ventures and look forward to hearing your success stories. If you wish to share your experiences with me, feel free to e-mail me at bruce@gizwebs.com.

Best of Luck,

Bruce C. Brown

CHAPTER 17

Recommended Google, Search Engine Optimization, & Business Reference Library

It is a good idea to build a quality reference library to assist you with your overall e-commerce online marketing portfolio, SEO, and general business planning. While there are plenty of excellent books on the market, try adding the following to your library. All are available through Atlantic Publishing Company, at **www.atlantic-pub.com**.

How to Use the Internet to Advertise, Promote and Market Your Business or Web site—With Little or No Money

Interested in promoting your business or Web site, but don't have the big budget for traditional advertising? This book will show you how to build, promote, and make money off of your Web site or brick and mortar store using the Internet, with minimal costs. Let us arm you with the knowledge you need to make your business a success! Learn how to generate more traffic for your site or store with hundreds of Internet marketing methods, including many free and low-cost promotions.

This new book presents a comprehensive, hands-on, step-by-step guide for increasing Web site traffic and traditional store traffic by using hundreds of proven tips, tools, and techniques. Learn how to target more customers to your business and optimize your Web site from a marketing perspective. You will learn to target your campaign, use keywords, generate free advertising, search-engine strategies, learn the inside secrets of e-mail marketing, how to build Web communities, co-branding, auto-responders, Google™ advertising, banner advertising, eBay® storefronts, Web-design information, search-engine registration, directories, and real-world examples of what strategies are succeeding and what strategies are failing.

ISBN: 9780910627573 • $24.95

The Complete Guide to Google Advertising— Including Tips, Tricks, & Strategies to Create a Winning Advertising Plan

Are you one of the many who think Google™ is simply a search engine? Yes, it is true that Google™ is the most popular search engine on the Web. More than 275 million times a day, people use Google™ and its related partner sites to find information on just about any subject. Many of those people are looking for your products and services. Consider this even if you don't have a Web site or product. There are tremendous opportunities on the Internet and money to be made using Google™.

Google™ has created numerous marketing and advertising products that are fast and easy to implement in your business including AdSense, AdWords, and the Google™ APIs. This book takes the confusion and mystery out of working with Google™ and its various advertising and marketing programs. You will learn the secrets of working with Google™—without making costly mistakes. This book is an absolute must-have for anyone who wants to succeed with advertising on Google™. This book teaches you the ins and outs using all of Google™'s advertising and marketing tools. You will instantly start producing results and profits.

In addition to the extensive research placed in the book, we spent thousands of hours interviewing, e-mailing, and communicating with hundreds of successful Google™ advertising experts. This book contains their secrets and proven successful ideas, including actual case studies. If you are interested in learning hundreds of hints, tricks, and secrets on how to implement effective Google™ marketing campaigns and ultimately earn enormous profits, then this book is for you.

ISBN: 9781601380456 • $24.95

Online Marketing Success Stories: Insider Secrets from the Experts Who Are Making Millions on the Internet Today

Standing out in the turmoil of the Internet marketplace is a major challenge. There are many books and courses on internet marketing; this is the only book that will provide you with insider secrets. The reason - we asked the marketing experts who make their living on the Internet every day – and they talked. Online Marketing Success Stories will give you real life examples of how successful businesses market their products online. The information is so useful you can read a page and put the idea into action!

With e-commerce expected to reach $40 billion and online businesses anticipated to increase by 500 percent through 2010, your business needs guidance from successful internet marketing veterans. Learn the most efficient ways to bring consumers to your site, get visitors to purchase, how to up sell, oversights to stay away from, and how to steer clear of years of disappointment.

We spent thousands of hours interviewing, e-mailing, and communicating with hundreds of today's most successful e-commerce marketers. This book is a compilation of their secrets and proven successful ideas. If you are interested in learning hundreds of hints, tricks, and secrets on how to make money or more money with your Web site, then this book is for you.

Instruction is great, but advice from experts is something else, and the experts chronicled in this book are earning millions. This new, exhaustively-researched book will provide you with a jam-packed assortment of innovative ideas you can put to use today. This book gives you the proven strategies, innovative ideas, and actual case studies to help you sell more with less time and effort.

ISBN: 9780910627658 • $21.95

The Ultimate Guide to Search Engine Marketing: Pay Per Click Advertising Secrets Revealed

Is your ultimate goal to have more customers come to your Web site? You can increase your Web site traffic by more than 1,000 percent through the expert execution of pay-per-click advertising. With PPC advertising you are only drawing highly qualified visitors to your Web site! PPC brings you fast results and you can reach your target audience with the most cost effective method on the Internet.

Pay-per-click, or PPC, is an advertising technique that uses search engines where you can display your text ads throughout the Internet keyed to the type of business you have or the type of products you are promoting. Successful PPC advertising ensures that your text ads reach the right audience while your business only pays for the clicks your ads receive!

Master the art and science behind pay-per-click advertising in a matter of hours. By investing a few dollars you can easily increase the number of visitors to your Web site and significantly increase sales! If you are looking to drive high quality, targeted traffic to your site, there is no better way than to use cost-per-click advertising. Since you only pay when someone actually clicks on your ad, your marketing dollars are being used more effectively and efficiently compared to any other advertising method.

By 2010, online marketers will spend $7 billion on PPC advertising (JupiterResearch). Thousands of companies will waste precious advertising dollars on ineffective or poorly organized PPC campaigns. There is an art form to this method of advertising, and that is what this book is all about. In this book, we show you the secrets of executing a successful, cost-effective campaign.

The key to success in PPC advertising is to know what you are doing, devise a comprehensive and well-crafted advertising plan, and know the relationships between your Web site, search engines, and PPC advertising campaign methodology. This exhaustively researched book will provide everything you need to know to get you started on generating high-volume, high quality leads to your Web site. It will teach you the six steps to a successful campaign: Keyword Research, Copy Editing, Setup and Implementation, Bid Management, Performance Analysis, Return on Investment, and Reporting and Avoiding PPC Fraud.

In addition, we spent thousands of hours interviewing hundreds of the most successful PPC masters. This book is a compilation of their secrets and proven successful ideas. Additionally, we give you hundreds of tips and tricks to ensure your Web site is optimized for maximum search engine effectiveness to drive business to your Web site and increase sales and profits. In this book, you will find actual case studies from companies who have used our techniques and achieved unprecedented success. If you are interested in learning hundreds of hints, tricks, and secrets on how to implement pay-per-click advertising, optimize your Web site for maximum search engine effectiveness, develop a cost-effective marketing campaign, and ultimately earn enormous profits, then this book is for you.

ISBN: 9780910627993 • $ 24.95

The Complete Guide to E-mail Marketing: How to Create Successful, Spam-Free Campaigns to Reach Your Target Audience and Increase Sales

Researchers estimate that by 2008 e-mail marketing revenues will surpass $1.8 billion annually. Are you getting your share? According to Jupiter Research, 93 percent of U.S. Internet users consider e-mail their top online activity. E-mail is a fast, inexpensive, and highly effective way to target and address your audience. Companies like Microsoft®, **www.amazon.com**, Yahoo!®, as well as most Fortune 1000 firms are using responsible e-mail marketing for one simple reason. It works! And it generates profits immediately and consistently!

In this book you will learn how to create top-notch e-mail marketing campaigns, how to build stronger customer relationships, generate new qualified leads and sales, learn insider secrets to build your e-mail list quickly, deal with spam filters, and the optimum days and times to send your e-mails.

You will have step-by-step ways to:

- Build your business quickly using responsible, ethical e-mail marketing

- Leverage your current Web site using auto responders

- Write effective e-mail advertising copy

- Develop newsletters

- Write winning subject lines

- Get high click-through rates

- Format your messages

- Put the subscription form on your site

- Use pop ups

- Use single or double opt-in subscriptions

- Increase the response rate of your offer dramatically

- Format your e-mail so that it will be received and read

- Choose between text or HTML e-mail

- Reduce advertising expenses

- Have measurable marketing results with instant feedback

- Automate the whole e-mail marketing process

In addition, we spent thousands of hours interviewing, e-mailing, and communicating with hundreds of successful e-mail marketing experts. This book contains their secrets and proven successful ideas, including actual case studies. If you are interested in learning hundreds of hints, strategies, and secrets on how to implement effective e-mail marketing campaigns and ultimately earn enormous profits, then this book is for you.

ISBN: 9781601380425 • $24.95

How to Open and Operate a Financially Successful Web-Based Business (With Companion CD-ROM)

With e-commerce expected to reach $40 billion and online businesses anticipated to increase by 500 percent through the year 2010, you need to be a part of this exploding area of Internet sales.

If you want to learn about starting a Web business, how to transform your brick and mortar business to a Web business, or even if you're simply interested in making money online, this is the book for you.

You can operate your Web-based business from home and with very little start up money. The earning potential is limitless. This book will teach you all you need to know about getting started in your own Web-based business in the minimum amount of time. This book is a comprehensive, detailed study of the business side of Internet retailing. Anyone investigating the opportunities of opening a Web-based business should study this superb manual.

While providing detailed instruction and examples, the author teaches you how to draw up a winning business plan (The Companion CD-ROM has the actual business plan you can use in MS Word™), basic cost control systems, pricing issues, legal concerns, sales and marketing techniques, and pricing formulas. You will learn how to set up computer systems to save time and money, how to hire and keep a qualified professional staff, meet IRS reporting requirements, plan sales, provide customer service, track competitors, do your own bookkeeping, monthly profit and loss statements, media planning, pricing, and copywriting. You will develop the skill to hire and fire employees without incurring lawsuits, motivate workers, apply general management skills, manage and train employees, and generate high profile public relations and publicity. You will have the advantage low-cost internal marketing ideas and no-cost ways to satisfy customers and build sales. Learn how to keep bringing customers back, accomplish accounting, do bookkeeping procedures and auditing, as well as successful budgeting and profit planning development.

This manual delivers literally hundreds of innovative ways demonstrated to streamline your business. Learn new ways to make your operation run smoother and increase performance, shut down waste, reduce costs, and increase profits. In addition, you will appreciate this valuable resource and reference in your daily activities and as a source of ready-to-use forms, Web sites, and operating and cost-cutting ideas that can be easily applied to your operation.

ISBN: 9781601381187 • $39.95

The Secret Power of Blogging: How to Promote and Market Your Business, Organization, or Cause with Free Blogs

Blog is short for Weblog. A Weblog is a journal (or type of newsletter) that is updated often and intended for the general public. Blogs generally represent the personality of the author or the Web site. In July 2006, the Pew Internet & American Life Project estimated that the US "blog population has grown to about 12 million American adults," some 8 percent of US adult Internet users. The number of US blog readers was estimated at 57 million adults (39 percent of the US online population).

If you have a product, service, brand or cause that you want to inexpensively market online to the world then you need to look into starting a blog. Blogs are ideal marketing vehicles. You can use them to share your expertise, grow market share, spread your message and establish yourself as an expert in your field, for virtually no cost. A blog helps your site to rank higher in the search engines. This is because Google™ and the other search engines use blogs because of their constantly updated content.

Tiny, one person, part-time businesses use blogs as well as companies like Microsoft®, Apple®, Nike®, Amazon.comSM, Yahoo!®and General Motors® Most Fortune 1000 firms are using responsible blogs and blog marketing as well as advertising on blogs for one simple reason — it works! And, it generates profits immediately and consistently! In addition, many blogs earn additional revenue by selling advertising space on their niche targeted blog.

In this book you will learn how to create top-notch Blog marketing campaigns, how to build stronger customer relationships, generate new qualified leads and sales, and learn insider secrets to build your readership list quickly.

In addition, we spent thousands of hours interviewing, e-mailing, and communicating with hundreds of successful Blogging experts. This book contains their secrets and proven successful ideas, including actual case studies. If you are interested in learning hundreds of hints, strategies, and secrets on how to implement a highly effective Blog marketing campaigns and ultimately earn enormous profits, then this book is for you.

ISBN: 9781601380098 • $24.95

Word of Mouth Advertising Online & Off: How to Spark Buzz, Excitement, and Free Publicity for Your Business or Organization-With Little or No Money

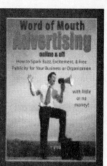

Word-of-Mouth Marketing, "WOMM" as it is commonly known, is the least expensive form of advertising and often the most effective. People believe what their friends, neighbors, and online contacts say about you, your products, and services. And they remember it for a long, long time.

Word-of-mouth promotion is highly valued. There is no more powerful form of marketing than an endorsement from one of your current customers. A satisfied customer's recommendation has much greater value than traditional advertising because it is coming from someone who is familiar with the quality of your work.

The best part is that initiating this form of advertising costs little or no money. For WOMM to increase your business, you need an active plan in place and do what is necessary to create buzz. If your business is on the Web, there are myriads of possibilities for starting a highly successful viral marketing campaign using the Internet, software, blogs, online activists, press releases, discussion forums and boards, affiliate marketing, and product sampling. Technology has dramatically changed traditional marketing programs. This book covers it all.

This all sounds great, but what is the catch? There really is none, except you must know what you are doing! This groundbreaking and exhaustively researched new book will provide everything you need to know to get you started creating the "buzz" — free publicity about your product or service whether online or off.

In this easy to read and comprehensive book you will learn what WOMM is, how to get people talking about your product or service, how to get your customers to be your sales force, how to get WOMM to spread quickly, how to automate WOMM, how to create a blog, create awareness, and how to amplify it. The entire process is covered here: marketing, dealing with negative customer experience, writing online press releases, creating a customer reference program, bringing together a fan club or loyalist community, naming VIPs, using flogs (photos), and spurring evangelism among influential people. Included are tactics that pertain especially to non-profits, including reputation management.

In addition, we have gone the extra mile and spent an unprecedented amount of time researching, interviewing, e-mailing, and communicating with hundreds of successful WOMM marketers. Aside from learning the basics you will be privy to their secrets and proven successful ideas.

Instruction is great, but advice from experts is even better, and the experts chronicled in this book are earning millions. If you are interested in learning essentially everything there is to know about WOMM in addition to hundreds of hints, tricks, and secrets on how to put WOMM marketing techniques in place and start earning enormous profits, then this book is for you.

ISBN: 9781601380111 • $24.95

How to Open & Operate a Financially Successful Web site Design Business: With Companion CD-ROM

According to a 2007 survey by Netcraft, there are more than 108 million Web sites worldwide. Every Web site needs to be designed. The Pricing & Ethical Guidelines Handbook published by the Graphic Arts Guild reports that the average cost of designing a Web site for a small corporation can range from $7,750 to $15,000. It is incredibly easy to see the enormous profit potential.

Web design businesses can be run part- or full-time and can easily be started in your own home. As such, they are one of the fastest growing segments of the Internet economy. This new book will teach you all you need to know about getting your own Web site design business started in the minimum amount of time.

Here is the manual you need to cash in on this highly profitable segment of the industry. This book is a comprehensive and detailed study of the business side of Web site design. It should be studied by anyone investigating the opportunities of opening a Web design business and will arm you with everything you need, including sample business forms, contracts, worksheets and checklists for planning, opening, and running day-to-day operations, plans and layouts, and dozens of other valuable, time-saving tools that no entrepreneur should be without.

While providing detailed instructions and examples, the author leads you through finding a location that will bring success, drawing up a winning business plan (the Companion CD-

ROM has the actual business plan that can be used in MS Word), buying (and selling) a Web design store, pricing formulas, sales planning, tracking competitors, bookkeeping, media planning, pricing, copy writing, hiring and firing employees, motivating workers, managing and training employees, accounting procedures, successful budgeting, and profit planning development.

By reading this book, you will become knowledgeable about basic cost control systems, retail math and pricing issues, Web site plans and diagrams, software and equipment layout and planning, legal concerns, sales and marketing techniques, IRS reporting requirements, customer service, direct sales, monthly profit and loss statements, tax preparation, public relations, general management skills, low and no cost ways to satisfy customers and build sales, and low cost internal marketing ideas, as well as thousands of great tips and useful guidelines.

The manual delivers literally hundreds of innovative ways to streamline your business. Learn new ways to make your operation run smoother and increase performance. Shut down waste, reduce costs, and increase profits. Business owners will appreciate this valuable resource and reference it in their daily activities as a source for ready-to-use forms, Web sites, operating and cost cutting ideas, and mathematical formulas that can be easily applied. The Companion CD-ROM contains all the forms in the book, as well as a sample business plan you can adapt for your own use.

ISBN: 9781601381439 • $39.95

The Complete Guide to Writing Web-Based Advertising Copy to Get the Sale: What You Need to Know Explained Simply

Since the advent of the Internet and since more and more people are making purchases online, writers have had to adapt to composing copy for the Web. Contrary to what many people think, writing for the Web and writing for print are not the same and involve very different skill sets. Instead of struggling to find the right words, copywriters should read this new book from cover to cover to discover how to write sales-generating copy.

The Complete Guide to Writing Web-based Advertising Copy to Get the Sale will teach you how to make your copy readable and compelling, how to reach your target audience, how to structure the copy, how to visually format the copy, how to forget everything you ever learned about writing, how to pull in visitors, how to convince visitors to buy, how to outline and achieve your goals, how to create a customer profile, how to create a unique selling position, how to include searchable keywords in the copy, how to convert prospects to paying customers, and how to compose eye-catching headlines.

In addition, you will learn about the trends in Web-based advertising, the categories of advertising, and the important information that needs to be included in your copy, such as what you are selling, what sets your product apart from the competition's, where you are located, what makes your product affordable, and why you yourself would buy the product. You will also learn about writing in the inverted pyramid style, the do's and don'ts of Web-based advertising, and key phrases to incorporate in your copy. We will also provide you with some common mistakes to avoid and tips for writing, revising, and proofreading.

By incorporating the principles in this book, you will take your Web-based advertising copy from boring to brilliant, while boosting your sales and increasing your customer traffic.

ISBN: 9781601382320 • $24.95

Internet Marketing Revealed: The Complete Guide to Becoming an Internet Marketing Expert

Internet Marketing Revealed is a carefully tested, well-crafted, and complete tutorial on a subject vital to Web developers and marketers. This book teaches the fundamentals of online marketing implementation, including Internet strategy planning, the secrets of search engine optimization (SEO), successful techniques to be first in Google™ and Yahoo!, vertical portals, effective online advertisement, and innovative e-commerce development. This book will help you understand the e-business revolution as it provides strong evidence and practical direction in a friendly and easy-to-use self-study guide.

Respected author and educator Miguel Todaro has created a complete introduction to Internet marketing that is instructive, clear, and insightful. This book is the result of several years of research and deep professional experience implementing online solutions for major corporations. Written in an instructive way, you will find fundamental concepts explained along with detailed diagrams. Many short examples illustrate just one or two concepts at a time, encouraging you to master new topics by immediately putting them to use.

Furthermore, you will find a variety of teaching techniques to enhance your learning, such as notes, illustrations, conceptual guidance, checklists of learned topics, diagrams, advanced tips, and real-world examples to organize and prioritize related concepts. This book is appropriate for marketing professionals as well as

Web developers and programmers who have the desire to better understand the principles of this fresh and extraordinary activity that represents the foundation of modern e-commerce.

Finally, you will learn and understand why big and mid-size corporations in North America have redistributed more than $15 billion of their advertising budgets from traditional promotional activities to Internet marketing initiatives. Discover how you can be part of this successful business highway that is redefining the future of the world's digital economy.

ISBN: 9781601382658 • $24.95.

The Complete Guide to Affiliate Marketing on the Web: How to Use and Profit from Affiliate Marketing Programs

Affiliate marketing is a highly profitable online advertising method in which Web site merchants pay independent third parties to promote the products or services of an advertiser on their Web site. In other words, affiliate marketing involves posting a company's banner on your Web site or blog and attempting to send visitors to their Web site. If someone clicks on that banner or goes to that site and buys something, you will be paid a commission. While some affiliates pay only when a sale is made, some selling big ticket items like cars, credit cards, travel, and so forth have modified the model and pay for qualified leads. Affiliate marketing is now viewed as a key component of a company's online marketing strategy.

Affiliate marketing is an advertising technique that originally was developed by Amazon.com℠. In this new book you will learn how to master the art and science behind affiliate marketing in a matter of hours. By investing a few dollars you can easily increase the number of visitors to your Web site and significantly increase sales. If you want to drive high quality, targeted traffic to your site, there is no better way than affiliate marketing. Since you only pay when a sale is made, your marketing dollars are being used more effectively and efficiently compared to any other advertising method.

The keys to success in affiliate marketing are knowing what you are doing, devising a comprehensive and well-crafted advertising plan, and knowing the relationships between your Web site, search engines, PPC advertising, and campaign methodology. This exhaustively researched book will provide everything you need to know to get you started on generating high-volume, high quality leads. You will learn the six steps to a successful campaign: keyword research, software needed, copy editing, setup and implementation, performance analysis, return on investment, and reporting and avoiding PPC fraud.

In addition, we spent thousands of hours interviewing hundreds of today's most successful affiliate marketing masters. This book is a compilation of their secrets and proven successful ideas. Additionally, we give you hundreds of tips and tricks to ensure your Web site is optimized for maximum search engine effectiveness, which will drive business to your Web site and increase sales and profits. You will find actual case studies from companies who have used our techniques and achieved unprecedented success. If you are interested in learning hundreds of hints, tricks, and secrets on how to implement affiliate marketing, optimizing your Web site for maximum search engine effectiveness, developing a cost-effective marketing campaign, and ultimately earning enormous profits, this book is for you.

ISBN: 9781601381255 • $24.95

Amazon Income: How Anyone of Any Age, Location, and/or Background Can Build a Highly Profitable Online Business with Amazon

The Internet affiliate program industry is one of the largest and fastest growing digital revenue generators in the world, with more than $65 billion in total income brought in during the 2006 fiscal year. It is because of programs like Amazon's Associate program, which has been around for more than a decade, and allows casual, every day users of the Internet to install widgets and links on their Web sites that link back to Amazon products. Users like you can earn commissions of up to 15 percent on products that your Web site visitors purchase when they visit Amazon. With the world's largest online retailer as a potential source of income, you can make generate endless streams of income as a result.

No matter where you are from, how old you are, and what your background is, you can build and run a highly profitable business with Amazon℠. This comprehensive book is written to show you exactly how to do so. You will learn every detail necessary to complete the transformation from casual Internet user to Amazon guru in just a matter of weeks, making unfathomable amounts of money by selling Amazon℠ products, your own products, starting a store, promoting outside projects, and making referrals.

In this book, you will learn how the Amazon℠ business model works and how much money they will pay you in multiple different ways. You will learn how to build a traffic funneling Web site with dozens of free tools such as blogs, podcasts, videos, and social networks that will allow you to increase the number of visitors you can send to Amazon in no time for minimal investment. You will learn how to take advantage of the Amazon℠ Kindle program and its revolutionary take on digital distribution of books and newspapers. You will learn what you can do to start your own store in the Amazon Marketplace, selling products at set prices to anyone in the world in much the same way you could on eBay® with substantially more freedom.

Learn how to publish your own books on Amazon℠ with little to no investment and use the features Amazon℠ provides, such as Search Inside and digital distribution to reach more people faster than you could anywhere else. In addition, learn how you can take advantage of multimedia services on Amazon such as Advantage that allow you to publish your own music, videos, and professional titles around the globe. Learn how to use Amazon℠ Connect effectively to promote your products and reach potential customers and how Amazon provides dozens of additional methods by which you can advertise your products without outside investments.

You will learn how to choose a niche to market towards and what you need to create in your Web site to make your visitors more willing to click your links and purchase the products you are promoting or selling on Amazon℠. Hours of extensive research and interviews with the top Amazon℠ associates and independent authors have given us countless pieces of advice that will ensure your marketing and promotion methods allow you to generate traffic, promote products, and convert sales at a rate that will help you build a successful business in no time. If you have been looking for the resource that will undoubtedly help you break free of the shackles of your job and start working from home, this guide is that resource and Amazon is your ideal income source.

ISBN: 9781601382993 • $24.95

Ad: For Web advertising, an ad is almost always a banner, a graphic image, or a set of animated images (in a file called an animated GIF) of a designated pixel size and byte size limit. An ad or set of ads for a campaign is often referred to as "the creative." Banners and other special advertising that include an interactive or visual element beyond the usual are known as "rich media."

Ad impression: An ad impression, or ad view, occurs when a user pulls up a Web page through a browser and sees an ad that is served on that page. Many Web sites sell advertising space by ad impressions.

Ad Rotation: Ads are often rotated into ad spaces from a list. This is usually done automatically by software on the Web site or at a central site administered by an ad broker or server facility for a network of Web sites.

Ad Space: An ad space is a space on a Web page that is reserved for ads. An ad space group is a group of spaces within a Web site that share the same characteristics so that an ad purchase can be made for the group of spaces.

Ad Stream: The series of advertisements viewed by the user during a single visit to a site.

Ad View: An ad view, synonymous with ad impression, is a single ad that appears on a Web page when the page arrives at the viewer's display. Ad views are what most Web sites sell or prefer to sell. A Web page may offer space for a number of ad views. In general, the term "impression" is more commonly used.

Affiliate: The publisher/salesperson in an affiliate marketing relationship.

Affiliate Directory: A categorized listing of affiliate programs.

Affiliate Forum: An online community where visitors may read and post topics related to affiliate marketing.

Affiliate Fraud: Bogus activity generated by an affiliate in an attempt to generate illegitimate, unearned revenue.

Affiliate Marketing: Revenue sharing between online advertisers/merchants and online publishers/salespeople, whereby compensation is based on performance measures, often in the form of sales, clicks, registrations, or a hybrid model. Affiliate marketing is the use by a Web site that sells products of other Web sites, called affiliates, to help market and sell the products, earning the affiliate some form of commission for referrals, leads or sales conversions. Amazon.com℠, the book seller, created the first large-scale affiliate program, and hundreds of other companies have followed since.

Affiliate Merchant: The advertiser in an affiliate marketing relationship.

Affiliate Network: A value-added intermediary providing services, including aggregation, for affiliate merchants and affiliates.

Affiliate Software: Software that, at a minimum, provides tracking and reporting of commission-triggering actions, such as sales, registrations, or clicks, from affiliate links.

Banner: A banner is an advertisement in the form of a graphic image that runs across a Web page or is positioned in a margin or other space reserved for ads. Banner ads are usually Graphics Interchange Format (GIF) images. In addition to adhering to size, many Web sites limit the size of the file to a certain number of bytes so that the file will display quickly. Most ads are animated GIFs since animation has been shown to attract a larger percentage of user clicks. The most common larger banner ad is 468 pixels wide by 60 pixels high. Smaller sizes include 125 by 125 and 120 by 90 pixels. These and other banner sizes have been established as standard sizes by the Internet Advertising Bureau.

Beyond the Banner: This is the idea that, in addition to banner ads, there are other ways to use the Internet to communicate a marketing message. These include sponsoring a Web site or a particular feature on it, advertising in e-mail newsletters, co-branding with another company and its Web site, contest promotion, and finding new ways to engage and interact with the desired audience. Beyond the banner approaches can also include the interstitial and streaming video infomercial. The banner itself can be transformed into a small, rich media event.

Behaviorally Targeted Advertising: A method of compiling data on Web visitors, such as surfing history, gender, age, and personal preferences, to later target them with tailored ads.

Black Lists: Block mail from known spam sources.

Booked Space: The number of ad views for an ad space that are currently sold out.

Brand, Brand Name, and Branding: A brand is a product, service, or concept that is publicly distinguished from other products, services, or concepts so that it can be easily communicated and usually marketed. A brand name is the name of the distinctive product, service, or concept. Branding is the process of creating and disseminating the brand name. Branding can be applied to the entire corporate identity as well as to individual product and service names. In Web and other media advertising, there tends to be some kind of branding value, regardless of whether an immediate, direct response can be measured from an ad or campaign. Companies like Proctor and Gamble have made a science out of creating and evaluating the success of their brand name products.

Caching: In Internet advertising, the caching of pages in a cache server or the user's computer means that some ad views will not be known by the ad counting programs, which is a source of concern. There are several techniques for telling the browser not to cache particular pages. On the other hand, specifying no caching for all pages may mean that users will find your site to be slower than you would like.

Campaign: A campaign consists of one or more Ad Groups. The ads in a given campaign share the same daily budget, language and location targeting, end dates, and distribution options.

Click: A click is when a visitor interacts with an advertisement by actually clicking their mouse point on the advertisement.

Click Stream: A click stream is a recorded path of the pages a user requested in going through one or more Web sites. Click-stream information can help Web site owners understand how visitors are using their site and which pages are getting the most use. It can help advertisers understand how users get to the client's pages, what pages they look at, and how they go about ordering a product.

Click-Through: A click-through is what is counted by the sponsoring site as a result of an ad click. In practice, click and click-through tend to be used interchangeably. A click-through, however, seems to imply that the user actually received the page. A few advertisers are willing to pay only for click-throughs, rather than for ad impressions.

Click Rate: The click rate is the percentage of ad views that resulted in click-throughs. Although there is visibility and branding value in ad views that do not result in a click-through, this value is difficult to measure.

Co-Branding: Co-branding on the Web often means two Web sites, Web site sections, or features displaying their logos, and thus their brands, together so that the viewer considers the site or feature to be a joint enterprise.

Cookie: A cookie is a file on a Web user's hard drive (it is kept in one of the subdirectories under the browser file directory) that is used by Web sites to record data about the user. Some ad-rotation software uses cookies to see which ad the user has just seen so that a different ad will be rotated into the next page view.

Cost-per-Action (CPA): What an advertiser pays for each visitor that takes some specifically defined action in response to an ad beyond simply clicking on it. For example, a visitor might visit an advertiser's site and request to be subscribed to their newsletter.

Cost-per-Click (CPC): The amount of money an advertiser will pay to a site each time a user clicks on an ad or link.

Cost-per-Lead: This is a more specific form of cost-per-action in which a visitor provides enough information at the advertiser's site (or in interaction with a rich media ad) to be used as a sales lead. Note that you can estimate cost-per-lead regardless of how you pay for the ad; in other words, buying on a pay-per-lead basis is not required to calculate the cost-per-lead.

Cost-per-Sale: Sites that sell products directly from their Web site or can otherwise determine sales generated as the result of an advertising sales lead can calculate the cost-per-sale of Web advertising.

Cost-per-Thousand (CPM): Cost per thousand ad impressions; an industry standard measure for selling ads on Web sites. This measure is taken from print advertising. The "M" is taken from the Roman numeral for "thousand."

Creative: Ad agencies and buyers often refer to ad banners and other forms of created advertising as the creative. Since the creative requires creative inspiration and skill that may come from a third party, it often does not arrive until late in the preparation for a new campaign launch.

Conversion Rate: The percentage of site visitors who respond to the desired goal of an ad campaign compared with the total number of people who see the ad campaign. The goal may be, for example, convincing readers to become subscribers, encouraging customers to buy something, or enticing prospective customers from another site with an ad.

CTR: Click-through rate. The cost of one click-through for a banner ad.

Demographics: Demographics are data about the size and characteristics of a population or audience; for example, gender, age group, income group, purchasing history, and personal preferences.

Domains: Registered domain name (with name server record).

Double Opt-In: A message is automatically sent to the person who has been signed up for a mailing list, asking whether they want to be added to the list. Unless they actively reply positively, their name is wiped from the list, and they never get another message.

Dynamic Ad Placement: The process by which an ad is inserted into a page in response to a user's request.

Electronic Mailing Lists: Also referred to as listservs; sometimes used to send advertising messages because they reach a list of subscribers who have already expressed an interest in a topic.

Filtering: The immediate analysis by a program of a user Web page request in order to determine which ad or ads to return in the requested page. A Web page request can tell a Web site or its ad server whether it fits a certain characteristic, such as coming from a particular company's address or that the user is using a particular level of browser. The Web ad server can respond accordingly.

Fold: "Above the fold," a term borrowed from print media, refers to an ad that is viewable as soon as the Web page arrives. You do not have to scroll down or sideways to see it. Since screen resolution can affect what is immediately viewable, it is good to know whether the Web site's audience tends to set their resolution at 640 by 480 pixels, at 800 by 600, or higher.

Harvesting: Using automated scripts known as "bots" to identify the correct syntax of e-mail addresses on Web pages and newsgroup posts and copy the addresses to a list.

Header Analysis: Identifies headers that do not conform to RFCs, a strong indication of spam.

Host: A computer system with a registered IP address.

Hit: A hit is the sending of a single file, whether an HTML file, an image, an audio file, or another file type. Since a single Web page request can bring with it a number of individual files, the number of hits from a site is a not a good indication of its actual use (number of visitors). It does have meaning for the Web site space provider, however, as an indicator of traffic flow.

Impression: According to the "Basic Advertising Measures," from FAST, an ad industry group, an impression is "the count of a delivered basic advertising unit from an ad distribution point." Impressions are how most Web advertising is sold, and the cost is quoted in terms of the cost per thousand impressions (CPM).

Insertion Order: An insertion order is a formal, printed order to run an ad campaign. Typically, the insertion order identifies the campaign name, the Web site receiving the order and the planner or buyer giving the order, the individual ads to be run (or who will provide them), the ad sizes, the campaign beginning and end dates, the CPM, the total cost, discounts to be applied, and reporting requirements and possible penalties or stipulations relative to the failure to deliver the impressions.

Internet: The millions of computers that are linked together around the world, allowing any computer to communicate with any other that is part of the network.

Inventory: The total number of ad views or impressions that a Web site has to sell over a given period of time. Inventory is often figured by the month.

Keyword Matching Options: There are four types of keyword matching: broad matching, exact matching, phrase matching, and negative keywords. These options help you refine your ad targeting on Google search pages.

"Junk" E-mail: E-mail messages sent to multiple recipients who did not request it and are not in the right target audience.

Keyword: A word or phrase that a user types into a search engine when looking for specific information.

Keyword Searches: Searches for specific text which yield relevant search results in search engines.

Maximum Cost-per-Click (CPC): With keyword-targeted ad campaigns, you choose the maximum cost-per-click (Max CPC) you are willing to pay.

Maximum Cost-per-Impression (CPM): With site-targeted ad campaigns, you choose the maximum cost per thousand impressions (Max CPM) you are willing to pay.

Media Broker: Since it is often not efficient for an advertiser to select every Web site it wants to put ads on, media brokers aggregate sites for advertisers and their media planners and buyers, based on demographics and other factors.

Media Buyer: A media buyer, usually at an advertising agency, works with a media planner to allocate the money provided for an advertising campaign among specific print or online media — such as magazines, TV, or Web sites — and then calls and places the advertising orders. On the Web, placing the order often involves requesting proposals and negotiating the final cost.

Meta Tags: Hidden HTML directions for Web browsers or search engines. They include important information, such as the title of each page, relevant keywords describing site content, and the description of the site that shows up when a search engine returns a search.

Newsgroups: Topic-specific discussion and information exchange forums open to interested parties.

Non-Permission Marketing: An e-mail message that is or appears to be sent to multiple recipients who did not request it, even though they may be in the right target market.

Opt-In E-mail: E-mail containing information or advertising that users explicitly request (opt) to receive. Often, a Web site invites its visitors to fill out forms identifying subject or product categories that interest them and about which they are willing to receive e-mail from anyone who might send it. The Web site sells the names, with explicit or implicit permission from their visitors, to a company that specializes in collecting mailing lists that represent different interests. Whenever the mailing list company sells its lists to advertisers, the Web site is paid a small amount for each name that it generated for the list. You can sometimes identify opt-in e-mail because it starts with a statement that tells you that you have previously agreed to receive such messages.

Page Impressions: A measure of how many times a Web page has been displayed to visitors. Often used as a crude way of counting the visitors to a site.

Page Requests: A measure of the number of pages that visitors have viewed in a day. Often used as a crude way of indicating the popularity of a Web site.

Paid Search: The area of keyword, contextual advertising, often called pay-per-click.

Page View: A common metric for measuring how many times a complete page is visited.

Pay-per-Click: In pay-per-click advertising, the advertiser pays a certain amount for each click-through to the advertiser's Web site. The amount paid per click-through is arranged at the time of the insertion order and varies considerably. Higher pay-per-click rates recognize that there may be some "no-click" branding value as well as click-through value provided.

Pay-per-Lead: The advertiser pays for each sales lead generated. For example, an advertiser might pay for every visitor that clicked on a site and then filled out a form.

Pay-per-Sale: Pay-per-sale is not customarily used for ad buys. It is, however, the customary way to pay Web sites that participate in affiliate programs, such as those of **www.amazon.com** and **www.beyond.com**.

Pay-per-View: Since this is the prevalent type of ad buying arrangement at larger Web sites, this term tends to be used only when comparing this most prevalent method with pay-per-click and other methods.

Payment Threshold: The minimum accumulated commission an affiliate must earn to trigger payment from an affiliate program.

Proof of Performance: Some advertisers may want proof that the ads they have bought have actually run and that click-through figures are accurate. In print media, tear sheets taken from a publication prove that an ad was run. On the Web, there is no industry-wide practice for proof of performance. Some buyers rely on the integrity of the media broker and the Web site. The ad buyer often checks the Web site to determine the ads are actually running. Most buyers require weekly figures during a campaign. A few want to look directly at the figures, viewing the ad server or Web site reporting tool.

Psychographic Characteristics: This is a term for personal interest information that is gathered by Web sites by requesting it from users. For example, a Web site could ask users to list the Web sites that they visit most often. Advertisers could use this data to help create a demographic profile for that site.

Reporting Template: Although the media have to report data to ad agencies and media planners and buyers during and at the end of each campaign, no standard report is yet available. Fast, the ad industry coalition, is working on a proposed standard reporting template that would enable reporting to be consistent.

Return on Investment (ROI): The bottom line on how successful an ad or campaign was in terms of what the returns (often sales revenue) were for the money expended (invested).

Rich Media: Rich media is advertising that contains perceptual or interactive elements more elaborate than the usual banner ad. Today, the term is often used for banner ads with popup menus that let the visitor select a particular page to link to on the advertiser's site. Rich media ads are generally more challenging to create and to serve. Some early studies have shown that rich media ads tend to be more effective than ordinary animated banner ads.

Run-of-Network: A run-of-network ad is one that is placed to run on all sites within a given network of sites. Ad sales firms handle run-of-network insertion orders in such a way as to optimize results for the buyer consistent with higher priority ad commitments.

Run-of-Site: A run-of-site ad is one that is placed to rotate on all non-featured ad spaces on a site. CPM rates for run-of-site ads are usually less than rates for specially-placed ads or sponsorships.

Search Engine Marketing (SEM): Promoting a Web site through a search engine. This most often refers to targeting prospective customers by buying relevant keywords or phrases.

Search Engine: A special site that provides an index of other Web site addresses listed according to key words and descriptions in the original page.

Search Engine Optimization (SEO): Making a Web site more friendly to search engines, resulting in a higher page rank.

SPAM: An unwanted e-mail message sent in bulk to thousands of addresses to try to advertise something.

Spam Posts: Messages posted to e-mail discussion groups, chat rooms, or bulletin boards that are off topic or distinctly promotional.

Splash Page: A splash page, also known as an interstitial, is a preliminary page that precedes the regular home page of a Web site and usually promotes a particular site feature or provides advertising. A splash page is timed to move on to the home page after a short period of time.

Sponsor: Depending on the context, a sponsor simply means an advertiser who has sponsored an ad and, by doing so, has also helped sponsor or sustain the Web site itself. It can also mean an advertiser that has a special relationship with the Web site and supports a special feature of a Web site, such as a writer's column, a Flower-of-the-Day, or a collection of articles on a particular subject.

Sponsorship: Sponsorship is an association with a Web site in some way that gives an advertiser some particular visibility and advantage above that of run-of-site advertising. When associated with specific content, sponsorship can provide a more targeted audience than run-of-site ad buys. Sponsorship also implies a synergy and resonance between the Web site and the advertiser. Some sponsorships are available as value-added opportunities for advertisers who buy a certain minimum amount of advertising.

Targeting: Purchasing ad space on Web sites that match audience and campaign objective requirements. **Http://techtarget.com**, with over 20 Web sites targeted to special information technology audiences, is an example of an online publishing business built to enable advertising targeting.

Unique Visitor: A unique visitor is someone with a unique address who is entering a Web site for the first time that day (or some other specified period). Thus, a visitor who returns within the same day is not counted twice. A unique visitors count tells you how many different people there are in your audience during the time period, but not how much they used the site.

User Session: A user session occurs when someone with a unique address enters or re-enters a Web site each day (or some other specified period). A user session is sometimes determined by counting only those users that have not re-entered the site within the past 20 minutes, or a similar period. User session figures are sometimes used to indicate "visits" or "visitors" per day. User sessions are a better indicator of total site activity than "unique visitors," since they indicate frequency of use.

View: A view is, either an ad view or a page view. Usually, an ad view is what is meant. There can be multiple ad views per page view. View counting should consider that a small percentage of users choose to turn the graphics off (not display the images) in their browser.

Visit: A visit occurs when a Web user with a unique address enters a Web site at some page for the first time that day (or for the first time in a lesser time period). The number of visits is roughly equivalent to the number of different people that visit a site. This term is ambiguous unless the user defines it, since it could mean a user session or it could mean a unique visitor that day.

White Lists: Guarantee delivery of known good addresses.

Yield: The percentage of clicks versus impressions on an ad within a specific page.

BIBLIOGRAPHY

Eroshenko, Dmitri and Michael Bloch. "How to Defend your Website Against

Click Fraud," ClickLab, United States, 2004.

Wikipedia. October 2008. Wikipedia, The Free Encyclopedia. 8 Oct. 2008

<en.wikipedia.org/wiki/wiki.Google>.

Google Code. December 2008. Google, Inc. 16 Dec 2008

<code.google.com>.

Google AdWords. December 2008. Google, Inc. 18 Dec 2008

<adWords.google.com>.

Google Code University. December 2008. Google, Inc. 18 Dec 2008

<code.google.com/edu/>.

Blogger. October 2008. Google, Inc. 14 Oct 2008

<www.blogger.com>.

Google AdSense. December 2008. Google, Inc. 13 Dec 2008

<adSense.google.com>.

Marketing Terms. January 2009. Crucial Marketing. 06 Jan 2009

<www.marketingterms.com>.

Google Webmaster Tools. November 2008. Google, Inc. 04 Nov 2008

<www.google.com/webmasters/>.

Bruce C. Brown is an award-winning author of eight books as well as an active duty Coast Guard officer, where he has served in a variety of assignments for nearly 25 years. Bruce is married to Vonda and has three sons: Dalton, Jordan, and Colton. His previous works include *How to Use the Internet to Advertise, Promote and Market Your Business or Website with Little or No Money*, winner of a 2007 Independent Publisher Award, as well as *The Ultimate Guide to Search Engine Marketing: Pay Per Click Advertising Secrets*

Revealed, winner in the USA Best Books 2007 Award program. He also wrote *The Complete Guide to E-mail Marketing: How to Create Successful, Spam-free Campaigns to Reach Your Target Audience and Increase Sales*, *The Complete Guide to Google Advertising: Including Tips, Tricks, & Strategies to Create a Winning Advertising Plan*, *The Secret Power of Blogging: How to Promote and Market Your Business, Organization, or Cause With Free Blogs*, *Returning From the War on Terrorism: What Every Veteran Needs to Know to Receive Your Maximum Benefits*, and *The Complete Guide to Affiliate Marketing on the Web: How to Use and Profit from Affiliate Marketing Programs*. He holds degrees from Charter Oak State College and the University of Phoenix. He currently splits his time between Land O' Lakes, Florida and Miami.

His books have been consistent best-sellers and have received prestigious awards such as the "Best Book – **USBookNews.com**," "Winner – Independent Book Publisher (Silver/Gold)," "INDIE Excellence Awards," and "Book of the Year – Foreword."

INDEX

B

L

M

N

O

P

R